Kumu Kahua Plays

Kumu Kahua Plays

EDITED BY
DENNIS CARROLL

UNIVERSITY OF HAWAII PRESS
Honolulu

To the Kumu Kahua Boards
1971–1982

The plays published in this volume are subject to royalties. No performances may be given without the permission of the playwrights, who may be contacted c/o Kumu Kahua, Kennedy Theatre, 1770 East-West Road, University of Hawaii at Manoa, Honolulu 96822.

Oranges Are Lucky copyright © 1980 by Darrell H. Y. Lum. *Oranges Are Lucky* was first published in a slightly different version in *Talk Story: An Anthology of Hawaii's Local Writers*, edited by Eric Chock et al. (Honolulu, 1978) and in *Sun: short stories and drama* by Darrell H. Y. Lum (Honolulu, 1980).

In the Alley was previously published in abridged form in *Talk Story: An Anthology of Hawaii's Local Writers*, edited by Eric Chock et al. (Honolulu, 1978).

Library of Congress Cataloging in Publication Data
Main entry under title:

Kumu Kahua plays.

    1. American drama—Hawaii.   2. American drama—20th century.   I. Carroll, Dennis, 1940–   II. Kumu Kahua (Theatre group)
PS571.H3K85   1983   812'.54'0809969   82–23724
ISBN 0–8248–0805–3

CONTENTS

PREFACE

THE PLAYS collected in this volume are strikingly varied in theme and dramatic arrangement yet have three obvious features in common. They are all local plays—that is, they have all been written by residents of Hawaii and deal in some way with life in Hawaii. They have all stood the test of theatrical production, some more than once. And they have been produced by Kumu Kahua ("Original Stage"), an organization affiliated with the University of Hawaii Drama Department which exists to produce locally written plays and theatre pieces.

In terms of style and subject matter, the plays in this volume fall naturally into pairs: *Ashes* and *Reunion* are realistic dramas that deal with identity problems of Japanese Americans; *Oranges Are Lucky* and the *All Brand New Classical Chinese Theatre* both add a touch of surrealism to their dramas about the identity problems of Chinese Americans; Hawaii's social problems are dealt with in *Paradise Tours* and *In the Alley;* and the last two plays, although written for a contemporary audience, draw on classic models—*The Travels of Heikiki* follows the structure of the historical pageant play, and *Twelf Nite O Wateva!* is a pidgin adaptation of Shakespeare's play.

The plays typify other local plays in that they tend to emphasize their character's internal conflicts as much as the conflicts that surround them. The fact that these plays have "cinematic" structures much looser than those of "well-made" plays, and that the conflicts in these plays tend to be resolved happily may owe something to the unique Hawaiian milieu and the legend of aloha described by writers such as Dennis Ogawa, Gavan Daws, Ed Sheehan, Bob Krauss, and Edward Joesting.

In preparing this anthology I was faced with the problem of standardizing the transcription of the pidgin in the plays. Pidgin orthography is still in a transitional stage because there is much disagreement between linguists and creative writers over how it should be rendered. I owe many thanks to Carol Odo, who produced for the book a glossary of pidgin words which also outlines pronunciation features of the language.

It is impossible to list the names of the many people who have contributed in some way over the last few years to the development of local drama in general and to Kumu Kahua in particular; however, I would like to acknowledge a few.

This anthology was subsidized in part by a financial bequest from the now defunct Hawaii Public Theatre. During its existence that theatre had a policy of encouraging local playwrights and had commissioned several plays. It passed on its assets to Kumu Kahua as the theatre group whose philosophy and aims were closest to its own. I wish to thank the current Kumu Kahua board members— Jan Dee Abraham, Michelle d'Albrecht, Penny Bergman, Suzanne Brown, Barbara FitzSimmons, Tom Hitch, Barbara Kelly, Richard MacPherson, Russell Omori, and Pamela Viera—for voting to support this volume and for their encouragement during its preparation.

For help in uncovering the fullest and most complete performing versions of the plays, which sometimes existed in a bewildering number of different versions, I am indebted to Professor Edward Langhans, Dando Kluever, Leslie Freundschuh, and James Nakamoto, as well as to the playwrights themselves. For helpful editorial advice at an early stage I would like to thank Katharine Brisbane, General Editor of Currency Press, the Australian drama publisher.

The introduction to this anthology is partly based on the article by Dennis and Elsa Carroll, "Hawaiian Pidgin Theatre," which appeared in the March 1976 issue of _Educational Theatre Journal._ In connection with the Introduction I wish to thank the Board of the Honolulu Community Theatre for allowing publication of research findings from their archives. Permission to examine the archives was originally granted by Mr. Norman Wright.

Honolulu, 1982

INTRODUCTION

UNTIL KUMU KAHUA was founded in September 1971, there had never been a Honolulu theatre group established solely for the encouragement of Hawaii's playwrights. The original group of eight graduate students and myself hoped that we would eventually develop a touring theatre where audiences of all ages and walks of life could recognize themselves and their problems, aspirations, and fantasies. In 1981 we celebrated our tenth anniversary. We have presented forty original full-length plays and twenty-six short plays and theatre pieces, and most of these have been offered in the Laboratory Theatre of the University of Hawaii's Drama Department. Preference has been given to plays that depict the milieu of Hawaii and to those that are unconventional in form or style.

Kumu Kahua is part of the history and development of local drama in Hawaii, itself an interesting and neglected topic. This drama can be divided into two main categories: plays in standard English that deal with historical subjects such as the myths and legends of pre-Cook Hawaii, and that tend to be modeled after the pageant form; and contemporary ethnic plays that are often comic and that use Hawaiian pidgin.

Before World War II, the historical pageant play was more successful than the ethnic play. Some of the major ethnic groups in the islands—the Japanese, Chinese, Filipinos, and Hawaiians—were content with their own cultural activities and did not seek entertainment in the theatre, apart from efforts by the Chinese and Japanese to establish classical theatre forms from their native traditions. None of the groups attempted to deal theatrically with the anxieties of assimilation in an alien culture.

The reconstitution of Japanese and Chinese theatre forms in Hawaii may have aided the early development of the historical play, especially by way of their material, exotic settings, and performance conventions. In the early years of the century, there were Japanese and Chinese amateur dramatic societies that sometimes imported troupes of professional actors. One such society gave a performance of *Othello* in Japanese as early as 1912, and was contemplating a Chikamatsu.[1] In 1919, a professional kabuki actor, Shusui Hisamatsu, settled in Hawaii and organized the Shinsei Gekidan (New Voice Theatrical Troupe), which toured the Pacific coast. When adaptations of Japanese plays were written in the 1920s and 1930s, he and his wife were sought as consultants on kabuki-derived conventions.[2] A similar situation existed for Chinese theatre. From 1920 to 1930, a Peking opera troupe performed continuously at Maunakea Street in Honolulu, and by the 1930s there were two important Chinese dramatic associations in Honolulu. The Tan Sing Dramatic Club, the most active, not only performed its own productions, traditional as well as modern adaptations, but also coached actors and musicians for work in other productions.[3] In the 1930s, the most important of these sumptuously set and costumed productions were put on by the Theatre Guild at the University of Hawaii, supervised by Arthur E. Wyman.

The greatest influence on the spectacular historical play was the theatrical form most associated with the Hawaiians: the pageant. Pageants were introduced in Hawaii in the late nineteenth century but had been presented regularly since 1913, roughly the date when they became the rage across the entire United States.[4] The pageants in Hawaii were often associated with floral parades and usually depicted the landing of Kamehameha at Waikiki in the conquest of Oahu. Although the productions took place on Kamehameha Day (June 11), during the next few years other themes were selected from Hawaiian history and mythology. A contemporary description indicates what the Hawaiian participants, responsible for every detail in the pageant, brought to their performances: ''The subjects appealed to them, and the self-possession and pride of the race enabled the several features to be presented with pleasing naturalness, without any semblance of restraint or stiffness, yet well maintaining the dignity and barbaric pomp of ancient royalty.''[5]

One of the most significant pageants was organized by the Kaahumanu Society and presented at Kailua-Kona. It depicted the meeting of the rival kings Kamehameha and Kaumualii of Kauai and their choice of peace over war. This pageant was more elaborate than an earlier version produced in Honolulu. The meeting of Kaumualii and Kamehameha was dramatized on an actual beach, and a large number of warriors and attendants and a huge flotilla of canoes were part of the scene.[6]

By the 1920s the pageant form became associated with other ethnic groups and historical subjects. It also began to adopt a more conventional form requiring more writing and rehearsals: it included original narration, a written scenario of mime, business and action in several episodes, and songs that could be learned quickly or were already known by the choral groups recruited for the occasion. Frequently the setting was outdoors, costumes were elaborate and authentic, and the size of the cast ran well into the hundreds. The history of the Hawaiian Mission Society, for example, was depicted in a spectacular pageant in Manoa Valley, with lyrics and music written in conventional western style by Ethel Damon and Jane L. Winne.[7] In the 1930s the University Theatre Guild regarded their annual pageant as the "Hawaiian" theatrical event of the season. They were usually written by haoles,[8] the casting crossed racial boundaries, and the pageants became increasingly associated with the Lei Day beauty contest at the University.[9]

In 1935 the Lei Day pageant was replaced by *Ke Kuapuu Alii* (The Royal Hunchback), "something entirely new in dramatics," the "first full-length Hawaiian play."[10] The play was written by Roland R. Shepardson, an instructor at Kamehameha Schools, and the cast was entirely of Hawaiian or part-Hawaiian descent. The play dealt with the personal and ideological struggles of two twelfth-century Hawaiian kings, the gentle Kanipahu and the aggressive Kamaiole, and was written in a kind of neo-Shakespearean verse.[11] The play had thirteen scenes which were accommodated on three settings built side by side in an area lit as need-

ed. Over three thousand attended the single, May 2 performance
in the recently opened Andrews Amphitheatre at the University.[12]

This event was in a sense the birth of the historical kind of local
play. The contemporary pidgin play had to wait another decade,
because pidgin was not regarded as a respectable vehicle for social
intercourse, let alone artistic expression. It was used only occasion-
ally in popular songs and entertainment, and even less often in surviving local plays written before World War II.[13]

The first amateur theatrical organizations founded in twentieth-
century Hawaii were not receptive to any contemporary work in
pidgin. These organizations included the student group at the
University, from 1913 on; the Footlights (later called the Honolulu
Community Theatre), founded in 1915; the Lanai Players, founded in 1917; the Wilbur Players and the Maui Players. They were
elitist organizations as much designed to cement social solidarity
and inculcate acceptable social behavior as to create live theatre.
The repertory of these groups was similar to that of other neocolo-
nial middle-class communities in America and the British Empire.
It was conventional but by no means trivial, and included works by
Shaw, Wilde, Galsworthy, and Coward. Few of the playwrights
were American, but that was hardly surprising since O'Neill, Rice,
Barry, and other first-generation contemporary American playwrights did not really establish themselves until the mid-1920s.
Footlights produced some original plays, but these seem to have
been Shavian in tone and style; none of them dealt directly with
the local scene.[14] The situation changed a little in the 1930s when
the University Theatre Guild did some topical sketches in its
Scrambled Sandals revues and put on two musical comedies by
Claude Albion Stehl that "not only lampooned Honolulu's pet
officials but also pet institutions."[15] Much of this material harked
back to turn-of-the-century music hall, however, and music was
borrowed from Arthur Sullivan. The only surviving early plays of
Hawaiian contemporary life were published in the University magazine *The Quill.*

After the Pearl Harbor attack of 1941, Hawaii's theatre catered
to an influx of servicemen, but few of these productions were local
in emphasis. There were some "Hawaiian-style" variety acts in

benefit shows, but they mostly exploited the cliches of nightclub entertainment.[16] In January 1945 a topical revue written by two Navy men, William Corrigan and David Hughes, made something of an impression. *Waikiki Diary* was a string of amusing sketches and musical numbers about sailors on leave in Waikiki. The locations of the play included the Kaukau Korner, the Moana Hotel Lobby, Kalakaua Avenue, and the interior of a crowded war-time bus. Apparently because of the treatment of contemporary local scenes, a reviewer called the production an "innovation in Honolulu theatre history," and she recommended that it should be revived after the war "as a sort of reminder that all things change."[17]

For local drama, things did change with a happy vengeance in the immediate postwar years. The year 1947 saw the production of the last great local pageant, *Ke Kula Nui* (The Big School); the production of a new historical play, *The Harp in the Willows;* and perhaps most significant of all, the first production of a contemporary pidgin play, Bessie Toishigawa's *Reunion*.

Ke Kula Nui was written by Willard Wilson, in whose playwriting class *Reunion* had emerged. It presented an allegorical depiction of the beginnings of the University of Hawaii in seven episodes with six hundred performers. One scene dealt with the contributions of various races to Hawaiian culture. Groups of Hawaiians, Chinese, Filipinos, Japanese, Portuguese, Russians, Koreans, Spanish, Samoans, Scots, and Norwegians eventually intermingled and were shown pledging their allegiance to the United States flag.[18]

The important local historical play of 1947, *The Harp in the Willows,* was written by the new assistant director of the Honolulu Community Theatre at the time, John Kneubuhl. Elroy Fulmer, Gregg Sinclair, and others had expressed hopes that it would become a "true *Community* theatre which could be used by everyone."[19] This ideal guided the local theatre movement. Kneubuhl came to Hawaii from Samoa at the age of twelve to seek an education. From December 1946 he emphasized in his writing the need to create a genuinely local theatre, and he promulgated the slogan "Pacific plays for Pacific playwrights."[20] He had planned to start a theatre workshop in Kalihi in which "local talent" could "evaluate its social heritage."[21] A radio workshop was started with KULA, and for a time the Community Theatre seemed to have been solidly behind Kneubuhl's plans.

Kneubuhl envisioned local drama as including historical and legendary subjects from the entire eastern Pacific Basin. Fulmer, who was director of the Community Theatre, endorsed his ideals and wrote that "every effort should be made by the HCT to attract, find, and train the few writers who can interpret the qualities that influence life in the Pacific area."[22] Kneubuhl was also aware of the value of Hawaii's cultural variety and said, "We want to have a far greater representation of the various groups that make up island society, and we hope for the day when they can appear solely in plays for them and by them."[23]

The Harp in the Willows falls firmly into the category of the spectacular, historical kind of local play. It deals with the first five years in the career of the missionary Lorenzo Lyons, whose diocese was the huge parish of Waimea on the island of Hawaii in the early nineteenth century. Hawaiians and part-Hawaiians made up a large part of the cast, and there were extensive passages of untranslated Hawaiian dialogue and verses of Hawaiian hymns composed by Lyons himself. Backstage after the shows, the cast provided visitors from the audience with impromptu entertainment.[24] In 1947 the Community Theatre performed a second Kneubuhl play, *The City is Haunted,* a contemporary play with tinges of expressionism. Set in a downtown park, the play portrays postwar Honolulu haunted by a guilt that helped to resurrect ghosts from its past.[25] The characters include a group of Japanese American veterans, children, a Hawaiian mother, and her Communist son.

Reunion, a play which uses pidgin in its characters' dialogue, was a success to audiences who delighted in its familiarity, and to reviewers who praised it. The play is about the adjustment to civilian life of Japanese American veterans who return from war covered in glory.[26] Directed by Joel Trapido, this production marked the beginning of a slight but steady stream of indigenous prize-winning plays done by the University Theatre Group. This development continued up to 1961, the year that Edward Sakamoto's *In the Alley* was produced. It is arguable that none of the other plays achieved the quality of these two. Clara Kubojiri's *Country Pie* (1953) is a touching portrayal of a young Japanese American family struggling with poverty and in-law interference; Aldyth Morris' *The Sign* (1951) is a well-crafted historical play about the birth of Kamehameha; Kuuana Bell's *The Malo Maker* (1953) is an amusing parody of historical play cliches; and James Mishima's *Hoomalimali* (1955) is an ingeniously framed picture of a Hawaiian beach-boy hardened by the depredations of lustful Waikiki tourists. The Theatre Group did not, however, seek to emphasize local drama in its programming. The plays dealing with the local scene were lumped together in bills with Chekhov, Ionesco, and locally written plays about Pennsylvanian football heroes and Alaskan incest.

A decline in local drama, certainly in its theatrical production, is noticeable throughout the 1950s and early 1960s. There are several possible reasons for this. By the 1950s, the second generation of American playwrights headed by Arthur Miller and Tennessee Williams had ensured the entrenchment of a mainstream American drama centered on Broadway, which came to the forefront of English-language drama. At the same time, the classical American musical reached its heyday. Theatre outside New York in America was less healthy than it had been in the 1930s, despite successes such as that of Margo Jones' work in Dallas and Glenn Hughes' work in Seattle. The trend was felt at the Honolulu Community Theatre. The big musicals were very popular with local audiences, and increased rental and organizational costs in the 1950s forced the theatre to concentrate on proven mainstream fare to ensure box-office success.[27] John Kneubuhl's departure for Hollywood in 1949 robbed the local theatre of an articulate and passionate spokesperson, and he was not immediately replaced by other playwrights capable of forging local material into full-length plays. The University of Hawaii Theatre Group, under the leadership of Earle Ernst and Joel Trapido, pioneered the staging of authentic English-language kabuki—with multiracial casts—and of challenging European and American plays. The Community Theatre staged some musicals with South Pacific or oriental settings, and a couple of their plays produced with the Chinese Civic Center and the Japanese Chamber of Commerce examined separate ethnic groups in exotic or old-country settings but did not focus on their interaction in modern Hawaii. The successful drive to statehood in 1959, the massive physical development of Hawaii, and the resulting population explosion all partly explain the lack of emphasis on local drama and theatre.

During the 1960s, however, the Community Theatre produced two significant full-length plays, both in the historical tradition. Artist Jean Charlot's *Naʻauau* (The Light Within) was a rather arch attempt at introducing lighter touches into drama characteristically very solemn; the play's uncertainty of tone, however, was underlined by an inadequately rehearsed production.[28] In the following season (1963–1964), Aldyth Morris' *The Damien Letter,* a historical drama about Robert Louis Stevenson and Damien, was performed to more significant effect.

An important development in the 1960s was the production of several local children's plays based on Hawaiian legends and the Hawaiian milieu by the Honolulu Theatre for Youth, founded in 1955. In 1960 Jeffrey Fleece's *Kalau and the Magic Numbers* was performed, and it was revived twice in the decade; and in 1963 and 1964 two plays by Mary S. Bell, *Ke Alii Umi* and *Escape at Lahaina Roads,* were produced.[29] Fleece used nonintrusive modern American speech rather than the inflated language favored by other playwrights dealing with similar material.

By the time Kumu Kahua was founded in 1971, the number of local drama productions had shrunk drastically—the Theatre Group had even suspended regular production of the playwriting competition prize-winners. But during the following decade there was a recovery because of several factors both local and international. Mainstream American drama went into eclipse with the faltering powers of Williams, Miller, and Albee. Dissatisfaction with establishment theatre, particularly of the realistic kind, kindled interest in experimental, nonrealistic forms, and minority groups developed an "alternative" theatre. After the Vietnam War, much of the energy of the political theatre was channeled into ethnic theatre, and the Black, Hispanic, and Chicano theatres flourished. At the same time vigorous local drama was also developing in Canada, Australia, and other English-speaking countries earlier held in thrall by Broadway and London.

In Hawaii there was a marked new interest in the contemporary pidgin play. Pidgin had become a badge that separated "locals" from resident haoles and tourists of all races. This new assertiveness was connected with anxiety about overdevelopment, the abuse of the environment, and the increase in crime and racial tension. Stinging social satire became a common means of disposing of the venom this anxiety created.

Kumu Kahua was in the vanguard of the rise in pidgin theatre during the 1970s. Especially notable is the 1974 success of James Grant Benton's *Twelf Nite O Wateva!* Another significant development was the meteoric rise in the mid-1970s of the comedy group Booga Booga, a coined pidgin expression meaning "oil, grease."[30] At first the group consisted of eleven people—six actors, a four-man band, and a technical man—but it reached its definitive form with three male actors, Ed Kaahea, Rap Reiplinger, and James Grant Benton. The twenty sketches that formed the group's repertory were all in pidgin, and most of them satirized island lifestyles, often with a tart abrasiveness and a heady sense of danger; other sketches were farcically innocuous tall tales. Booga Booga broke up in 1978. A move to Waikiki was not a success, but Reiplinger became a local solo attraction in his own right and has several records to his credit. Benton and Kaahea contributed in other ways to local theatre in the final years of the 1970s.

The Honolulu Theatre for Youth was another important development in the 1970s. In 1974 it produced a "modern legend" for children, *Mo'o,* by Peter Charlot. In the following year, Wallace Chappell employed an ensemble of talented actors and used the Paul Sills–Viola Spolin "story theatre" techniques in developing several theatre pieces with Hawaiian and Pacific subject matter. *Maui the Trickster* (1974) was certainly the liveliest theatricalization to date of the kind of material usually preserved in the amber of the historical pageant play. Two years later, Chappell applied similar techniques to the whole of the Pacific area in *Tales of the Pacific,* which toured the mainland.

The summer of 1976 was the high point in local drama's history since 1947. Funds from the Bicentennial Year appropriation made possible the revival of *Twelf Nite O Wateva!* by the newly formed Hawaii Theatre Festival (later the Hawaii Public Theatre). Under

Chappell's direction the play was performed on an outdoor archi-
tectural stage to large audiences. The University of Hawaii Theatre
Group produced Aldyth Morris' *Damien,*[31] a moving monodrama
on the life of the leper priest, and the fruit of at least fifteen years'
definition and redefinition of Damien in at least three earlier
plays. In a TV version with Terence Knapp, it reached audiences
nationwide and garnered national awards. The Leeward Community College Theatre produced *Hotel Street,* a group-created musical directed by David Johnson which examined the past history and
present state of the colorful and notorious "red light" area of
Honolulu. The year 1976 was also a very good one for Kumu
Kahua, which performed two important new pidgin plays before
large audiences.

The late 1970s, however, saw a decline in local theatre. Audiences, and even performers, felt that the emphasis on pidgin had
become excessive and perhaps exploitive. There was less exuberance. Nationally, the "rough" production techniques of the alternative theatre and the surreal cartoon style of the early 1970s fell
out of fashion, and there was a return to contemplative realism.
Once again America's mainstream playwrights such as David Rabe
and David Mamet were leading the way, and others such as Sam
Shepard and Lanford Wilson were writing more conventional plays
than they had in the early 1970s, thereby garnering establishment
reputations. Broadway and many new repertory theatres outside
New York co-opted much of the talent from the alternative theatre, and many ethnic theatre groups in America became more
mainstream, even commercial, in their objectives.[32]

There were bright spots. Tremaine Tamayose wrote several plays
about local social problems which toured community colleges, uni-
versities, and schools. *It's School Brah* (1976) dealt with high
school dropouts; *Lovetown* (1976), with drugs and sex abuse;
'Onolulu (1977), with racism in schools; and *Big Boys Don't Cry*
(1980), with the development of criminal behavior in males. In
addition, *Sexpectations,* a lively examination of sex role stereo-
typing, was created in a joint effort by Dando Kluever, Carol
Honda, and Elizabeth Wichmann. These productions were toured
through the General Assistance Center for the Pacific, a government agency.[33]

Interest in Hawaiiana was also roused by two other monodramas by Aldyth Morris, one on Stevenson and the other on Cook; by a drama about generational conflict, *O'o,* written by Peter Charlot and produced at the Leeward Community Theatre in 1978; and by *Mark Twain in the Sandwich Islands,* a historical play for children written by Michael Cowell and produced by the Honolulu Theatre for Youth in 1980.

In spring 1982, it appears that local pidgin theatre is again alive. The original Booga Booga has just reformed. Edward Sakamoto's *Manoa Valley,* a nostalgic look at Hawaii at the time of statehood, attracted sell-out audiences to Kennedy Theatre. And with the help of two grants from the State Foundation for Culture and the Arts, Barbara FitzSimmons has started a new arm of Kumu Kahua called the Kumu Performing Company, which will tour the neighbor islands with proven local plays.

There are also signs that local playwrights are attempting more complex characterizations and exploring the use of pidgin as more than a device to suggest male group assertiveness or provide satirical digs and easy local color. Other local subjects that await theatrical exploration include the lives of colorful individuals, political and social movements, various immigrant groups, and many contemporary issues. For example, the Samoans and Vietnamese, Hawaii's newest immigrants struggling for full acceptance in the community, remain uninvestigated, as does the world of the middle-class haole, who has appeared too often in local drama as an aloof historical personage, callow sexual opportunist, or paternalistic racist. Surely time will alter all of this. People in Hawaii are more mobile, probably better educated, certainly more in touch with international issues than before. But at the same time, partly because of this, they seem more aware of what makes Hawaii a unique place. Ultimately, it is through this awareness that playwrights will continue to build a stimulating local drama.

NOTES

1. *Honolulu Advertiser,* 6 December 1912.
2. Edwin G. Burrows, *Hawaiian Americans* (New Haven, 1947, reprinted ed., Archon Books, 1970), p. 185.

3. Ibid., pp. 178–79.

4. "Hawaiian Pageants," *Thrum's Hawaiian Annual,* 41 (1915):70.

5. Ibid., pp. 73–74.

6. Ibid.

7. Ethel Damon, *The Hawaiian Mission Centennial Pageant,* 1920, Hawaiian and Pacific Collection, Hamilton Library, University of Hawaii.

8. Caucasians.

9. *Ka Palapala,* 17 (1932) through 21 (1936) are annual reports on the pageants.

10. *Ka Palapala,* 20 (1935):112–13.

11. *Honolulu Advertiser,* 1 May 1935.

12. *Honolulu Advertiser* and *Honolulu Star-Bulletin,* 3 May 1935.

13. George S. Kanahele, ed., *Hawaiian Music and Musicians: An Illustrated History* (Honolulu, 1979), p. 298.

14. The Footlights originated from playreadings in the homes of the affluent "first families" of Honolulu. The archives of the Honolulu Community Theatre include scrapbooks with material concerning these early days. Norman Wright's brochure *Honolulu Community Theatre: A Brief History* (Honolulu, 1975) includes notes on the original plays and playwrights.

15. *Ka Palapala,* 22 (1937), unpaginated.

16. Lucille Breneman's M.A. thesis, "A History of the Theatre in Honolulu During the Second World War 1941–46" (University of Hawaii, 1949), discusses the theatrical explosion during these years.

17. *Honolulu Star-Bulletin,* 26 January 1945.

18. Ibid., 26 March 1947. The text of the pageant is in the Hawaii and Pacific Collection, Hamilton Library, University of Hawaii.

19. Gregg M. Sinclair, *Amateur Theatre in Honolulu* (brochure published in 1941).

20. John Kneubuhl, program note to *The Harp in the Willows,* February 1947, p. 12.

21. Kneubuhl, "Honolulu Community Theatre—a Preview," *Paradise of the Pacific,* 58 (December 1946):13.

22. Honolulu Community Theatre Archives, "Director's Report—1946 Season."

23. John Kneubuhl, "A Letter to a Broadway Playwright," *Paradise of the Pacific,* 61 (December 1947):68.

24. "Harp in the Willows," *Paradise of the Pacific,* 59 (March 1947):10.

25. J. Leslie Dunstan, "The City is Haunted," *The Friend,* 118 (February 1948):7–11, 32.

26. Dennis Ogawa, *Kodomo No Tame Ni—For the Sake of the Children: The Japanese-American Experience in Hawaii* (Honolulu, 1978), p. 325. It is interesting, however, that as late as 1942 Japanese Americans were exhorted not to use pidgin. By 1948 the turnaround was so great that the 442nd Veterans' Association

in Honolulu secured the services of Kneubuhl to "pidginize" and direct *The Sound of Hunting,* Harry Brown's Broadway play about army life.

27. The Honolulu Community Theatre Archives attests to the problems of rising costs and fluctuating audiences.

28. *Honolulu Advertiser,* 29 April 1962. The play has been published in Jean Charlot's *Three Plays of Ancient Hawaii* (Honolulu, 1963), pp. 1–87.

29. See *Honolulu Theatre for Youth: Twenty-Fifth Anniversary Year* (Honolulu, 1980) which lists all the theatre's productions.

30. Conversation with Edward Kaahea, Honolulu, April 1975.

31. Published in Honolulu in 1980, the play was presented in an earlier, multi-character version by Kumu Kahua in 1973.

32. The implications of the move of various ethnic theatres toward mainstream audiences are discussed by Oscar Giner in "Valdez' *Zoot Suit,*" *Theatre* 10, no. 2 (Spring, 1979):123–128.

33. Conversation with Tremaine Tamayose, Honolulu, February 1981.

Kumu Kahua Plays

Ashes

EDITOR'S NOTE

The action of *Ashes* might at first appear static and "undramatic" because the ten scenes of the play are not tightly connected through cause and effect and cover a considerable period of time; but their disjointed, spaced-out rhythm is deliberate. There is external conflict in the play, but it is a diversion. Hackneyed ideological and generational issues give a mother and daughter an excuse not to resolve the more painful conflict within each of them that is the real center of the play's action: coming to terms with the father's death.

At the end Yuki decides that her mother and brother need her guidance and love within the framework of what is familiar to them, so she stays at home. She resolves to move the ashes out of the living room, not because she has rejected them but because she is at last able to move beyond them. Not so her mother. The middle-aged woman comes into the room, does not notice that the ashes have been removed from their pedestal, and addresses the empty space.

ASHES *was first produced by Kumu Kahua at Kennedy Lab Theatre for a season beginning on November 11, 1972.*

Cast

YUKI	*Pamela Chong*
RUTH	*Jan Yuen*
BURT	*Kenneth Ogi*
TURK	*Wallace Landford*
SADAKO	*Linda Sun*
WALTER	*Yungsoh Pak*
JANET	*Janice Nomura*
MIKE	*Edward Baxa*
JERRY	*Keene Matsunaga*

Directed by Dennis Carroll
Sets and lighting by James Utterback
and Charles Myers III

Ashes

BY
LYNETTE AMANO

Characters
(in the order in which they speak)

YUKI, *22*
BURT, *17*
MOTHER (Ruth), *late 40s*
TURK, *early 40s, Ruth's brother*
SADAKO, *early 40s, Turk's wife*
JANET, *late 30s, Ruth's sister*
WALTER, *late 40s, Janet's husband*
JERRY, *17, a friend of Burt's*
MIKE, *17, a friend of Burt's*

The action takes place in Honolulu, 1971. The play has nine scenes and covers a period of three months. (Scene Five was added for the revival production in 1981.)

SCENE ONE

The living room of a modest house in Honolulu.

The room is austerely furnished, its simplicity accentuated by the almost symmetrical placement of the furniture. Up left is a door to the bedrooms and the rest of the house; up right is a door to the kitchen. Up center is a large sofa, and directly in front of it is a low coffee table. Flanking the table, angled inward, are simple chairs with wooden arms. There is an isolated chair right center balanced on the left-center side by a futon, record rack, and small record player.

Down center in the "fourth wall" there is a large window. Down left, also in the "fourth wall," is the front door to the house and the porch area.

[*Early evening. The door opens and* MOTHER, YUKI, *and* BURT *enter the living room dressed in black*]

YUKI: Well, so that was that. [*Sits*] Boy, am I hungry.

BURT: Is that all you can think of . . . food?

YUKI: Is there anything better? I didn't get a chance to eat anything there . . . especially after thanking everyone. Besides, my stomach was in knots . . . how could I?

MOTHER: Better get undressed, children. The others will be here soon.

BURT: The salt . . . we forgot the salt!

YUKI: We don't need it now, do we? I mean, we're the family, and it's only Daddy.

MOTHER: I thought I told you to leave the salt outside the porch.

YUKI: I forgot.

MOTHER: How could you forget? [*Goes to the kitchen*]

YUKI [*yelling after her*]: Well, you forgot too, didn't you?

BURT: Will you shut up? You know what she's going through. Just keep your damn mouth closed.

YUKI: Shut up yourself! Why the hell do you always have to yell? You never stop yelling . . . that's your whole problem!

MOTHER [*returning from the kitchen with salt*]: Children, stop it. Can't you two ever stop fighting? Especially now? Come on, here's the salt.

[YUKI *and* BURT *follow* MOTHER *to the door. They all stand on the porch, pour some salt into a hand and throw it over their shoulders. They do this twice, once over each shoulder. As each of them completes this ritual, they enter the house*]

MOTHER: Oh, we shouldn't have forgotten the salt . . .

BURT: It's too late now, we did it anyway.

YUKI: You've got a nerve saying that . . . especially at a time like this.

MOTHER: That's enough, Yuki. You shouldn't have forgotten the salt. It makes me feel bad things.

YUKI: Hummph. [*Pauses*] Look, Mom, it's only Daddy. Do you think his ghost will haunt us? Just because of the salt?

MOTHER: Don't be silly, Daddy wouldn't do that to us.

YUKI: That's exactly what I mean.

MOTHER: Hurry up and undress. They'll be here soon.

YUKI: I just hope they bring the rest of the food.

BURT: Well, we didn't take all those pots and pans down there for nothing, stupid.

[YUKI *ignores* BURT *and goes to the bedroom. As* MOTHER *tries to straighten the living room,* BURT *removes his coat and tosses it onto the sofa. He removes his shoes and socks, leaves them where he's dropped them, and comfortably settles down to read a comic*]

MOTHER: No matter how hard I try to keep this house clean, it's always messy. Burt! Hang up your coat . . . and pick up your smelly socks and put them in the hamper. And you never put your shoes away. Always tossing everything around this house. Now hurry up and hang your coat before it gets dirty.

BURT: Aw, ma, how can it get dirty? I just took it off!

MOTHER: It'll get dusty.

BURT: What do you think we're doing? We breathe dust every single day of the year, and we only clean our noses once in a while.

MOTHER: Stop talking dirty. You always talk dirty.

BURT: I don't. It's all in your mind.

MOTHER: Always dropping things all around the house. Look—you even spilled the salt.

BURT: Mom, will you leave me alone! Can't you ever stop nagging? Even today?

MOTHER: I don't nag. I'm just telling you. I want you to be a decent boy. Do you think I want everyone to know you're sloppy?

BURT: I'm not sloppy. I'm comfortable.

YUKI [*enters the room barefoot, wearing shorts and a T-shirt*]: Mom, you'd better change your clothes.

BURT: Yeah, before they get dirty.

MOTHER: I'm not through straightening out the house.

YUKI [*looking through records*]: Where's my new Lennon album?

MOTHER: You can't play records today. We're in mourning.

YUKI [*slightly embarrassed*]: Oh . . . I forgot.

BURT: It's not here anyway. I loaned it to Jerry.

YUKI: You loaned it to Jerry? Without asking permission? Boy, you've got some nerve!

BURT: I figured we wouldn't be able to play it anyway. Don't worry, you'll get it back.

YUKI: It better not be scratched.

BURT: Boy, and the way you talk about materialism.

YUKI: That's different. This is only a record. At least I don't waste my money on booze and other dumb things.

BURT: That's different. I spend my money on a good time. Good talk, good drink, easy chicks, good friends—fun. I'm living.

[*Off, a horn toots.* MOTHER *enters the living room and goes to the window*]

MOTHER: They're here already. Burt, go outside and help them carry in the food. Yuki, help Burt. [YUKI *and* BURT *exit*] Oh, just look at this place. What a disgrace!

[MOTHER *hurriedly straightens a few papers and magazines and frantically picks up* BURT'*s coat, shoes, and socks. Goes to bedroom*]

YUKI [*calling from outside*]: Hey, Mom! Open the door!

[MOTHER *returns quickly, opens the door, and helps* YUKI *with a large box*]

MOTHER: My goodness, look at all this food. Take it into the kitchen, Yuki.

[*As* MOTHER *and* YUKI *go to the kitchen,* BURT *enters carrying another huge box and is followed by* WALTER, TURK, SADAKO, *and* JANET, *who are carrying boxes, pots, and pans*]

MOTHER [*from the kitchen*]: Bring it all in here.

[*They all go to the kitchen. The first one to reenter the living room is* BURT. *He sits down on the sofa and puts his head back*]

BURT: Well, I guess she put my "messy" things away.

[TURK *enters*]

TURK [*seating himself on an adjacent chair*]: Well, it's been a quiet day, huh?
BURT: Yeah. It was a nice funeral.
TURK: Sure was a lot of people. The bon-san had to chant a long time.
BURT: Took almost a half hour for the osho-ko.
TURK: Clocked it, huh? [BURT *nods*] Yeah, it was long.
BURT: I'm glad we didn't have the same priest obaa-chan had. [*Laughs*]
TURK: That was a bad one. He was too old . . . his lungs didn't have enough power.

bon-san: priest
osho-ko: a section of a funeral service in which the priest chants, and the relatives and friends of the deceased place incense near the coffin as a final token of respect
obaa-chan: grandmother

BURT: Man, you don't know how hard I tried not to laugh. He sounded like a chalk on a blackboard going dit-dash-dit-dash. Except in Japanese, it was nnng-gnnnng-nggg-nggggg!

[*They laugh. From the kitchen come sounds of talk and clattering of pans*]

TURK [*after a thoughtful silence*]: Listen, Burt. With your old man gone . . . you know . . . things will be different. I mean, they'll go on pretty much the same . . . but, well, hell, he's gone. I never thought he'd kick the bucket so quick. [*Slightly cheerful*] Look, if you need anything . . . you know . . . money, don't ask your mother, okay? You come to me, okay?

BURT: Thanks, Uncle Turk. But it's okay.

TURK: No, no. You come to me. I don't want you to bother your mother.

BURT: I think I can get some social security checks. Anyway, that's what Uncle Walter told me.

TURK [*looking toward the kitchen*]: He should be in the restaurant business . . . but he's so tight he wouldn't even want to serve food.

BURT: But he did tell me about social security checks until I was twenty-two.

TURK: Yeah, yeah, I know about that, but I'm talking about immediate money . . . spending money. A guy needs money in his pockets, you know.

BURT: Uh-huh. But things are different now.

TURK: You still got your job?

BURT: Yeah. I just wish it paid more.

TURK: Don't worry about that. A job is a job. In time, you'll get raises.

BURT: Ha! I've been there for over a year and what did I get? A five cent raise? I tell you, it's dirty. I break my ass lifting those crates, unloading those stupid containers, and delivering to Kailua—for what? The thing that gets me is that I'm only a part-timer and those full-timers just sit on their asses.

SADAKO [*entering from the kitchen*]: What's that about asses?

BURT: Nothing. I was just talking about my work.

SADAKO [*sits by* TURK]: Oh, yeah, how's the banana business?

BURT: Hey! Don't knock my banana business. I know my line. I know my bananas too.

TURK: Just what have you learned, eh?

BURT: I know all about 'em. Bluefield, Apple, Chinese, Chiquitas. Chiquitas sell out fast. Boy, you don't know how many container loads of them we get . . . you wouldn't believe it!

MOTHER [*entering with* YUKI]: The food's all out on the table. Turk, Sadako, go and help yourself. You must be tired and hungry. Come on, Burt, go and eat something.

BURT: I am not hungry.

MOTHER: You haven't eaten anything since breakfast. We have to keep our strength up or we'll get sick. And that means more bills to pay.

BURT: Look, Mom, I'll eat when I'm hungry, okay?

MOTHER: Look at your sister—she's eating.

BURT: She's always eating.

YUKI: Dry up!

TURK: Better watch it, Yuki, or you'll be ready for the sumo tournaments.

YUKI: I don't care if I get fat—just as long as I'm happy. And you should talk, Uncle Turk—just look at you!

TURK: What are you talking about? I'm a fine shape of a man.

SADAKO: Really? What happened? [*Points to his belly*] Did your chest fall down?

TURK [*as* BURT *and* YUKI *laugh, gestures as if to hit her*]: Get out of here.

SADAKO: I bow to your every command. What do you want to eat? Sashimi, noodles, sushi, salad, ham, namasu, mochi, what?

TURK: A little bit of everything. And get me a beer.

[SADAKO *exits*]

namasu: pickled vegetable salad

YUKI: She really gives it to you. If you treated her better in public, she'd be treating you like a king.

TURK: Why should I? There's only one way to treat a woman—kid her around a little bit, but show her who's boss.

BURT: Right on!

YUKI: Shut up! That's what I mean about you guys. You give the single wahines all the attention. Your own wives can go to hell.

TURK: That's where they belong. At least I don't beat her up, like in the old days.

YUKI: You're kidding.

TURK: No. It was good for them. My father used to beat up my mother. Oh, he didn't hit her hard, so there were no marks left. It was just something to keep them in line.

BURT: It was a good idea. I intend to knock my wife around after I get married.

YUKI: *If* you get married. I intend to warn any girl who thinks you're so hot.

[*The others enter the living room and sit*]

JANET: Goodness, what were you all talking about?

YUKI: Wife-beating.

JANET: You're kidding.

YUKI: Aunty Sadako, did Uncle Turk ever beat you up?

SADAKO: He tried.

TURK: I knew I should have finished you off in your sleep. Yak, yak, yak. That's all you women are good for.

SADAKO: Don't mind him, he's just too embarrassed to tell you anything. He just likes to try it when he's drunk, but he's never laid a finger on me.

MOTHER: I never knew he tried to beat you up, Sadako. Turk, you're terrible! What a disgrace to the family. Oh, the neighbors must have heard everything.

SADAKO: They did. But it was no big deal . . . they just saw me running for the hills.

JANET: Sadako was always a fast runner as a girl.

WALTER: Yes, always knew Sadako had fast legs.

MOTHER: This is terrible.

SADAKO: Ane-san, it happened years ago, when he was physically fit.

BURT: Ever thought about going on the Newlywed Game?

[BURT *and* YUKI *laugh*]

MOTHER: Burt! Yuki! You mustn't joke about married people, especially if they're your relatives.

JANET: You know young people. . .

MOTHER: I'll never understand them. They should be serious, instead of joking all the time. Why, I was working since I was seventeen . . .

BURT: Are we going to hear about all that again?

JANET: It's true. Your mother worked hard all her life.

MOTHER: And I gave every cent to my father too. I only kept fifty cents for the movies and other things.

TURK: She used to come home every month and give all of us kids haircuts.

JANET: And she'd bring comics, toys, candies for us too. We just used to wait every month out by the road for her.

[*Silence*]

TURK: Burt, how about getting me another beer? One for the road.

MOTHER [*as* BURT *exits*]: You're not leaving yet, are you?

SADAKO: No, but soon. You all have to get some rest.

MOTHER: But I'm not tired.

WALTER: Of course you are. You may not know it yet but you're going to feel it if you don't get some rest.

JANET: Walter's right, Ane-san.

[BURT *returns with* TURK*'s beer*]

BURT: Here's one for the road, Uncle Turk.

SADAKO: Just remember, that's your last one. You have to drive, you know.

---

ane-san: term used when addressing older sister

WALTER [*to* MOTHER]: When will the urn be ready?

MOTHER: We're supposed to pick it up on Tuesday.

BURT: Where am I supposed to pick it up? The main mortuary or the small one?

MOTHER: Mr. Morita said to go to the small one. They're going to deliver it there.

WALTER: That's good. It'll save us the long drive to the country. Having two branches so far from each other—one in the city and one in the country—is a perfect example of poor planning.

BURT: Well, people die in the boondocks too, you know.

YUKI: Yeah, but all these developers are moving into the countryside. In another century burials will be a crime.

WALTER: I'm just glad I bought my plot ten years ago.

TURK [*to* MOTHER]: Are you going to have a seventh-day service?

MOTHER: Yes, Wednesday night.

WALTER: Janet, I think we'd better be leaving.

JANET: Sorry we have to leave so soon, Ane-san. But you know how expensive babysitters are, and you *must* get your rest. We'll see you on Wednesday night.

YUKI: Do we still have to wear black?

MOTHER: Of course. The immediate family will have to wear black. It's the only proper way to do things.

SADAKO: Come on, Ruth. I'll help you with the dishes.

MOTHER: You don't have to, Sadako. I need something to do.

TURK [*to* SADAKO]: Get your things, we're going.

SADAKO: Now? Don't be silly. I'm helping your sister with the dishes. We haven't even started on the mess.

[TURK *gets* SADAKO's *things.* WALTER *and* JANET *move to the door*]

WALTER: I'll call you up about the papers later, Ruth. All right?

MOTHER: I don't know how to thank you for all your help. I wouldn't have known what to do.

TURK [*to* SADAKO]: Hurry up. I want to get some sleep.

SADAKO: Humph. What about this mess? Why won't you lend a hand with it? Why don't you help your sister, you lazy bum!

JANET [*covering her embarrassment*]: I'll call you up tomorrow. Goodnight, Yuki, Burt. Sadako, call me tomorrow. Bye Turk.

[WALTER *and* JANET *exit*]

TURK [*to* SADAKO]: Do you want to walk home?
MOTHER: Go on home.
SADAKO: I'm sorry, Ruth. You know how he is when he gets drunk.
MOTHER: I know, I know.
TURK [*waving out to* JANET *and* WALTER]: Yak, yak, yak, yak. You'll be seeing each other tomorrow. So cut all this crap.

[*All move to the door.* MOTHER, BURT, *and* YUKI *wave good-bye to guests.* BURT *and* YUKI *move back into the room.* MOTHER *remains at the door. Silence.* YUKI *and* BURT *sit.* MOTHER *turns away from the door, moves into the room, sits. None of them move. Silence*]

Blackout

SCENE TWO

[*Three days later. The urn is resting on a white tablecloth that is covering a small, makeshift table in the center of the room. There is a candle burning in front of it. It is six o'clock in the evening.* WALTER, YUKI, *and* MOTHER *are seated on the sofa. The coffee table is strewn with papers*]

WALTER: It's essential that these papers be signed. I've asked for seven copies of the death certificate, and once you get them, you'll have to mail them to the insurance companies and the State Tax Office.
MOTHER: Don't we need a lawyer?
WALTER: No. All you have to do is go to the small estate court and they'll do everything. It's cheaper too. These lawyers charge about twice as much for the same job.
YUKI [*as* MOTHER *signs the papers*]: Do I have to go with Mom? I mean, to the estate court?

WALTER: If you want to. You could learn a couple of things with that visit, it would be quite educational. But your mother will be able to do it herself.

YUKI: Hey, you'd better withdraw Daddy's money from the bank.

WALTER: She can't. Your father's account is frozen until the court clears it.

YUKI: What do you mean "frozen?"

WALTER: It means that no one can touch the money. The bank won't issue it, not even to the wife.

YUKI: Well, Uncle Walter, just what are we supposed to use for money? Air?

WALTER: Don't worry about that. I'll take care of everything until you set yourselves up. Besides, I deposited the monetary gifts from the funeral into a joint checking account for you and your mother. That will tide you over for a while.

MOTHER: Walter, I just don't know what we'd do without you. Thank you so much for your help.

WALTER: Oh, it's nothing. I mean, what is a family for? Just don't worry about anything. [*Gathers his papers and glances at his watch*] Six-thirty already?

YUKI [*looking thoughtfully at the urn*]: It's hard to believe that Daddy is in there.

MOTHER: I know. We didn't even have a chance to talk. Everything happened so fast.

WALTER: Where's Burt?

MOTHER: Oh, he went to his judo class.

WALTER: Good, good. I'm glad to see he's continuing his attempt in physical fitness.

[YUKI *says nothing.* WALTER *takes it as a snub*]

MOTHER: Uncle Walter was talking to you, Yuki.

YUKI: Oh. Sorry.

[TURK *enters*]

TURK: The door was open, so . . .

YUKI: Howzit, Uncle Turk! Where's Aunty?

TURK: Where she's supposed to be. Home. Eh Walter, what's up?

WALTER: Nothing but business.

TURK: I see you got the urn, huh?

MOTHER: Yes. Burt picked it up this morning. Isn't it nice?

TURK: I guess so. I don't know much about urns. [*Goes over and examines it*] Hey, isn't the date of death wrong?

MOTHER [*rushing to the table excitedly*]: Where? Oh, no! What's the matter with those people! I've got to call Mr. Morita! [*Exits*]

WALTER: Well, we'll just have to change it after services tomorrow.

TURK: Yeah, but how can they make a mistake like that? Man, that engraver must have been asleep.

YUKI: Well, at least Daddy's inside it, isn't he? I mean, they wouldn't make a mistake about that, would they?

TURK: If they did, people would find out about it sooner or later.

YUKI: What?

TURK: If they filled an urn with the wrong ashes, or buried a guy in the wrong place, a ghost would turn up.

YUKI: A ghost? Uncle Turk, you've flipped. I never thought you believed all this hocus pocus.

TURK: Why don't you ask Walter? His cousin's house was haunted.

WALTER: That's not exactly true.

TURK: It was a tree. A lychee tree. In the front yard of Walter's cousin's house. Walter's cousin was picking lychee with a mango picker, see, but all the big fruit was at the top, so he decided to climb the tree. Anyway, he fell down. He fell down. And that guy swears he was pushed. Then Walter's brother climbed the tree. That night he swears something was sitting on his chest and he couldn't move or breathe. That guy was scared. That's when I came into the picture. I said someone was buried under it. Walter's cousin put a picket fence around the tree after the priest blessed it. We can still pick lychee, but we can't climb it. He used to burn incense all the time.

YUKI: Ghost? Crazy lychee tree? [*Gestures to the urn*] All I asked you was whether or not you thought Daddy was in there.

TURK: Yes. Part of him.

YUKI: Part of him?

TURK: You don't think all of him is in there, do you?

YUKI: Well, yeah. Why not?

[MOTHER *enters the living room carrying a tray with a teapot, teacups, and an assortment of crackers*]

MOTHER: Honestly, that man! He just wouldn't believe me when I told him the engraver had made a mistake. He insisted that I wait until he checked the records. How could they give the engraver a wrong date? Don't they ever listen?

[MOTHER *pours the tea with great care. She doesn't make one direct pour but stops mid-way and then pours again*]

YUKI: Daddy is in the urn, isn't he?

MOTHER: Of course he is. Who else could it be. Walter, here, have a cup of tea.

WALTER: Thank you. Did Mr. Morita straighten everything out?

MOTHER: Yes. Burt will have to deliver the urn to him tomorrow morning. Would you like some sen-bei? [*The bowl is passed.* MOTHER *pours tea for* YUKI *and herself.* TURK *refuses*] Walter, how's your tea?

WALTER: It's a bit lukewarm.

MOTHER: Oh, I'm so sorry. I left it off the burner. Well, cold tea is even better for the body.

WALTER: In any case, I should go. Janet and I have plans for the evening, and it's getting late. Why don't you come with me to the car to look at those other papers? That'll save me the trouble of coming back to the house again.

MOTHER: Oh, oh. That's very true. Of course. You're so busy and taking all this time . . .

[MOTHER *and* WALTER *exit*]

YUKI [*to* TURK]: What did you mean when you said that only a part of Daddy was in there?

sen-bei: tea cookies

TURK: Well, it's true. His bones aren't in that little urn, you know.

YUKI: Then where are they?

TURK: I don't know about that. I never did wait around to see that part.

YUKI: What are you talking about?

TURK: Once I sneaked into a crematorium. I was only a boy then, and my friend's father worked the furnace. He and I hid behind some big wooden boxes and we watched this body being burned. I'll never forget it. Dan's father turned the furnace on. The heat! We stayed there, we kept quiet. They wheeled in a coffin. I hid my eyes when they placed it into the furnace, I was too scared to look. The men left. Dan and me went over to the glass window they had on the furnace. The body jumped. It actually jumped. We were scared, we ran away, then we came back and watched it burn. It kept jumping all the time. Plulp! Plulp! Plulp! Like lava, bubbling up and popping . . . it just kept moving. [*Goes to the urn*] I know his body kept moving too. Strange, huh? what a little heat can do to a body?

YUKI: Are you telling me the truth?

TURK: Why would I lie to you? Let me finish. The cremated man was also Japanese. The next day we hid again and watched them place the ashes in the urn. Did you know they start from the feet up? Just so he'll be a whole man again in his new world. The ashes of the feet go into the bag first, then slowly up, until the head.

YUKI: How come you never told us about this?

TURK: Who wants to know? [*Pauses*] I wonder if they still do it the same way. [*Pauses. Looks at his watch*] I gotta go. You know your aunty. She'll probably tell me I was out chasing some wahine.

YUKI: Goodnight.

[TURK *leaves.* YUKI *goes to the door. Off,* TURK *says goodbye to* MOTHER *and* WALTER. YUKI *stands by the door, glances at the urn, and, still in the grip of* TURK's *story, sits.* MOTHER *comes in the living room*]

MOTHER: I had such a nice talk with your Uncle Walter, Yuki. Oh, he's so helpful. I don't know what I would've done without his help.

YUKI: Hey, Mom? Was Uncle Turk sober tonight?

MOTHER: I can't tell after all these years. He's pretty good at hiding it, so you can never tell. Once it was different . . . but that was long ago. [*Exits to the kitchen*]

YUKI [*looking after* TURK]: I believe you. [*Turns to the urn*] Yeah, for once . . . I really believe you.

Blackout

SCENE THREE

[*Two months later. The urn is now on a pedestal table by the window.* BURT, MIKE, *and* JERRY *are seated on the living room floor. All is quiet when the scene opens, and they are looking at each other playfully*]

MIKE: Frank Zappa.

BURT: Think you got me, huh? Okay . . . Zsa Zsa Gabor.

JERRY: Gregory Peck.

MIKE: Preston Foster.

BURT: Hey, I got a good one! Francis X. Bushman.

JERRY: Who's that?

MIKE: Yeah.

BURT: A silent screen star.

JERRY: B? We're running out of B's. Burgess Meredith?

MIKE: M . . . M . . . M. Oh, I got one. Milton Bradley, Jr.

BURT [*kicking* MIKE]: That's a game company, shit-head. Stop thinking about the B's.

MIKE: Okay . . . Milton Berle.

JERRY: Bill Dana.

MIKE: Darryl Zanuck!

BURT: You and your Z's!

[YUKI *enters through front door*]

YUKI: Hi. What are you guys doing?

JERRY: Playing ''Big Mouth.'' Burt's stuck with Z.

YUKI: Oh, that's easy. Zsa Zsa Gabor!

BURT: We already said that. Either shut up or leave.

YUKI: Thanks for the choice. I'll play.

BURT: Zachary Taylor.

JERRY: Thomas Hardy.

YUKI: He's a writer, not an entertainer or in show business.

JERRY: Shit! Tom Jones, then.

YUKI: Jeffry Hunter.

MIKE: Huntz Hall.

BURT: I haven't heard of him in years . . . Harry Belafonte.

JERRY: We said that.

BURT: Oh, no, we didn't!

[MOTHER *enters the living room, looks at everyone, then walks toward the kitchen*]

YUKI [*following* MOTHER]: Hey. Call me when it's my turn.

MIKE: Your turn, Jerry, and you've got an H, Burt.

JERRY: Hermione Gingold.

BURT: Who?

JERRY: Hey! Yuki!

YUKI [*coming out briefly*]: What?

MIKE: G.

YUKI: Gene Autry. [*Goes back to the kitchen*]

MIKE: Anthony Quinn.

BURT: Q . . . whose name starts with a Q?

MIKE: Ready for a G, Burt?

[*As* BURT *tries to think of an answer, parts of an argument are heard from the kitchen*]

JERRY: That was it, huh?

BURT: I can't think if you're yakking.

MOTHER [*off*]: Never mind! If you're so interested in that game, then stay out there.

MIKE: Come on, Burt.

MOTHER [*off*]: Look, am I expected to feed the world? I don't
have enough!
YUKI [*off*]: Look, will you keep your voice down! I said, okay.
Forget it, huh?
BURT [*embarrassed*]: Q . . . uh . . . uh . . . Quin . . .
MOTHER [*off*]: They have homes, you know.
BURT: I can't think of a damn thing.
MOTHER [*off*]: What do you expect me to do?
YUKI: Will you drop it?
BURT: Q . . . Quincey Jones. Whew.
JERRY: Jack Cassidy. Uh, Yuki? [*Louder*] Yuki?

[*Uneasy silence.* YUKI *enters the living room*]

YUKI: Whose turn is it?
JERRY: Yours. Didn't you hear me call you?
YUKI: Uh, no. [*Pause*] What's the word?
JERRY: C.
YUKI: Charles Laughton.

[*As the game progresses, the responses become more mechanical. The tone of enjoyment disappears, and there are no breaks between the answers. It is obvious that the whole mood has been destroyed*]

MIKE: Lloyd Bridges.
BURT: Barry Fitzgerald.
JERRY: Florence Ziegfield.
YUKI: Zasu Pitts.
MIKE: Paul McCartney.
BURT: Michael Redgrave.
JERRY: Roy Rogers.
YUKI: Rodney Dangerfield.
MIKE: Danny Thomas.
BURT: Toshiro Mifune.
JERRY: Marlon Brando and I quit. I'm tired.
MIKE: Me too. Two hours is a lot of hours.
BURT: Is it? We've gone on longer before.
JERRY: Yeah, but . . .
MIKE: We gotta go. You know—the usual stuff.

BURT: Okay. I'll see ya.

JERRY: You dropping by?

BURT: Yeah, I guess so. Same place, huh?

JERRY: Yeah. Come quick, huh? Don't want to waste any time.

MIKE: If we're not there . . . we'll be over at my place.

JERRY: Anyway, you know what we'll be doing. No sweat involved. Everything's cool.

BURT: Same place, same thing. Yeah, I know.

MIKE: Don't wait too long. Otherwise, nothing'll help your
throat. Too dry. Just hurry up, for once.

[MIKE *and* JERRY *exit.* YUKI *remains where she is*]

YUKI: Humph . . . They didn't even tell me goodbye.

[BURT *remains standing by the door. He looks in the direction
of the kitchen, then gets a cushion and angrily throws it
down*]

Blackout

SCENE FOUR

[*One hour later.* BURT, YUKI, MOTHER *in the living room*]

MOTHER: Burt, did you take out the garbage?

BURT: No.

MOTHER: When are you going to do it, then?

BURT: Later.

MOTHER: Do I always have to tell you when to do things?

BURT: No, you just love to tell me.

YUKI [*putting down her book*]: For Christ's sake, can't we have
any peace around here?

MOTHER: I didn't start it. Can I help it if I have lazy children?

YUKI: No, you were just blessed, that's all. And we're not children.

MOTHER: You haven't shown me anything else.

BURT: You haven't let us show you anything. You know everything.

MOTHER: That's true.

YUKI: See? That's exactly what we mean.

BURT [*to* YUKI]: Just drop it before it gets worse. It always does.

YUKI: Easier said than done.

MOTHER [*after a short silence, not looking up from her knitting*]: Why is everything my fault?

YUKI: Does there have to be someone at fault?

MOTHER: I'm sick of all this stupid talk.

YUKI: You brought the whole thing up.

MOTHER [*indicating* BURT]: You. Why can't you eat dinner at the right time? You always have your friends over . . . don't they know when we have dinner?

BURT: Oh, no, here we go again. [*Pauses*] No, why should they know when we're having dinner? They came to see me, not to ask me about dinner.

MOTHER: All I asked was if you took out the garbage.

YUKI: Christ! [*Puts down her book*] I'm sick of all this talk. Senseless, dumb fights. That's how talk always ends. You talk about religion and sooner or later you're in an argument with somebody. You talk about philosophy and the same thing. But in this family, it's talk about garbage that does it!

MOTHER: The trouble with you, Yuki, is that you just can't learn to be a good Japanese girl. Why don't you just listen to everything I tell you and keep quiet? I'm only telling you for your own good. Who else is going to do it? No one cares for you like your own parents. Why don't you ever do what I tell you —nicely? Just how do you ever expect to get married?

YUKI: Who knows, who cares? I guess I'll just put an ad in the paper. Wanted: good-looking male, preferably tall, virile, young, blond, blue eyes . . . no experience necessary.

MOTHER: Now I know what college has done for you. One semester, and you think like a tramp.

YUKI: I'm just kidding.

[BURT *and* YUKI *are both disgusted and amused that* MOTHER *doesn't understand the joke*]

MOTHER: I'm not telling you not to have friends over, but I must have my privacy. Besides, we're still in mourning.

YUKI: Please, let's not overuse that excuse.

MOTHER: What excuse? It's the truth: we're still in mourning.

BURT: Yeah, but you expect us to act as though the funeral was taking place again. Do you want us to give up our friends, everything?

MOTHER: When did I say that? I don't expect anyone to come over, but they come when they have free time.

BURT: You're not listening to me.

MOTHER: Of course I am. I have ears. I'm listening.

BURT: You're not listening.

MOTHER: There you go, yelling again. Can't you ever talk without yelling?

BURT: You never hear me unless I do.

YUKI: Mom, you're talking about one thing and Burt's talking about something else. You're not on the same level. Just forget everything, okay? [*Pauses*] Mom, you said that people would come over when they had free time, right?

MOTHER: Only if they wanted to.

YUKI: Well, where's Sadako, Turk, Janet, and Walter? How come they never come over anymore?

MOTHER: Why, they work . . . they're too busy and tired.

YUKI: Why haven't they been coming over? Do you realize that they came only when Daddy died? Did they come to the forty-ninth day service? Huh?

MOTHER: Janet and Walter had to go to another funeral, and Sadako and Turk both had the flu.

YUKI: Yeah, I bet. What relatives we have! Dear Uncle Walter . . . and his septic personality! [*Rises and acts out movements*] He would enter the front door naturally, without the flair of Loretta Young, and walk, walk, walk, walk around this house . . . like he had hebejebes. He should make his entrance with white gloves. Quite proper.

BURT: And meanwhile, back at the ranch . . . Aunty Janet and her quiet sweetness would sit dumbly . . .

YUKI: In the corner. She's definitely a corner type! And she'd smile once in a while, just to let us know she's still alive and she belongs to the forty-nine-percent-less-cavities group. And

ex*press*ive when it comes to telling a story. On her P's and Q's
—right to the letter!

BURT [*imitating* JANET]: However, she'd get the message over to
Walter sooner or later that [*breaking back to himself*] she'd
like to get the shit out of here!

YUKI: Egggg-xactly!

MOTHER: I knew college would do this.

YUKI: Wrong again, Mom! Try kindergarten! Sit back and enjoy
this show! I'm giving you an accurate description. Of course,
you do know, don't you? And Uncle Turk! I mustn't forget
him. Oh, he's a fine figure of a man. But has to be full every
minute!

BURT: You can't tell if he's sober . . . not even by his breath.

YUKI: How could you? The alcohol finally turned into blood! One
hundred proof.

BURT: And whiskey breath. Or rum? Smell one, smell 'em all.

YUKI: And poor scatter-brained Sadako.

BURT [*acting it out with* YUKI *vaudeville style*]: "I sleep with a
six-pack of Primo between us."

YUKI: "How about some kids?"

BURT: "No can!"

YUKI: "The alcohol killed the spermatozoa."

BURT [*new idea*]: "We got kids!"

YUKI: "Yeah! I'd like to introduce my children, Pupu . . ." [*gestures to one side*].

BURT: "And Chaser" [*gestures to the other side*].

[*They laugh.* MOTHER *rises*]

MOTHER: Yuki, Burt. You're talking about your only relatives!

YUKI: Please, don't remind me. I only wish Daddy had relatives,
instead of your stagnant side of the family.

MOTHER: Oh, this is stupid!

BURT [*rising*]: Everything is stupid or silly to you. Even us. [*Exits*]

MOTHER: Why do you two always do these stupid things? Do you
want to hurt me?

YUKI: Of course not. We're joking, Mom, but you always take
things so seriously.

MOTHER: Life is serious.

YUKI: Right. Life is serious . . . more serious than death, because it's harder to live than it is to die. Everyone knows this but you.

MOTHER: This is silly.

[BURT *enters*]

YUKI: Hey, you going somewhere?

BURT: You bet. The biggest thing of my life. See you all later. [*Goes to the door*]

Blackout

SCENE FIVE

[*A half hour later.* MOTHER *is going through a large box of old letters.* YUKI *enters with a knapsack*]

YUKI: Well, Mom, I'm going. [*Starts for the door*]

MOTHER: Where? I wanted you to help me sort through Daddy's things.

YUKI [*sighing*]: Mom, I volunteered to help you do that a month ago.

MOTHER: But that was too soon! I couldn't do it then.

YUKI: Well, I can't do it now.

MOTHER [*looking at all the things*]: Do you have an art class . . . so late?

YUKI [*smiling*]: Well, you can call it that. I'll be working on some posters. Sort of an emergency.

MOTHER: Yuki, we never talk like we used to.

YUKI: Mom, look. I'm sorry about what happened earlier. You'll just never understand me, and I guess I can't understand you either.

MOTHER: But it shouldn't be that way between mother and daughter.

YUKI [*looking at front door anxiously*]: A friend is going to pick me up . . .

MOTHER: Where are you going?

YUKI [*quickly changing the subject*]: What's all this? [*Starts reading a letter. Sits next to* MOTHER] Boy, is this stuff old! Who's Emiko-chan?

MOTHER: She and Daddy wrote to each other after her family left for Japan. I can't believe he kept all these old letters! Emiko-chan and her family moved back to Japan so that she could study at Waseda.

YUKI: You mean she used to live here?

MOTHER: Yes. According to your obaa-chan, she was born here, but her family decided to move back so that all the children could go school in Japan.

YUKI: Why? Weren't the schools here good enough?

MOTHER: They didn't think so. Besides, school is a lot harder in Japan.

YUKI: Oh, Mom! It's hard for me now.

MOTHER: That's because your mind isn't on studying. [*Changes the subject*] Here's a letter dated 1938 from one of your daddy's old school teachers.

YUKI: Wow! He kept in touch with them, huh?

MOTHER: Daddy was a very smart man. This man was his English teacher . . . a good haole man.

YUKI: There you go again.

MOTHER: What did I say?

YUKI: "A good haole man."

MOTHER: He was! Daddy always said so.

YUKI: He was a good teacher . . . that's what counts.

MOTHER: For a haole.

YUKI: Where is my ride?

MOTHER: He writes to your dad for years and years and never signs his real name . . . just his initials. I don't know why these haoles always do that.

YUKI: It's a thing teachers do—writers do this a lot. It's like a tradition—nothing harmful.

MOTHER: When have Japanese writers done this? Have you ever seen a Japanese writer do something like that?

YUKI: I haven't read anything by a Japanese author.

MOTHER: Why not?

YUKI: I haven't an interest in things Japanese.

MOTHER: Are you ashamed of your heritage?

YUKI: No, I'm not.

MOTHER: What's wrong with the University, anyway?

YUKI: Mom, if I was interested in Japanese literature—fine. But I'm not! It gives me nothing, I don't get a kick out of it.

MOTHER: Who is picking you up?

YUKI: A friend.

MOTHER: I wish you'd stay home and help me more.

YUKI: With what? You like things done your way. You don't like the way I do anything.

MOTHER: That's not true. I'm trying to teach you to do things the right way. That's all.

YUKI: Take me as I am or not at all!

MOTHER: There! That's what I mean! Your attitude! With Daddy gone, you should be thinking of me . . . of the family! The family is what counts . . . not your friends! Not so soon!

YUKI: Well, life goes on! I am in school. I have to think of that! I have friends, so I think of them! I don't want to be buried alive! You can't think of me being alive!

MOTHER: Of course we're alive. We're talking, aren't we?

[*Off, a car horn toots*]

YUKI: I'll help you, Mom, always, but I have got to go on doing what I'm doing.

MOTHER: Yuki! Yuki! Who are you going with? [*Rushes to the door, looks out*] I can't see who that is. [*Turns back into the house, moves to couch*] What am I going to do with that girl?

Blackout

SCENE SIX

[*Late afternoon of the following day.* MOTHER *is knitting by the window. No one else is home*]

MOTHER [*addressing the urn*]: You know, people have been so
nice to me. I'm making a hat for nephew John. It's the same
style I made for you, just a little smaller. Walter says John
won't wear it. But I'm making it just the same. I'm so tired. I
wouldn't be so bad if I had someone to talk to. The children
listen sometimes, but they're not you. I don't mind, though.
Remember how you'd say you were listening when you really
didn't hear a word I said? They're just like you. [*Rises and
walks to the urn*] The candle's out again. It doesn't last very
long. I change the candle, give you water and tea . . . coffee
in the morning . . . rice at night. I am doing everything I
can. I haven't been putting any sugar in your coffee, though.
Too much sugar isn't good . . . too fattening. Remember
how your father used to tell you that? I wish you'd listened to
him then . . . now it's too late. Wasn't the forty-ninth-day
service beautiful? Such a nice bon-san. I wonder where Yuki
and Burt are. I wish they'd hurry home. [*Straightens the
tablecloth and returns to her chair*] I forgot to tell you that
Mr. Kim died four days ago. I read it in this morning's paper.
Such a young man. About the same age.

Blackout

SCENE SEVEN

[*Mid-morning the next day. When the scene opens, the living
room is empty.* BURT *comes in, puts a record on, lights a
joint. Pause. He hears noise off, swallows joint, fans air with
his hand*]

TURK [*off*]: Ruth? [*Slight pause. Enters*] Eh, Burt!
BURT: Hi, Turk. What are you doing here?
TURK: Oh, I just thought I'd drop by . . . see how you were
doing. Uh, where's your mom?
BURT [*shrugging*]: She's gone out. [*Goes to the kitchen*]
TURK [*sitting down*]: Where's Yuki?
BURT: I don't know. I thought she was home. [*Throws* TURK *a
beer. Long pause*]

TURK: You okay?

BURT: Yeah. Why'd ya ask a question like that? Do I look sick?

TURK: Nah. Maybe kinda strange, but not sick.

BURT: Yeah, I know what you mean.

[*Uneasy silence.* BURT *stares off into space and* TURK *just watches him*]

TURK: Need some dough?

BURT: Who doesn't? Nah . . . I don't. When you got too much of it, you only lose it. If you don't spend it on booze, you spend it on chicks.

TURK: Yeah. I'm thinking of going to Kona . . . fishing. Wanna go?

BURT [*gets a little excited, but stops himself*]: Uh . . . not this time.

TURK: It won't cost much. I'll treat you!

BURT [*smiling*]: Nah. [*Pauses*] Don't get me wrong . . . I wanna go, honest, but not right now.

TURK: Okay. [*Pauses*] You think Yuki would like to go?

BURT: I don't know . . . go and ask her. [*Pauses*] Man, you must be loaded . . . Mom told me that you went to Molokai two weeks ago.

TURK [*laughing*]: Yeah, I went hunting. Didn't shoot a damn thing. All the deer ran away when they heard me coming through the bushes. I just gotta lose some weight! [*Pauses*] Yeah, that was a nice trip. Man, you should've seen this dame I met there. Whooohhh! Man, was she stacked . . .

BURT [*interested, he smiles*]: Oh, yeah? What ya do?

TURK: Can you see me in a pup tent with that broad? Jesus, there's no room to move! Picture it. A Hawaiian sunset. Molokai. She suddenly appears against the setting sun.

BURT: Silhouette, huh?

TURK: Yeah. Sideview. [*Laughs lecherously.* BURT *grins*] Well, we talked. She had a husband, see, but she gave me the old green light. "What about your husband," I said. "He's in Halawa jail," she said. Hoo-eee! It was dark by then. I worked our way through the bushes. There was a glint in her eye. She was panting. Her hand was moist. Then we saw the

pup tent looming out of the dark. Man, did I go through a lot
of trouble. She made me clear away all the pebbles on the
ground with a flashlight. Then . . .

BURT: Yeah?

TURK: She was okay. Yeah . . . she was okay. All I have to do is
keep up my good run in craps. I was never much of anything
. . . always ended up with snake eyes . . . but wow! I've
been lucky lately.

BURT: Yeah . . .

[YUKI *enters the house*]

YUKI: TURKEY! What's up? [*Hugging* TURK *around the neck*]
You know, I've really missed you!

TURK [*embarrassed*]: Oh? . . . Oh. Well, wea you been?

YUKI: Ahh, just fussing around. Nothing much to do, really.

TURK: Wanna go to Kona?

YUKI [*excited*]: Kona? What? You're asking me? *Me?*

TURK: Well, I got only one grown-up niece. And as sure as hell, I
ain't taking Janet and Walter's mangy bunch!

YUKI: How sweet! When you going?

TURK: This weekend.

YUKI [*disappointed*]: Oh. Shucks! I can't. I got something
planned already.

TURK: Well, break it. A treat like this doesn't come around the
corner every day, you know.

YUKI: Yeah, I know. Oh, fuck!

TURK: What did you say?

YUKI: Oh, nothing.

TURK: Since when have you started talking like that?

BURT: Since always.

YUKI: Yeah. I just don't say it in front of my ''relatives.''

TURK [*tapping her on the shoulder*]: Eeehhh. You're all right
. . . you're all right!

YUKI: I am?

TURK: Goddamn right you are!

[TURK *and* YUKI *enjoy this moment together*]

YUKI: Uncle Turk! Such language!

[BURT *turns off the record. This breaks the light mood, and* TURK *looks more seriously at* YUKI]

TURK: Have you been thinking more about what I told you?

[YUKI *nods and looks down*]

Blackout

SCENE EIGHT

[*Evening of the following day. Sundown.* YUKI *is filling a box with odds and ends and taping it down.* BURT *is reading the sports section. Voices are heard off stage*]

JANET [*off*]: Yuki! Ruth! Anyone home?
YUKI [*to* BURT]: It's the jet set.

[MOTHER, WALTER, *and* JANET *enter the living room and cross it*]

JANET: Hello, Ruth. My, you're looking wonderful!
MOTHER: Janet and Walter. Come in, come in. My, you're all dressed up. Are you going somewhere?
JANET: Later on.
MOTHER: How nice. It's been such a long time since we've seen you. [MOTHER *takes their coats.* JANET *sits;* WALTER *walks nervously about*]
YUKI [*stage whisper to* BURT]: This must be what they call a token visit.
BURT: Yeah.
JANET: My, Yuki, you look . . . really comfortable.
YUKI: I know.
JANET: Burt, how's your job?
BURT [*playing the game*]: Fine, fine.
JANET: Well, Ane-san, I hope you're keeping your strength up.
MOTHER: Well, I don't really have my appetite back, but I try to eat as much as I can.

[*Signals between* BURT *and* YUKI]

JANET: Oh, that's terrible. Isn't it, Walter.

WALTER: Yes. Say, Ruth, how long are you planning to keep the urn here?

MOTHER: Oh, as long as I'm able to care for it.

WALTER: Hmmm.

JANET: I know how lonely it is for you, but you mustn't think about it. Oh, Sadako called me today. She said she wanted to drop by but she couldn't. She's been so tired.

MOTHER: I know.

JANET: You do?

MOTHER: Yes. I've stopped by her house a few times . . . she wasn't home.

JANET: She should come to see you! She's home all day.

MOTHER: She's busy. She has a house to run.

JANET: That's no excuse. She doesn't have any children.

[YUKI *exits*]

MOTHER: By the way, I'm almost through knitting that cap for John.

JANET: Really? How nice! What color is it?

MOTHER: Navy blue.

JANET [*in a whiney voice*]: Oh, his favorite color is green.

MOTHER: You really should have told me.

JANET: I must have forgotten.

MOTHER [*after an awkward pause*]: I really miss him, Janet.

JANET [*uncomfortably*]: I can imagine . . .

MOTHER: It's natural, I guess. It's just that I'm so lonely. [BURT *exits to the kitchen*] It's too bad the TV's broken. I'll have to get it fixed. Daddy was watching it the night he died. But then he always watched TV, didn't he? I don't have a man working around the house anymore.

JANET: Well, try not to think about it.

MOTHER: What?

JANET [*almost soap-operatically*]: You can't go back to the past.

MOTHER: But all those years . . . you can't forget overnight.

[YUKI *enters the living room and takes the box*]

YUKI: Well, I'm off.

MOTHER: Where are you going?

YUKI: Off to be arrested! [*Marches out of the house*]

JANET: What was all that about?

MOTHER: I don't know. Something stupid and crazy. You know Yuki and her scatterbrained ideas.

JANET [*sits. Slight pause*]: Doesn't she have a haole boyfriend?

MOTHER [*shocked*]: What? [*Trying to be protective*] Well, she has a lot of friends, but I don't know about a haole boy. I mean, she can't help it if her friends are haole.

JANET: Do you remember the night we saw them, Walter?

WALTER: Vaguely.

JANET: I told her that night . . . how long ago was it, Walter? Three or four months ago?

WALTER: That's a good approximation.

JANET: I told her that night . . . not to marry one of those haole boys.

MOTHER: What haole boys?

JANET: Oh, no one in particular. Just plain haole. I told her, "Yuki, whatever you do, don't marry a haole." And do you know what she said? She said, "Oh, no, Aunty Janet, I'm going to marry a negro." Well, actually she said "black." But it's the same thing, you know.

MOTHER: What a thing to say!

JANET: I was so embarrassed! Walter and I were with some friends of ours when we saw her.

MOTHER [*interested*]: Where?

JANET: Oh, where was it? Walter, do you remember where we saw Yuki and that haole boy?

WALTER: Waikiki, wasn't it?

JANET: Oh, yes. We went to see this movie. And we saw them holding hands and walking down Kalakaua with their arms around each others' waists! [*Shakes her head*] Oh—and the way they were dressed! I just couldn't believe it, I just couldn't believe it!

MOTHER: Go on, go on, Janet!

JANET: Well, we tried to be nice, if you know what I mean. We were with the Gilroys from San Francisco . . . some business associates of Walter's. And since they're haoles—but of course the really good kind—I had to make do with everything. Anyway, I said "Hello." And when the Gilroys were talking to whatever-his-name-was, I talked to Yuki, and that's when she said what she said! I have no idea whether the Gilroys heard her . . . she talked so loud. I swear I can still hear everything as clear as a bell!

MOTHER: Why didn't you tell me this sooner?

JANET: I forgot. Besides, after the funeral and all, I just couldn't say anything. You really should do something about that girl.

MOTHER: I know.

[BURT *enters the room from the kitchen*]

BURT: Yuki! [*Calls toward the bedroom*] Yuki!

MOTHER: She's gone.

BURT: Oh. I was going to give her a ride.

JANET: You can still catch her if you hurry.

MOTHER: Janet, you don't think . . .

JANET: No. Don't think of it, Ruth! Otherwise you'll go stir-crazy. She wouldn't!

MOTHER: But last week, do you know what she said? She said, "Guess who's coming to dinner!"

JANET: No, no! [*Laughs in a forced way*] That's got to be that crazy sense of humor of hers. She wouldn't . . . I mean, so soon after her father's death!

BURT: What's this all about?

MOTHER: Aunty Janet was telling me about Yuki and this haole boy she saw her with. Do you know anything about him?

BURT: Which one?

MOTHER: Which one? Don't you know?

BURT: No, do you?

MOTHER: Of course I don't!

BURT: Well?

JANET: Burt, what do you know about her boyfriend?

BURT: Tall, short, skinny, fat, blond, black . . .

JANET: Black?! She has a negro boyfriend?

BURT: Sure. Don't you know it's the ethnic thing to do? She's also got them in pink, blue, polka dots, and stripes.

JANET: Since when has she been going out with this negro?

BURT: What nee-grow?

JANET: The one you're talking about!

BURT: I was talking about his hair.

JANET: His hair!

MOTHER: What a relief . . . You shouldn't joke about something like this, Burt.

JANET: You see, Ruth, I told you you had absolutely nothing to worry about. I always knew Yuki would never do a thing like that to our family.

MOTHER: You should see the kind of people she's going out and mixing up with. And she actually brought some of them to the house!

JANET: Some of them never take a bath!

BURT: Christ . . .

MOTHER: If Daddy were alive, she wouldn't dare to behave this way.

BURT [overlapping and topping her]: She'd be doing the same thing.

MOTHER: She's so out of hand.

JANET: Spare the rod and spoil the child.

MOTHER: Walter, what do you think I should do?

WALTER: She should be whipped!

[Silence. Everyone looks at WALTER]

JANET: Uh, oh . . . what time is it? My goodness, how time flies. We've got to be off. The Goldsteins will be waiting for us. Some business friends of Walter's. They just flew in from Chicago. More leis. They're international Jewish. I ate my first, ah, what was it, Walter?

WALTER: Lox.

JANET: Yes, lox. It was so good. I mean, it didn't seem at all like Jewish food. Ruth, did you know you can tell if they're Jewish by their names? I was so surprised! All you have to do is see if their names end in "stein." It's so easy.

BURT: Could be German, you know.

WALTER: Janet, we must go!

JANET: Yes. We have to meet them at their apartment for night-caps. Or was it cocktails? It's so much fun. Well, goodbye, Burt. Take care, Ruth.

BURT: Goodbye.

MOTHER: Thank you for coming. Goodbye, Walter.

[WALTER *and* JANET *exit.* BURT *says several distinctly sarcastic goodbyes as they leave*]

BURT [*as a parting shot*]: Have a nice day!

MOTHER: It was so good of them to drop by.

BURT [*mockingly*]: "Nee-grow." "Goldsteins." "All you have to do is look for 'stein.' "

MOTHER: Well, it was nice of them to come over. [*Goes to the kitchen*]

BURT: There's just got to be a way. [*Looks at the urn, walks to the table, picks up some joss sticks*] Eternal rest . . . what a laugh.

Blackout

SCENE NINE

[MOTHER *enters from the bedroom and picks up her knitting. A few seconds later,* YUKI *comes in the front door*]

YUKI: Whew! What a day! . . . God, what a day! [*Places her knapsack and a rolled-up poster by the window*]

MOTHER: There's some juice in the icebox.

YUKI: I'll settle for some plain, cold water. [*Goes to the kitchen*]

MOTHER: Where were you?

YUKI [*off*]: What?

MOTHER: I said, where were you? [YUKI *comes in with the water, sits, downs it in a gulp.* MOTHER *shows irritation*] Where have you been today? When I went to your room this morning, you were gone.

YUKI: I went to the valley.

MOTHER: Valley? What valley?

YUKI: Jesus, Mom, haven't you been reading the papers? The valley. I thought for sure the police would arrest us today.

MOTHER: Police?! What are you doing? Your name will be in all the papers! You'll have a police record—it's worse than having a traffic ticket, you know!

YUKI: There's nothing to get excited about, Mom. Getting arrested is nothing.

MOTHER: I bet it's the group you're running around with. . . I knew it would lead to this—jail!

YUKI: Jail?! What this is is a show of togetherness. Old and young people are joining hands and standing up to the lousy developers and landowners. The whole thing is a plot, it's happening all the time, and it's happening in the valley now. And we're just not going to let them get away with it . . . not by a long shot! [Holds up a "Save Kalama Valley" poster]

MOTHER: You're always getting yourself mixed up with the wrong kind of people.

YUKI: Wrong kind of people, my eye! The world is full of wrong kinds of people. Who knows . . . maybe we're just another person's wrong kind of people!

MOTHER: That's ridiculous! The Japanese are clever. No one can beat Japanese ingenuity!

YUKI: Poo, poo to that! Don't your ears ever curl up at talk like that? All this dumb third-world talk.

MOTHER: There's only one world—the one we're living in right now.

YUKI: Mom, do you know what I'm talking about?

MOTHER: Of course! You, almost a college graduate . . .

YUKI: I'm only a freshman . . .

MOTHER: Are telling me that with your education, you're frittering away time with useless people . . .

YUKI: I knew this was useless.

MOTHER: I'm your mother, I know what's best for you, no one else is going to care about you . . .

YUKI: I never can share anything with you . . .

MOTHER: . . . I'm your mother.

YUKI: . . . and you always say I never talk to you!

MOTHER: If Daddy were still here . . .

YUKI: He'd be listening . . .

MOTHER: . . . he'd know I'm right.

YUKI: . . . instead of getting excited like you.

MOTHER: I'm right—always! And one of these days you'll find that out.

YUKI: Why do you always talk before thinking?!

MOTHER: I can read you like a book. What I could tell people about you. But I never do, do I? I can keep secrets. I always protect you!

YUKI: Are you going back to the past again? Do you think I give a damn? You always make it such a heavy thing when it's minor, accidental, trite. A molehill is a mountain to you, borrowing turns into robbery, kissing into rape!

MOTHER: That's the only thing that interests you, isn't it?

YUKI: See? You're doing it again. Jesus.

MOTHER: I'm sick and tired of hearing that all the time. "Jesus" this, "Jesus" that!

YUKI: Who cares?!

MOTHER: That's why you went to church, huh?

YUKI: Why do I have to live with this? Not being listened to? Not being understood? Picked on day and night! I'm fed up. I'm getting out of this house for good! Do you hear me? I've had enough, I can't stand it anymore!

[MOTHER *is silent and she turns to look at the urn.* YUKI *slumps onto the sofa.* BURT *comes in and looks at one and then the other*]

BURT: Well, I'm home. [*Neither looks at him.* MOTHER *knits.* BURT *puts on a record*] That's a nice "Hello and how are you." [*Addressing* YUKI] Well, how'd it go today? [YUKI *gives a disgusted moan*] Yuki, what happened?

MOTHER: Are you going to yell too? [*Goes into the kitchen*]

BURT [*turns the stereo volume down. Softer*] Look, how'd it go today?

YUKI: Okay.

BURT: That's it?—okay?

YUKI: What do you want? A minute-to-minute account of everything? [*Pauses*] I got into a fight with her.

BURT: Again? When will you two ever let up.

YUKI: When I leave home, I guess. But don't you talk, brother
dear. [*Pauses*] I was just telling her about the valley and she
got all excited when I mentioned the word "police."

BURT: What did you think she'd say? "That's nice, Yuki. Don't
forget to call me when you need bail?" Use your head.

YUKI: Well, you know how she always comes after us, telling us
we never tell her anything. This time I did.

BURT: You going out again?

YUKI: In a while. I'll be there as long as I like.

BURT: Camp-out?

YUKI: Yeah. It'll be great. Things are really getting organized out
there. A lot of kids are gonna show up to help out.

BURT: Are you taking the tent?

YUKI: No. Janie brought hers and we're bunking together.
There's a lot to go 'round anyway. The police are all 'round
the place . . . they set up a barricade and everyone has to be
checked before they let you get in. Can you imagine? There
was some rumor going around about letting only the Hawaiians stay at George's place. I dunno what will happen. When
I left a while ago, there were so many kids there you wouldn't
believe it!

BURT: I lost my job.

YUKI: What?

BURT: Pipe down! I don't want Mom to know yet.

YUKI: Did you get fired?

BURT: No, laid-off. Because of that damn strike.

YUKI: Well, that can't be helped. I mean, it wasn't your fault.

BURT: That's not the point. Just why do you think I've been
breaking my ass at that lousy job? I needed every cent . . . I
wanted to get out of this place.

YUKI: And lose your maid and your cook?

BURT: I don't give a damn about that!

YUKI: How long have you been planning this?

BURT: Long before Dad died. But nothing turned out right. It's not what you think.

YUKI: Well, you've had your job for over a year, so you must have saved up a . . .

BURT: Hah!

YUKI: You did, didn't you?

BURT [*shaking his head*]: Uh-uh. Just where do you think I've been going with Jerry and Mike?

YUKI: How should I know? Since when do you tell me where you go and what you do?

BURT: We've been going to this joint.

YUKI: What is it? A pool hall?

BURT: That's kid stuff.

YUKI: Since when were you a man?

BURT: Knock it off, will you?

YUKI: Okay, I want to know. What is it? Whores?

BURT: I don't go for that.

YUKI: I bet. Dope?

BURT: Nah.

YUKI: You haven't been gambling, have you? [BURT *is silent*] You asshole! How dumb can you get!

BURT: Will you pipe down? Do you want her to hear?

YUKI: God, you're dumb. You tell me you need money to get out of here and you gamble yours away. Is that where you went last night?

BURT: Will you keep your voice down. I knew I shouldn't have told you, you're a regular PA system.

YUKI: Well, how much did you lose? [BURT *is silent*] Come on, it couldn't have been that much. What was it? Forty? Sixty? It wasn't over a hundred, was it?

BURT: Nope. You're far from it.

YUKI: It couldn't have been over two hundred.

BURT: I lost over five hundred dollars.

YUKI: GOD! You stupid, stupid sucker, you . . .

BURT: Knock it off, will you. It was my dough. I just can't figure it out . . . I was winning! The last time we played, I won a hundred and forty bucks.

YUKI: How much did Jerry and Mike lose?

BURT: I don't know. Forty or fifty.

YUKI: Didn't they tell you when to quit?

BURT: Yeah. A couple of times.

YUKI: Why didn't you listen?

BURT: Because I was so close. All I needed was another good pass and I would've scooped the pot!

YUKI: Man, are you stupid. They really set you up for the big kill. So they let you win the first couple of times . . . then the next time you come with a bundle—bang! They nail you!

BURT: You're wrong! I know these guys!

YUKI: At seventeen, the whole world knows you. [*Pauses*] You didn't lose everything, did you? [BURT *nods*] Boy, you've got some friends. They could have at least dragged you away.

BURT: It's not like that. If you're in a game with big stakes, you've got to stick it out.

YUKI: What are you going to do now?

BURT: I don't know.

[MOTHER *enters from the kitchen*]

MOTHER: Dinner's going to be late today.

BURT: It doesn't matter, I'm not hungry.

MOTHER: Not hungry? Are you sick? That's what you get for staying out late. If you get up early, and go to bed early, then you'll always be healthy. [*Smiles*] Did you know that after all that's happened, I finally have my appetite back?

Blackout

SCENE TEN

[*The next day, slightly before dawn.* BURT *has fallen asleep on the sofa. A small lamp is on. Someone is fumbling with the lock.* YUKI *enters with her knapsack and wearily dumps it by the door. She moves to the lamp and is about to turn it off when she sees* BURT *sleeping and changes her mind. She goes to the urn*]

YUKI: Well, I guess you know what happened, don't you. You would know. Something tells me that. [*Pauses*] I've had it. I really have. Nothing seems to be going the way I expected. Something always seems to change . . . when I'm in mid-flight. And I keep coming back to where I started. How'd you do it, huh? I wish I knew. [*Looks at* BURT] Look at him, sleeping like there's not a trouble in the world. You must have been there when his money went sailing away, huh? The dumb kid. [*Pauses*] Tell me—*why can't we have it?!*

BURT: Yuki?

YUKI: Yeah.

BURT [*waking up*]: Hey . . . uggh . . .

YUKI: Sit up. Are you going to be sick?

BURT: I'm okay. [*Sits up and away from her*] It all came up last night. Ohhh. I couldn't make it to the bedroom and I crashed here. [*Pauses*] Hey, I thought you'd be camping out there for the rest of the week.

YUKI: That's what I thought too. But things changed. They decided to keep only the Hawaiians there. Oh, I can dig that, it's right. But what about all the other kids who came out to lend a hand? That part sort of kills it.

BURT: Yeah? Couldn't you have camped out there anyway?

YUKI [*irritated and defensive*]: There were other things.

BURT: What things?

YUKI [*articulating sillily*]: Like mos-quit-oes, lack of lat-rines, toi-let pa-per, privacy, what have you.

BURT: What a weakling. Don't tell me you left because of those.

YUKI: No. I left because I wanted to crap in peace.

BURT: You really disappoint me, you know that?

YUKI: Listen, cat, don't you lecture me on disappointment. You've got some nerve. Real nerve. [*Pauses*] Besides, I got sick. They knew I was sick, they arranged the ride back for me. It must have been something I ate.

BURT: Yeah, I bet.

YUKI: Knock it off, will you. I'm going back later today . . . maybe tonight.

BURT: Or tomorrow, don't forget tomorrow.

YUKI: Okay, maybe tomorrow. Just because I got a little sick doesn't mean I have to give up this whole thing. [*Pauses*] You still planning on leaving?

BURT: Who knows?

YUKI: What are you going to use for money?

BURT: There must be a way. You got any? Maybe I could use that to get into another game.

YUKI: Wise up!

BURT: Okay, lay off. [*Subsiding weakly*] Oh . . .

YUKI [*sitting*]: God, that place was just crawling with bugs. And the stink. I was freezing with cold. Everything was such a mess. It wasn't at all what I expected.

BURT: Is anything?

YUKI: No, but we can hope, can't we. [*It gets lighter. They sit for a while*] Hey, Burt?

BURT: What?

YUKI: You believe in a soul?

BURT: Yeah, I guess so. Why?

YUKI: It's really interesting. Everybody has a different view on the soul. Just like that urn. It was once Daddy . . . but now it's just ashes, that's all. When he died, that was it. And yet we treat it like he's alive. To us, he is. To everyone else, he's ashes.

BURT: Do you think you should move it?

YUKI [*with a faint smile*]: I don't think he'd mind. [*Pauses*] It's really for us, isn't it?

BURT: What?

YUKI: Having it in the house.

BURT: How do you figure that?

YUKI: Well, religion isn't for the dead. How could it be? What can the dead get out of it? The Buddhists teach that once a man dies, his soul dies too. The Christians say there's a soul that goes on to Heaven . . . but the more I think about it, the less practical it seems. [*Takes the urn off the pedestal*]

BURT: I didn't know you were hooked onto this.

YUKI: I'm not. I don't think I am. But . . .

[YUKI *puts the urn on the coffee table. She and* BURT *stare at it. The room gets lighter*]

BURT: Do you think we should put it away? You know, in the plot.

YUKI: I've been thinking about that too.

BURT: Are you going to tell Mom?

YUKI: I think so. [*Pauses*] Do you think things will be any different when it's gone?

BURT: I don't know.

MOTHER [*entering*]: Yuki! Where have you been? Burt said something, but I didn't understand him.

YUKI: Well, I'm home now.

BURT: Yeah. Anyway, I'm hitting the sack. [*Exits*]

YUKI: Me too. Mom, don't wake me up. I want to have a long sleep. [*Exits*]

MOTHER: Someone forgot to turn off the light. And Yuki's knapsack. She's beginning to turn into a sloppy girl. [*Goes to the pedestal and addresses it as if the urn were still there*] Do you see what I go through every day, Daddy? The same thing, day in, day out. I don't know what I'm going to do with them. They're beginning to be just like you . . . and no one knows what I've been going through. No one.

Blackout

Curtain

Reunion

EDITOR'S NOTE

Reunion comically portrays the predicament of veterans who still have not found themselves after a year at home. The first production was praised for its affectionate reflection of familiar realities and for the pidgin dialogue—but differences between standard English and pidgin are used to underline a tension between individual and group, between private and public identity.

Though much shorter, *Reunion* is comparable to *Ashes* in that the action is rather static, with forward movement brought about through internal conflict in Taka and Masa. They resolve it when they come to realize that they are at least alive, unlike some of the soldiers they still remember; that they are in one piece, unlike Shig, who has a permanently damaged leg; and that unlike Jits and Duke, they are educated and further educable. They become newly aware of their potential to do more with their lives than spend them in sidewalk sessions of stag reminiscence. The real reunion occurs when they are united once again with their ideals and positive visions of the future.

REUNION *was first produced by the UH Theatre group at Farrington Hall, University of Hawaii, for a series of performances beginning May 7, 1947.*

Cast

TAKASHI	*Sam Sasai*
MIYO	*Louise Kishinami*
SHIGEYUKI	*Terry Adaniya*
MASAICHI	*Kenneth Saruwatari*
DUKE	*Bob Kadowaki*
JITS	*Ann Koga*

Directed by Joel Trapido

Revival by Kumu Kahua at Kennedy Lab Theatre for a series of performances beginning May 10, 1974.

Cast

MIYO	*Carol Honda*
TAKA	*Ron Nakahara*
MASA	*Jim Young*
SHIG	*Reid Min*
DUKE	*Brian Baptiste*

Directed by Ed Kaahea
Lighting by Dian Kobayashi Lopez and Darryl Kaneshiro

Reunion

BY
LISA TOISHIGAWA INOUYE

Characters
(in the order in which they speak)

TAKASHI (TAKA), *young veteran of the 442nd combat team*
MIYO, *his older sister*
SHIGEYUKI (SHIG)
MASAICHI (MASA)   *All veterans of the 442nd;*
DUKE   *Takashi's buddies, who fought*
JITSUO (JITS)   *with him in the same company*
MRS. MIYAMOTO, *his mother*
TERUKO, *his younger sister*

The street in front of the Miyamoto home in Kaimuki, a modest white house, built high above the ground. It has a neat porch with many steps leading up to it and a white picket fence surrounding both house and yard. There is a gate in the fence. It squeaks very loudly when opened. Time: One Sunday.

[*At curtain rise, the screen door of the house opens and* TAKA *comes out, bounds down the steps, opens the gate, and starts walking toward stage right. He stops, looks down at his shoes, then kneels down to tie the shoelace on one of his shoes. In the meantime, young* MIYO *also opens the screen door, comes out to the porch with a mop in her hand. She calls out from the edge of the porch in a shrill voice*]

MIYO: Ta-chan—Ta-chan!
TAKA [*still kneeling, turns his head*]: What?
MIYO [*firmly*]: Wea you going?
TAKA: Out.
MIYO: Everytime, everytime go out. Neva stay home! If you no come home early today, you no going get nutting to eat . . . you hia? [*Turns and goes into the house*]
TAKA [*mutters to himself*]: Aw, shut up! [*Rises to go, when he is hailed by someone from offstage left*]
MASA: Taka! Taka! Hey, Taka! [*Enters left*]
TAKA [*turning with a perplexed look on his face*]: Hey Masa! How come?
MASA: Aw, nothing to do so I thought I'd come over. Where to?
TAKA: Oh . . . I was thinking of going down to the library to fool around.
MASA: Thinking about going back to the U?
TAKA: Ah, I dono. [*Rubs his head, leans on the fence*] Might as well . . . nothing else to do. Come on, sit down. My old man's burned up with me. Last night we had a big fight. He called me a bum and a good-for-nothing. Almost told me to get out of the house. Was he mad! Whew! Guess I can't blame him, though. One year already since we came home and I still don't know what I want to do . . . I'm not working again.

MASA [*leans on fence*]: Yeah, you might as well go back to school. I hear lotta guys are back. Good fun, huh?

TAKA: Yeah, but what am I going to take up?

MASA: What were you taking last time?

TAKA: First was TC, next business and econ, next I dono.

MASA: Yeah, I'm kinda mixed up too.

TAKA: You too, Masa? Now, I thought you were the one who was going to be the doctor! Ever since I knew you, you were going to get an M.D. even if it killed you.

MASA: Yeah, I still want to continue in pre-med, but the way things are turning out . . . I don't know.

TAKA: Well, you can console yourself, you got a job. You're doing something.

MASA: Yeah, if you call it a job. $1.50 an hour pounding nails! Some fun. Give me a few years and mebbe I'll be foreman. [*Looks bitterly at his hardened hands*]

TAKA: You know, Masa, it isn't only Betty or women that's bothering me. I still wish I could find something I really wanna do, like you. You're damned lucky. You want to be a doctor and you're going to be one someday. Me, you know Masa, the Army gave me itchy feet. I want to buckle down, yet . . . I want to see some more. Now if I can find a woman who shares the same views, everything would be perfect! [*Clicks his tongue in his cheek*]

MASA [*smiles and shakes his head*]: Taka, you're the most unpredictable guy I ever knew. One minute you're serious like heck, the next, you act as if nothing in the world matters. [*Laughs*]

TAKA: Aww . . . I'm just too damned lazy to do anything, that's the whole trouble. Just one lazy baga.

MASA: You're just restless, Taka, like all the rest of us Sad Sacks. Why don't you go back to the U next semester? Maybe you'll find something to do. How about engineers? You never tried that, huh?

TAKA: No thanks. What a life! I'd get cross-eyed peering through that telescope day in and day out, and besides, I've done enough walking in the Army to last me a long time.

MASA [*laughs*]: Well, what about pre-med? You know, why don't you switch to the medics, then both of us could go to the States to finish up. Remember the night before we left Repple Depple in Naples? We talked about going to the States. You said you wanted to go to Illinois and I couldn't see it. I still don't—Michigan's the school, man! Gee, we sure were ambitious . . . the plans we made.

TAKA: Yeah, I remember. Kinda funny . . . no fight now. When you're over there, you sure do some wishful thinking. You know one guy I admire is Yoshi. I hear he's right on up at the University. He's in everything, full of fight. Ha, I remember the time we went on pass to Paris. We went to eat at a black market restaurant and they soaked us sixty bucks for two guys! Wow, never again.

MASA: Yeah, that French black market was terrific. One Frenchman offered me several hundred francs for my combat boots. [*Lifts his boot*]

TAKA: You should've sold them. But France, with all its Vosges mountains and wet and cold, is some place! Paris nice . . . I'm going back some day for more of that Champagne campaign.

[SHIG *enters from stage right. He limps, the result of severe injuries received in combat. He has only recently returned from a hospital on the mainland and still walks with a cane*]

SHIG: Hi. Watchu guys doing like two old ladies?

MASA and TAKA [*together*]: Hi, Shig!

TAKA: Wea you going?

SHIG: When I come up Kaimuki, wea you tink I go? No dumb questions, you! Wat you guys doing, eh?

MASA: Nothing, just chewing the fat.

SHIG: Boy, Honolulu one dead town, boy. No more nutting to do. Mo betta when I stay in New York.

MASA: Yeah, you shoulda got your discharge over there. I thought you going art school in N.Y.?

SHIG: Aw, da old lady tell me come home. Now no can go . . . too fool.

MASA: How about Chicago?

SHIG: No sir. Boy, das one pilau place and da cold wind! Tetsu guys shua can take it.

MASA: Oh, Tetsu guys went up? When?

SHIG: I dono. Coming-home-time I wen see him ova dea. We wen go look around the art school, den go eat. Boy, Tetsu fat baga now.

TAKA: How he got in?

SHIG: Aw, he smart, da guy. He wen regista befo he come home. Aw, anyway, I lazy go now. I going fool around li'l while.

MASA: Yeah, Shig, take it easy. Plenty of time. How's the leg?

[*They all look at* SHIG*'s leg*]

SHIG: Okay. Only when cold time, eh, inside sore. Da doc said going be sore while. No can walk fas, do' . . . Humbug. Mo betta cut om off.

TAKA: I dono Shig, I see Toku Motoyama walking around okay with his plastic leg, but he sure hates it.

MASA: Aw, well, he jus got it, dat's why. Wait till he gets used to it.

SHIG: Boy, I had good fun in da hospital. Da nurses, oh boy . . . some meats. Dey got a kick when I sing. One nurse especially ask me e—rytime, "go sing, go sing." Den she bring me candy and all kine stuff. Boy, her keed sista was some peach! Mama mia!

TAKA: You lucky bastard! Mo betta you stayed in the hospital.

SHIG: Yeah, come home no mo fun. Honolulu one small place, boy.

MASA: Sure, after New York, any place is small. I'd certainly like to be there now, huh?

SHIG: Huuh! Hey, Taka, dis guy talk like one kotonk! No? Yeah, I remomba in Shelby, one kotonk wahine used to chase him. Wat her name was? I foget, but Masa wen leave one broken heart, boy.

MASA [*embarrassed, he pushes* SHIG]: You're crazy.

TAKA: Yeah, what happened to the wahine, Masa? Maybe she's waiting, huh? [*Mimics* MASA. *He and* SHIG *laugh*]

MASA: Aw, she's only a friend.

SHIG: I dono about dat. In Shelby, boy, you la—dy killa! E—rytime dance, Masa right dea, boy, and mail call Hut 25, he da only guy get letter two time one week! [*He and* TAKA *laugh*]

TAKA: Hey, I never knew this, come on, Shig, tell me more.

SHIG: You know da time we went to Jerome fo da baseball game, eh, boy, firs ting we reach dea, Masa take off. We find him in da canteen wid one wahine. Eh, Masa, wat her name was? Mae? [*Turns to* MASA]

MASA [*blushing and feigning anger*]: I never knew a Mae.

[SHIG and TAKA *laugh*]

TAKA: Eh, Masa, you get sunburn or what, you face red!

[*More laughter. In the meantime,* DUKE *enters, walking with great strides from stage left. He is dressed in zoot-suit fashion: a pair of pin-striped black trousers with small cuffs; a pair of pointed black shoes; and a long gold chain, which dangles from one front pocket to the other. He wears a maroon-colored "Duke" shirt and his hair is "brilliantinely" shiny*]

DUKE: Wass da joke? Wass da joke, eh?

MASA: Hi, Duke!

TAKA: Eh, Duke, howzit!

SHIG: Oi, Paisan! Come esta!

DUKE: How's, howzit, paisanos?

TAKA: Where you going?

DUKE: Wassa matta, you no like I come see you, o wat? Wat you guys doing—laughing up? Man, I can hia you way down da bus stop!

SHIG: I was telling Taka about Masa and da wahines.

DUKE: Masa? Man! [*Guffaws*] Some guy, dat Masa. [*Points at* MASA] Ladies' man. [*Guffaws*]

MASA [*irritatedly*]: You guys sure can spread the bull.

DUKE [*with a mischievous grin on his face*]: Eh, Masa, who da signorita was who used to bring you ta-ma-go every morning in Leghorn? [*Makes a wolf whistle*] Bella signorina! Me, I tawt

shua dis time Masa got hooked! Man, man, everytime he go
drink wine wid da old man. [*Winks to others*] Eh, you know,
Masa, he no look like buddha-head, no? He look like hapa
. . . just like Sono Osato brada. Das why wahines go fo him,
das why.

[SHIG, TAKA, *and* DUKE *laugh.* MASA *blushes but grins never-
theless*]

MASA: What about you and the signora in Napoli? You know, the
     singing teacher . . .
DUKE: Da fat stuff? Strickly business, man, strickly business. I
     bring om one K-ration, she give one lesson. [*Begins to sing an
     Italian love song, amazingly in a rich tenor*] Good, eh?
TAKA: Too good, Duke!
SHIG: Boy, dose Italian signorinas sharp. One time we was looking
     fo cow near highway 66, sout' of Pistoin, eh, when we see one
     peachy signorina coming. She ask us fo candy, so we ask om fo
     amore. She tell us, "No for manjare." Sharp, boy.

[*They all laugh, especially* DUKE, *who is getting a great big
kick out of it*]

DUKE: Shua she going tell "for eat." Nobody like love up wid you
     ugly buddha-heads. [*Laughs loudly*]
TAKA: Hey, Duke, what you doing now?
DUKE: I working fo City and County Road Department. [*Leans on
     the fence and starts to fiddle with his long gold chain*]
SHIG: Wat! Still diggin' foxholes?
DUKE: Wassa matta—ass one good job. Scratch da road fifteen
     minute, take a blow half hour. Some life, man! [*They all
     laugh*] Wat you paisanos doing now? [MASA *makes a ham-
     mering motion and shows callouses on his hands*] Good fun,
     eh? How much you making?
MASA: $1.50 one hour.
DUKE: Man! You right on! You too, Taka? Still loafing?
TAKA: Yeah, still vacation. Terminal leave.
DUKE: Wassa matta, man? Mo betta you go join. Wass dat club
     dey got stateside? Oh yeah, 52/20. Das right, mo betta you

go start one 52/20 club in Honolulu, you molowa buddha-
head! Mo lazy den me!

TAKA: Never heard of that 52/20 club.

DUKE: How's da leg, man?

SHIG: Okay, no can walk good, do'.

DUKE: Yeah, man, you shua got om rough. Wat dey wen do in da
States?

SHIG: I dono, but dey put one stick inside.

DUKE: Yeah? [*Bends over to feel* SHIG's *leg*] Dat mortar shell shua
wen hit, man! Tanaka lose one eye, Shig almost lose his leg,
Yamamoto lose one piece scalp . . .

SHIG: Yeah, I wen see Tanaka in Washington. He said he no like
come home. I tink his wahine no like marry om.

DUKE: Crazy baga, if she no like om, man, I trow da kine wahine
away!

[MIYO *comes out to the porch and starts sweeping*]

MIYO: Ta-chan!

TAKA: What?

MIYO: Why don't you guys come inside and talk. Make noise outside!

[*All the men turn toward* MIYO]

DUKE [*waves in a Japanese fashion*]: Hello, Miyo-san. Do-
desu-ka?

MIYO [*bursts out laughing*]: Hello, Duke-san. Dozo agate kudasai. [*Smiles and beckons*]

DUKE: Arigato. Arigato.

MIYO: Masa and Shig, why don't you come in?

[MASA *and* SHIG *very shyly say thanks but remain where
they are*]

DUKE: You sista married?

do desu ka: how are you?
dozo agate kudasai: please come on in

TAKA: Nah. She going be old maid.

DUKE: Man, go shimpai me.

[*They all laugh*]

TAKA: You! You think I want one ugly baga like you for brother-in-law!

DUKE [*guffaws, slaps his knee; others laugh*]: You no tink me handsome guy. [*Gently pats a little wave in his hair*]

SHIG: You sista look like one kotonk in regimental headquarters. Boy, da bastard shua one to pull his rank. You pass om on da field and you no salute, eh, he call you back: "Corporal, don't you know, blah, blah" . . . da guy got no use fo me, boy.

DUKE: Yeah, jus like da benny-shave-tail in D Company. He talk beeg, eh, but when come time fo fight, Numba One go rear echelon. Man, li'l mo one buddha-head bus' om up. [*Spits through his teeth and nods his head*]

TAKA: Talking about rank, nobody can beat Okawa from first platoon. That son-of-a-bitch, just because he replace one first looey, he order us around like nobody's business.

DUKE: You mean da beeg baga . . . look like gorilla?

TAKA: Yeah.

SHIG: But one guy not dea was Lieutenant Toda. Boy, I like know how da hell one dumb Japanese like heem be officer. Everytime he get da names mix up. One time he almost make me do guard duty by mistake.

MASA: But the guy had a lotta guts though. Wiped out three jerry nests.

DUKE: Watchu talking—you silver star man. [*Pats* MASA *on the back*] You keep da star shiny, son?

[*All laugh*]

SHIG: Jits, da son-of-a-gun, he get one million-dollar wound. Tree months combat, eh, shrapnel scratch his feet, he no can walk, stretcher come take om. When he pass us he yell, "Hey paisanos, I got million-dollar wound." He no come back, da

shimpai: introduce

baga, he get jaundice afta dat. I tink maybe he swallow yellow shoe polish, no?

[JITS *comes slowly from left*]

JITS: Howzit?

[*The rest all greet him*]

DUKE: Eh Jits, how's da million dollar wound, man? [*Laughter*]
JITS: Right on, man, right on. [*Makes a circle with fingers*]
TAKA: You went your sister's?
JITS: Yeah, boy, da kid cry!
SHIG: Hey Jits, tell om about da million-dollar wound.
JITS: Dis Shige, how many times I gotta tell da same story . . .
MASA: Still working for engineers, Jits?
JITS: Yeah, Masa, still ova dea. You not going back to school?
MASA: Not yet, maybe bambai.
JITS: Wat about you, Taka, you not going back?
TAKA: I'm going back this semester.
SHIG: Wat you going take up?
TAKA: Oh, medics maybe.

[MASA *looks at* TAKA *in surprise*]

JITS: Wat? I tawt Masa hia was going be da doc. You too?
DUKE: Wassa matta, ass okay, eh?
JITS: Shua, shua. Chee, us no-brain guys no can go university. I
       give Masa and Taka credit.
SHIG: Yeah, if I go school, I tink I gotta start from first grade.
DUKE: First grade? Hahh, you no even can spell-out.
SHIG: Ah, shut up.

[*All laugh*]

JITS: You guys going States fo finish up?
MASA [*nods*]: We hope to.
JITS: Wea you going?
DUKE: Not Mississippi fo shua, wid dem chiggers.

[*Laughter*]

MASA: Naw. Taka's going to Illinois and I'm heading for Michigan.

JITS: Some ambitious guys! Eh, Shig, you going art school, eh?

SHIG: Long time mo yet. I tired now.

JITS: Me, I tink I get married.

DUKE: Dat's da stuff, you and me, dumb bagas, mo betta we get married, wat say, man? [*Slaps* JITS]

JITS: Yeah, but first we gotta find da wahines.

[*Laughter.* MRS. MIYAMOTO *and* TERUKO *come from stage right. Both are carrying packages. All the men laugh and greet them with nods*]

MRS. MIYAMOTO: Ma, Takashi, nashite uchie haira nai no? Takashi, mina tsurete aganasai?

[MASA *has opened the gate for her.* TERUKO, *who has been following her mother, is all smiles. She is a high school senior and quite pretty*]

TERUKO: Ta-chan, come in with the boys.

DUKE: Hello, Teru-chan, big ne-san now, huh? [MRS. MIYAMOTO *has already gone into the house.* TERUKO *laughs and runs upstairs*] You kid sista one cute kid. How old now?

TAKA: Seventeen, I think. Anyway, she's a senior in high school.

JITS: You interested, Duke?

DUKE: Shua, me, I like all wahines.

SHIG: No rob da cradle, you.

[*All laugh*]

TAKA: I think Masa has priority with Teru.

[MASA *looks at* TAKA, *quite astonished. They all begin teasing* MASA]

---

nashite uchie haira nai no: why don't you come on in; *mina tsurete aganasai:* bring everyone in
ne-san: older sister

JITS: Masa, da baga, waste time wid him around. Us guys no mo chance!

SHIG: Go home you. Boy! Even Taka's kid sista!

DUKE: Eh, Frankie, how you swoon om, anyway?

[MASA, *much abashed by the discovery that* TERUKO *is interested, blushes furiously*]

TAKA: I'm not spreading oil, the kid's got a crush on you, honest. [*They all laugh and punch* MASA] Masa, the swoon man!

JITS: Oh, Frankie!

SHIG: You send me, boy, you send me!

DUKE: Won't you show me how you do eet, signor?

TERUKO [*calling from the door*]: Ta-chan, okaa-san said for you folks to come inside for lunch.

DUKE: Eh, Teru-chan, watch out fo Masa, he's a ladykiller, you know.

[TERU *runs inside*]

TAKA: Eh, you guys, let's go inside eat.

JITS: Ah, my sista like me come back watch da kid today. I gotta go back.

TAKA: Oh, okay, Jits. Eh, Masa, stay, uh? How about you guys, Duke?

SHIG: Okay, I no mo nutting to do.

DUKE: Naw, bambai humbug fo you mada.

TAKA: Come on, Duke, next time I not going your house.

DUKE: Okay, okay.

JITS [*turning to go*]: I see you guys again. [*Exits left*]

TAKA: Okay, Jits, be seeing you.

SHIG [*waves his hand*]: Okay, Jits.

DUKE: Okay, paisan, so long!

[*All the men start to enter the gateway. They proceed on up the steps to the porch then indoors; but* MASA *and* TAKA *pause for a moment.* MASA *has stopped* TAKA *by holding his arm*]

okaa-san: mother

MASA: What was that crack about taking up pre-med? Were you just kidding, Taka, or are you really serious?

TAKA: Well . . . [*Rubs his head*] I dono, Masa, I'm not sure. But I was thinking . . . I never tried medicine before, although I used to think about it. Maybe if I got deep enough into it, it may be what I want to study . . . I used to like zoology. Besides, I like the idea of going to the States with you, even Michigan, you son-of-a-gun! [*Punches* MASA]

MASA: You sure are unpredictable, Taka, but I'm glad. You know, maybe I *can* get my brother to look after Mom for a while. He hates school so he won't be going to the U, and he's not getting married for a long time yet. Yeah, I'll talk to the kid tonight.

TAKA: Sure, Masa, he's making good money now, he can take good care of her for the time being. And, say, you can get disability compensation to help pull you through up in the States.

MASA: Disability compensation for what?

TAKA: For your malaria. That plus your sixty-five bucks subsistence oughta carry you for a while.

MASA: Yeah, but my malaria's not bothering me.

TAKA: Not now, but it came out once since you came home. Aw, what the hell. You got it and you might as well cash in on it!

MASA: Okay, okay. I'll go down the VA about it. But we have to work fast. If we send applications to the mainland now, we may be able to get in just about the time we're ready to go.

TAKA: Hey, I feel good already. I'm raring to go! You know, after we get our M.D.'s, we can open an office together. Just imagine, Masa, Miyamoto and Sakata, Physicians and Surgeons. [*Makes gestures with his hand indicating a sign*]

MASA [*laughing at* TAKA]: Wait a minute, we still have a long way to go yet! [*Laughs again at* TAKA*'s exuberance*]

TAKA: Hell, this is the first time I wanted to study since I came back. Michigan, here we come! [*Places his arm around* MASA, *opens the screen door and both go in*]

Curtain

Oranges Are Lucky

EDITOR'S NOTE

In *Oranges Are Lucky* the theme is cultural accommodation, and the external action, including the conflict with Ricky, is only a backdrop for the more important developments which take place within the main character.

Standard English and pidgin are used to distinguish Ah Po's private thoughts and reminiscences from her exchanges with her family. Her memories are related in a formal, neutral English to indicate that she is thinking in Chinese; this gives the memories and the life they construct a felt authenticity, and contrasts them to the more conventional social interchanges of the group, where pidgin is spoken.

Though the drama unfolds nominally in one place, the device of the spot-lit shifts to Ah Po when she is recalling her past "opens out" the action in time and space. The designer of the 1981 Kumu Kahua revival production emphasized the impact of these shifts by filling in the details of the restaurant—fan, screen, and especially the meal—as much as possible, and making the lighting change extreme. This enabled us to see better the disparity between Ah Po's past and present, the root of her inner conflict.

ORANGES ARE LUCKY *was first produced by Kumu Kahua and the Leeward Community College Drama Program at Leeward Community College Theatre for a season beginning on January 9, 1976.*

Cast

DEBBIE	*Melanie Meiling Ching*
JON	*Rod Goshi*
ESTHER	*Donna M. K. Spencer*
AH PO	*Phyllis Look*
DANE	*Mana Chung*
PETE	*Tom K. C. Kam*
RICKY	*Clayton Wai*
DENNIS	*Richard Kon*

Directed by Dennis Dubin
Lighting by Don Olson, Richard Kon, Rod Goshi
Make-up by Bryan Furor

Oranges Are Lucky

BY

DARRELL H. Y. LUM

Characters

AH PO, *grandmother, 81*
DEBBIE (Ah Yin), *granddaughter*
JON, *Debbie's Japanese boyfriend*
ESTHER, *daughter*
DANE (Ah Gnip), *the younger grandson*
PETE, *son-in-law, Esther's husband*
RICKY (Ah Jiu), *older grandson, Dane's brother*
DENNIS (Ah Yong), *a grandson*
WAITRESS

A small, simple Chinese restaurant. The walls are plain and bare except for a folding oriental screen painted and inlaid with garish scenes of Chinese village life. There is an electric fan in the corner with a couple of red ribbons fluttering from the wire shield. There is a round table, center stage, set for a nine-course dinner. Two other tables, similarly set, flank the main table.

[*At curtain rise,* DEBBIE *and her boyfriend,* JON, *are the first to arrive at the restaurant.* JON *is carrying a birthday cake in a cardboard box and a lei in a plastic bag*]

DEBBIE [*looks around, makes a face at the restaurant's plainness*]: Well, Bahk Hoo said dis place serves good food. Da main ting is dat dey give lots for our family.

JON: Yeah, your uncle always like dis kine no-class kine place. Remembah las' time he went pick da restaurant? He went pick someplace in Chinatown dat everybody come in and eat in their undershirt. Ass too much dat!

DEBBIE: Maybe we can put crepe paper or something, get one drugstore down da street . . .

JON [*sarcastically*]: And maybe we can get some of those toot horns and party hats and dose tings dat shoot out and uncurl when you blow 'em . . .

[JON *and* DEBBIE *sit at the table and look unhappy.* DEBBIE *takes off the flower in her hair and arranges it in the middle of the table as a centerpiece*]

JON: Look kinda had it, yeah?

DEBBIE: Shut up . . . you got da lei?

JON [*irritably*]: I got da lei, I got 'em.

[AUNTY ESTHER, UNCLE PETE, *and* AH PO *enter.* AH PO *is in a wheelchair and* PETE *is pushing her.* AH PO *looks about distractedly. She has a shawl and a lap blanket. She pulls the shawl closer to her shoulders, and clutches her handbag as she looks around*]

ESTHER [*reading the plates*]: Here, Ah Po. Hou Hou Chop Suey. Very Good Chop Suey. One ting fo sure, da pakes not shame when dey name restaurants. [*Looks around quickly*] It nice, Ah Po. Nice. Look, Debbie and Jon stay already.

[PETE *wheels* AH PO *into the middle seat of the center table.* JON *moves a chair out of the way.* DEBBIE *comes up and kisses* AH PO *on the cheek and presses an envelope into the woman's hand.* AH PO *does not recognize* DEBBIE *and looks around confused.* PETE *and* ESTHER *sit on either side of* AH PO]

DEBBIE: Happy birthday, Ah Po. This is Jon, my friend.
ESTHER [*whispering as she interprets for* AH PO]: Ah Debbie . . . Debbie boyfriend . . . Jon.

[ESTHER *takes the envelope from* AH PO*'s hand, rips it open, and records the amount of the gift in a notebook*]

ESTHER: Debbie, ten dollars.
DEBBIE [*corrects* ESTHER]: Das from me and Jon, Aunty.
ESTHER: Yeah, yeah. Debbie and Jon. [*Scribbles*]

[AH PO, *still confused, suddenly recognizes the voice and breaks into a smile. She reaches out and takes* DEBBIE*'s hand*]

AH PO: Ah Yin, eh. Tank you, eh . . . dough jay . . . tank you. Yahk chiahng . . . eat orangee? [AH PO *rummages about her feet as if there were a bag of oranges there. She offers* DEBBIE *an imaginary orange*] Nicee girl . . . nicee girl.
DEBBIE: No, Ah Po, I no like oranges. Bumbye come fat.
ESTHER [*laughing, repeats loudly to* AH PO]: She say bumbye she come fat . . .
AH PO [*leans toward* ESTHER *to catch her words*]: Ah . . . bumbye come fat like Ah Po. Ah Po fat, but she get good children, good grandchildren, even if dey all too skinny.

[JON *approaches* AH PO *with the lei. He bends over and presents it to her quickly, and pecks her on the cheek. He steps back next to* DEBBIE]

JON: Happy birthday . . . um . . . Ah Po?
ESTHER: Debbie boyfriend, Jon. [*Louder*] Debbie . . . Ah Yin . . . boyfriend, Jon. [*Scribbles in notebook*] Lei from Jon.

[AH PO *sticks out her hand formally for a handshake.* JON *comes forward and shakes it softly*]

AH PO: Tank you, tank you. [*Looks* JON *over, then whispers to* ESTHER] What kine boy?

ESTHER: Japanee boy, nice boy. Work shipyard with Pete. Nice boy, hard worker.

AH PO [*disapprovingly*]: Japanee boy? Get plenty Chinee boy, why she like Japanee boy? You shua he nice boy?

ESTHER: Yes, yes. He nice boy. Hard worker, Pete say.

[ESTHER *reaches over and fills a small teacup with tea, and motions to* JON *to serve it to* AH PO]

JON: Here, Ah Po. You like tea? I bring you tea.

AH PO: Ahh . . . yum cha . . . drink tea. I like tea, nice boy.

[AH PO *starts to rummage through her purse for lee-see, money wrapped in red paper to give as a gift. She cannot find any, so she pulls out a sheaf of red papers. She looks through her wallet but brings no money out, and folds an empty lee-see for* JON. JON *is uncomfortable as* AH PO *hands him the red paper*]

AH PO: Hia, you nicee boy . . . tank you, tank you.

JON [*starts to refuse the gift*]: No, no need nothing, it's your birthday.

DEBBIE: Take 'em Jon. Bumbye Ah Po tink you too good for her.

AH PO: Nice boy . . . nice Japanee boy. Ah Goong, you fahdah, Esther, before time he say, Japanee no good . . . no good marry Japanee. Must keep da family strong . . . alla same blood, keep 'em pure. I everytime tell him dat da Japanee buy at his store all da time and he still talk bad about dem. He say dat business dat, business okay but marry is different. Marry Japanee no good, business okay. He say Japanee like to spend dey money anyway, so mo bettah da Chinee man take from dem den da haole man. Chinee man mo fair den haole man store. Ah Goong he say dat but I watch him sometime when da Japanee man come buy meat, he leave da bone and plenny fat on top da meat. Or when he weigh da chicken, he leave da liver and gizzard and da chicken head on da scale. Chinee man come inside da store, neva mind Ah Goong

don't know da man, as long as Chinee man, he cut off da fat
and he no weigh da liver and gizzard, and he let anybody
Chinee come pick chicken feet from da scrap bin fo free.
Even he save da pig blood fo da Filipino man fo free everytime he kill pig. But da Japanee mans dat come inside da
store, he no give dem nutting. He say Japanee man no treat
wahine good, but da Japanee ice man always nice to me when
he come. He treat me good. Ah Goong he go wild if he tink I
talk to da ice man. He say we gotta teach our daughta right, so
no talk to Japanee. So I have to listen to him . . . He my husband so I have to listen. But I tink Japanee not so bad. Japanee smart fo grow garden. One time I ask da ice man how to
grow vegetable good. He tell me put egg shell inside da dirt
and put milk water inside da dirt. When Chew Mung, you
folks Ah Goong, eat da cabbage he ask me wea I learn how
grow so good cabbage. I like tell him from da Japanee ice man
but I no can say dat. I jes' smile and say it da secret of my garden. [*To* JON] You nicee Japanee boy. You take care of my
grandchild. You be nice husband to her. You my secret in da
garden.

JON: Tanks, Ah Po, tank you, but we not going get married
    yet . . .

ESTHER: Shhh . . . Jon, enough.

DEBBIE: Nuff already, Jon. She likes you, pau.

[*Lights dim, single spot on* AH PO]

AH PO: Shh, Ah Po . . . should not speak to the Japanese. Chew
    Mung will punish you and not permit you to play mah jong
    on Sundays. He will not let you buy sweet oranges or go into
    Chinatown to talk and shop. He will make you go to the
    temple every day and chant and pray with the bald-headed
    monks. All the monks are fat . . . there are no thin monks. It
    must be their poverty . . . ha! Do the monks cheat like how
    Chew Mung cheats the Japanese? Do they pray less for those
    who cannot make a big offering? Does the Buddha know?
    Sometimes when I kneel and chant and pray with my eyes
    closed tightly I can see the great Buddha's arm move. It is a

blessing to see the Buddha's arm move, just a fraction of an inch. A sign. I wonder if the monks see that, or perhaps it is they who make it move. Debbie has a Japanese boyfriend . . . She asks her Ah Goong for his blessing, Chew Mung. Will your eyes soften and move slightly in your way of saying "yes"? I shall go to the temple to see if the Buddha's hand moves. I think it will. I cannot defy you Chew Mung, I talked to the ice man. He taught me how to grow the vegetables . . . but you liked the vegetables. His Japanese soul is in those eggshells and milk water that fed the cabbages . . . and you ate them, Chew Mung. You ate the Japanese man's love for the plants. Does that make you part of the man's soul? Does that make your blood impure? [*Lights come up again*] You folks grandfahdah, your Ah Goong, going know dat I neva listen to him when we meet again in heaven. He not going to let me come until I pray some mo. You going do dat fo me? And afta one month you going back to da temple fo ask da monk if I wen go heaven okay. No let da fat monks cheat you. Maybe you going have to bring some mo offerings and fold and burn some mo dead peopo's money. Maybe mo den fo anybody else because I neva listen to my husband and I neva follow his word and I mock da fat monks and talk to da Japanee ice man . . . His vegetables dey grow so good . . .

ESTHER: Ah Po, Ah Po . . . Mama, enough already . . . stop. No talk dat kine.

[JON *is still standing at her feet, frozen, his hands clutching the red paper lee-see.* RICKY *and* DANE, *two brothers, enter.* DANE *has long hair and is comfortably dressed.* RICKY *is nattily dressed and chic.* DANE *approaches* AH PO *and gives her a red envelope. She looks around confused until* ESTHER *introduces* DANE]

ESTHER: Dis Ah Kong's youngest boy, Dane. [*To* DANE] What's you Chinese name? You know, Ah Goong name all you folks. Your grandfahdah give da Chinese name to all the grandchildren.

DANE: Hoong Gnip . . . Ah Gnip.

[AH PO *recognizes the name and reaches up to touch* DANE *and fingers his hair. She mutters something about hair*]

ESTHER: Ah Po say you should braid your hair into a queue like the old Chinese plantation workers. She say she used to put fish hooks inside da braid so when da Hawaiian kids tease and pull your fahdah's hair, they get poked in da hand.

DANE: Aw . . . Ah Po . . . maybe I cut for you? [*Makes a cutting motion*]

AH PO [*laughs*]: No cut . . . no cut. Nice hair, keep good hair. You fahdah no mo hair bumbye, so one son must have hair fo fahdah and son. Goodoo Boy. Tank you, dough jay, dough jay. Yahk orangee . . . eat orangee, lucky.

[AH PO *starts to rummage around again in her purse. Gives* ESTHER *the envelope.* ESTHER *opens and records the gift*]

DANE: No, Ah Po . . . umm yahk, no like.

AH PO [*offers an imaginary orange*]: Here yahk orange, goodoo boy . . . eat. Lucky.

DANE [*accepts* AH PO's *gift from her empty hands*]: Dough jay, Ah Po. Dough jay, tank you.

AH PO [*smiling to* ESTHER]: Dis boy always like eat orangee. Only when he eat orangee, he talk Chinee, he say "dough jay," he say "dough jay, Ah Po," no?

ESTHER [*patiently*]: Yes, Ah Po.

DANE: Aunty Esther, when you going ask Ah Po fo tell me about long time ago? You went tell her what I tol you? It important fo get 'em all down before she die. Da family tree, la dat. So dat everybody can tell how was in da olden days.

ESTHER: Yeah, yeah. No talk like she going die already. You only get her upset. She only talk about dat kine stuff when she feel like it anyway. Sometimes I tink she make up all her stories, so waste time. She cannot jes' sit and talk to you anyway, you lolo, in Chinese.

DANE: I know Aunty, ass why I need you fo help. All you gotta do is call me whenever she feel like talking. Or else, I lend you my tape recorder or you can jes' write 'em down afterwards.

ESTHER: Waste time dat kine. If we was royalty or something, maybe worth it. But you Ah Po only from one court official's family, small potatoes dat.

DANE: Yeah, but Ah Po feet dey was bound, eh? So dat must mean dey was kinda important, eh?

ESTHER: No mean nutting dat. Probably mean your great grandfather had big ideas. Jes' like your Uncle Pete, all bullshit ideas. Besides, if you so hot on dis kine family tree stuff, why you never learn Chinese in da first place?

DANE: Chee Aunty, dat was small-kid time. Everybody like be American, no good be China jack. You gotta fit when you small-kid time. I know was stupid dat, 'cause now I no can understand nutting. Yahk chiahng, yahk chiahng, eat oranges, ass all I know.

DEBBIE: Yeah, no? You know, before time, I thought Ah Po was one dumb dodo because all she ever ask me was "yahk" something, "eat orange or eat rice" la dat. And I always say "no," 'cause shame, eh?

JON [*teasing*]: No look like you *always* said "no."

DEBBIE: Shaddup, Jon.

DANE: Aunty Esther, you try ask Ah Po for me. C'mon Aunty, no tell me she no talk anykine stuff with you.

ESTHER: Ass all old stuff, no good talk about long time ago. No use, ancient history. You was right when you was small kid, da Chinese ways waste time, might as well be American. Too much dat kine talk no good for Ah Po. Bumbye she tink too much about dying and den she like go back China fo die. Nope, no good dat.

AH PO: Ah Gnip, Ah Gnip . . .

DANE: Yes, Ah Po.

AH PO: Ah Gnip, you cannot get married until Ah Jiu find one wife, okay? You wait fo him. Dat show respect.

DANE: Yes, Ah Po. You no need worry.

AH PO: Ah Jiu, wea Ah Jiu?

ESTHER: Ricky, come. Ah Po like talk to you.

PETE: Hey, Ricky, come have one beer.

RICKY: Okay, what you got?

PETE: Only Primo. I know you folks is Michelob people but ass all I got.

RICKY: Nah, Primo is good.

ESTHER: Ricky, Ricky, Ah Po like ask you something. Ah Po, dis Ricky over here, Ah Kong's number one son.

RICKY: Yeah, yeah. Howzit, grandma, how's it goin'. Oh, I get a little someting here fo you.

[RICKY *reaches into his wallet and withdraws a five, looks up to see* ESTHER *watching him, then withdraws another five-dollar bill. He spreads them out and presses them into* AH PO*'s hands*]

AH PO [*looks around. To* ESTHER]: Wea Ah Jiu? . . . Ah Jiu, Ah Kong's boy . . .

ESTHER: Right here, Ah Po.

RICKY: Yeah, I right here grandma. I right here . . . Ricky. I give you present. [*Points to* AH PO*'s hands*] Aunty, tell her ass me dat talking.

AH PO: Wea Ah Jiu? Firs, Ah Jiu find nice Chinee girl. Ah Jiu, you get married so Ah Gnip can marry. You numbah one boy, marry firs, den take care you fahdah . . .

ESTHER: Ricky, Ah Po ask if you married yet. She like you find one nice Chinee girl. I tink she like set you up with one rich widow at da temple. Not too nice body but plenny money! [*Laughs and tells her joke to* AH PO]

AH PO: Hai-lo . . . yes, get nice lady at da temple fo Ah Jiu. [*Turns serious*] What about da Yim's daughter? Nice girl fo you. She make plenny children fo you. She come from good family too. Ah Jiu, you like orangee? Yahk chiahng.

[AH PO *begins to rummage about again. Her hands open and drop the money on the floor. She offers* RICKY *an imaginary orange*]

RICKY: Ah Po, your money on da floor. I no like orange. I no like get married. [*Increasingly louder*] I no like Yim's daughter. I no like Chinee girls. [*Turns to* ESTHER] Eh, she senile already. I dunno why I bother, waste time. Pete, where my beer?

AH PO [*frightened by the ruckus*]: Ah Jiu, Ah Jiu.

RICKY: Ah Jiu . . . I dunno who Ah Jiu is. Ah Jiu no stay, grand-ma. [*Laughs cruelly*]

ESTHER [*to* AH PO]: Ricky . . . Ah Jiu, he work hard today. Ah Jiu give you lee-see, Ah Po. [*Bends over to pick up the money, puts it back into* AH PO*'s hand*]

AH PO: He no like Chinee girl? He no marry? Wassamalla him? Chinee girl good fo Ah Jiu. She cook fo him, she make plenny children fo him. Why he no like? Ah Goong name Hoong Jiu. Dat mean "successful businessman," and all da grand-children have da Chinese name "successful." Ah Jiu, every-time he quiet boy, no talk, him . . . Aie, I no bring coconut candy fo Ah Jiu. Maybe next time he tell me get married. You tell him no need be Chinee girl. Now modern days, okay marry Japanese, maybe haole, anykine girl okay. Ah Jiu get married, be happy, den Ah Gnip get married. I go temple and pray for Ah Jiu. Maybe da Buddha help me find one nice girl fo Ah Jiu. Bumbye no marry, no have children fo da fam-ily name . . . [*Lights dim*] Mama, who is that man who came to talk to Daddy? Am I to marry him, he is old! That is Chew Mung's father? Am I to marry Chew Mung? What is he like? Why cannot I see Chew Mung? Oh great Buddha, please make my husband happy and make me a good wife. They say he is a wise man. I hear so many things about Chew Mung. He comes from a scholar's family, he is a professor of philoso-phy, he can do calligraphy, he can write poems. He is the most important man in the world. But Mama, we are not rich. We have a good family name but I am not educated. What if Chew Mung does not like me? What if he disobeys his father and does not want to marry me? I cannot do calligraphy, we do not have many servants. My feet are bound. I do not know the wise sayings. I cannot be a good wife, Mama, say that I need not marry Chew Mung. Tell Daddy that I cannot marry, that I am barren and cannot have children. I will go to the temple to live. I will learn to cook for the monks. I cannot become an important lady in this family of good name. I can-not even become a simple farmer, my feet are useless. Say that to him. I cannot marry Chew Mung . . . [*Lights come up*] When I see you Ah Goong he look mean. He said da wisdom of our fahdahs is greatest and we gotta listen to dem. He brought me candy and sweet oranges. Ah Goong, he was a good man, he had a good name.

ESTHER: Ah Po, time fo eat. I tell da manager to start bringing da food, eh? Yahk fahn, Ah Po . . . time fo eat rice, Ah Po. Everybody sit down, the food is coming.

RICKY: Da old lady stop running off at da mout? Jeesus, might as well shoot me if I evah come la dat. Crazy, man. Old age, senile already.

DEBBIE [*trying to smooth things over*]: Ricky, come sit over here by us. You still working post office?

RICKY: Oh yeah, through rain and snow and sleet and hail.

DANE: And through goofing-off and pay raises and slow mail.

PETE: Chee, all you gov'ment workers da same. You tink you ripping-off Uncle Sam? Das me you ripping-off, ass my tax money.

DANE: I thot you was Uncle Pete.

PETE: I put da stamps on top da envelope and still take tree days fo my letter get across Pali. I used to have one carrier pigeon dat could fly across da Pali and back in ten hours. Dey oughta replace all you guys with a bunch of birds.

[*Everybody laughs*]

DANE: Dey already close, Uncle. All da carriers get bird brain anyway.

RICKY: You guys jes' jealous.

[*Waitress brings the first course*]

ESTHER: Bird nest soup everybody. Put your bowls close. Jon, you scoop out da soup. You da only one here not related so you can scoop da most even. Bumbye everybody say when I serve, get favortism. Dis bunch fo complain. Da first bowl go to Ah Po.

JON: Here Ah Po, da first bowl.

ESTHER: Ah Po, Jon-boy give you soup. He nice boy.

AH PO: Goodoo boy. You scoop fo you Ah Goong too. He like fresh parsley and wid one jigger whiskey inside.

PETE: Right, Ah Po . . . likker. Who like likker for put inside da soup? Bring you jigger, everybody bring you jigger. Ricky, where you jigger, you pilute, you drunkard?

RICKY: Right here.

ESTHER: Jon, no forget make bowls for Gary and his wife. And Cousin Dennis never come yet. Make one bowl for him too.

PETE: Who no mo likker? Debbie, put some tea inside your jigger so make 'em look like whiskey, so you can toast Ah Po. Okay, everybody ready? Okay, Ah Po. [*Everybody raises a jigger and stands*] To our Ah Po, who is eighty-one years old today. Happy birthday, Ah Po. [*Some start to sit, Pete stops them*] Wait, you guys, one mo round, gotta toast da soup. You gotta do dis right, bumbye bad luck.

DEBBIE [*to* JON]: My Uncle Pete famous for making da toasts. Dis way he get loaded by da fifth course and den, you watch, he going play Chinese junk-ena-po by da ninth course. Ass one game where da loser gotta drink one jigger. So my Uncle everytime lose on purpose. Funny, man, when get two guys trying fo lose on purpose.

PETE [*completes re-filling the jiggers*]: Okay, everybody, bottoms up to da soup.

RICKY, DANE, JON [*together*]: To da soup.

AH PO [*observing the toasting*]: Pete, you forget pour fo Chew Mung. You not supposed to drink until da children's goong goong went drink. [*Lights dim*] I have forgotten my place, Chew Mung. I will do as you say and pray for forgiveness. I do not think forgiveness will come until morning. I am sorry I disgraced you in front of your scholarly friends. You are of such a high position and I am so lowly. My feet are bound but it is not an indication of court life, it is a mistake. I am too lowly for you. There is a way for everything you say. And it is through these ways that we learn respect and the order of things. The children must have respect. I have to earn my respect by respecting you, Chew Mung. You are so solemn.

You only speak to me when I do wrong. And you speak in level and even tones . . . as you would do to a simple person or to a child. You wish the children to stay at home and to study as you study. You wish them to be doctors and poets and historians. They fear you, your children do. They mock and mimic your stern and solemn ways. They do not like school and the town talks of the professor's children who have no respect for their elders. Noisy, boisterous children who do not listen. They only ask why, why, why. Drink Chew Mung. Drink your whiskey and study your poems, and while you sleep, I shall comfort the children and play with them and put them finally to bed. Then I shall hold your head in my lap and look into your face to catch some of the wisdom that you give off in your sleep. I shall clip the hairs in your nose and your ears, and stroke the one long hair from your mole. You treasure it so . . . Chew Mung, I am not wise enough for you. You cannot discuss philosophy with me and I cannot discuss the children with you. [*Lights brighten*]

PETE [*loudly*]: Everybody put one shot whiskey inside da soup. Make 'em ono, boy. C'mon Debbie, jes' little bit, I no tell your mother. Dis going to make your complexion come smooth, give you rosy cheeks.

DEBBIE: Sure, Uncle, sure. Make me real drunk too, eh?

ESTHER: Where dose cousins of yours, Debbie? Their soup getting cold.

RICKY: Yeah, might as well I eat 'em. No good let 'em get cold. [*Silence*] Jeesus, you guys leave one bowl out fo grandpa. He's dead. You leave bowl out for people who probably not goin' come, maybe dey never goin' come. Why? 'Cause das da custom. Custom gotta have meaning, you guys gotta tink about what da meaning of tings. If tings don't have meaning, what's da use!

ESTHER: Ricky, serve you Ah Po tea. Use two hands now.

[DENNIS *enters, dressed in black with white patent leather belt and shoes. A jade medallion hangs from his chest*]

DEBBIE: Here comes da late kung-fu master. Eh, Dennis, where you was, out at some bar fighting evil?

DENNIS: Eh, howzit everybody. I sorry I late, Ah Po. Where da tea, I supposed to serve Ah Po tea, eh?

PETE: Aw, you just bucking for get one lee-see, you buggah.

[DENNIS *pours some tea and serves it to* AH PO. *He leaves an envelope in front of her on the table*]

DENNIS: Here, Ah Po, happy birthday. I sorry I late.

ESTHER: Ah Po, dis Ah Yong . . . Ah Yong.

DENNIS: Aunty Esther, tell Ah Po I sorry I late. Tell her I bring her some grapefruit, some boo-look. Nice kine. Tell her ass from da tree Ah Goong plant for my daddy when he get married and den my daddy plant for me when I got married. Still come out sweet dese buggahs.

[DENNIS *takes a few fruit out of a paper bag and passes it around the table. Each person holds it for a while, then it is passed to* AH PO]

AH PO [*confused as to where all the large fruit are coming from*]: Ai-ya? Boo-look . . . who get boo-look? Look like da boo-look you Ah Goong bring me when we get married . . . [*Lights dim*] We must stack the fruit in the window, Chew Mung, so that they can ripen and sweeten. I will stack them in pyramids of grapefruit and oranges and tangerines. The Chinese celebrate around citrus fruits. They are lucky fruit. To fruit is to have children and to be abundant. To be fruitful is to be prosperous. You wanted to be fruitful, Chew Mung. You were such an important person, but you saw a land of fruit. Hawaii, where there are trees that bear oranges the year long they told you. You left your friends in China, all the ones who came to you for advice because of your wisdom and your station and your education. Your friends with whom you discussed your calligraphy and your poetry. I told you to be a pioneer then, if it was your fate to go to Hawaii . . . You would give up your name and your station to go to America?

In America there are no classes. They do not listen to their elders. Respect is earned there, it is not automatic. They do not respect mere family names, they respect the person. Respect in America is better, it is earned and it is more reliable in the end . . . Sometimes I forget that when I expect the children and the grandchildren to listen to me. They are all good children, Chew Mung; you have not failed. I have failed because my feet were useless to you in the new land . . . I am a burden to you on this ship. It is a long journey and I insist that you carry me up and down the boat stairs because I am too slow to hobble after you up and down the decks . . . I left my home of oranges and fruits and sweet air to ride a boat to come with you to Hawaii, and to adventures I thought. I always thought I would be going to another land of oranges and grapefruit. That would show my simple parents. I refused to become like them. I was bored with the life of a court official's daughter. I was tired of your fruit, the fruit you brought me because it was how you were instructed to behave . . . I am tired of your fruit, Chew Mung! [*Picks up a grapefruit and throws it weakly*] I want adventures. I do not wish to watch your fruit ripen in my window . . .

[*Lights brighten. Everyone is eating heartily*]

ESTHER: Ah Po, eat chicken, hau yau chicken, oyster sauce chicken.

PETE: Drink, everybody, drink to the chicken. C'mon, Ricky, Dane, no scared 'em. Drink up. Dennis, I no need ask him twice, da pee-lute. Better hide da bottle from him.

DENNIS: Chee, you guys only tease, eh? My hands stay deadly weapons. You bettah watch out, they might jes' flick out dere and injure and maim you.

PETE: Ha, da only deadly ting about you is you mout . . .

RICKY: Or his futs. Dey silent and sneaky.

ESTHER: Shhh, you boys, enough.

DANE: Whoa, the next one here already. You guys better eat faster. Uncle, your toasts, dey slowing down, you not keeping up wit da courses.

ESTHER: You not forgetting to leave some on Gary and his wife plate, eh?

RICKY: Sure. And for Ah Goong, and for his Ah Goong and for the grandfather of his grandfather . . .

PETE: Ass Ricky getting smart? Cut off his likker supply, let him die of thirst.

RICKY [*gasping in mock horror*]: No, no, anyting but dat. Ah Po, Ah Po. I making plate for Ah Goong. He going enjoy his plate. [*Begins to pick at the plate set aside for Ah Goong*] Lemme test one piece here. Oh goong goong, dis buggah is ono. You oughta try one piece. What, you let me try for you? Okay. Eh, Ah Goong, you should be here whacking 'em in. Man, you get good life when you dead. Jes' like when we lug the roast pig up to Manoa cemetery every year, rain or shine. We always wait until the candles all burn down before we put da food away. Dose candles signify da repast of da dead. We burn dead people's money for you to spend in heaven, Ah Goong. We leave one bowl of food by da side of da gravestone for da caretaker of your grave and da guardian of your soul. You sucker, you sucking Ah Goong, you suck us dry with your Chinese ways. Waste time, Ah Goong, waste time! [*Louder and louder. The table is dead quiet*] Ah Po, you good-for-nutting. Nobody can understand you and you no can understand us. So what's the use, you're just as good as dead.

ESTHER: Ricky, keep quiet. Ah Po no can understand you when you mad.

AH PO: Ah Jiu, yahk orangee, yahk fruit. You eat, have good luck . . . you eat . . .

ESTHER: Pete, start getting the cake ready so we can sing Happy Birthday.

JON: I help you put da candles.

PETE: You went bring eighty candles? Mo bettah just put one propane torch on top dis cake. We go just put some so dat Ah Po get something fo blow out.

AH PO: When your Ah Goong say we come to Hawaii, I say good, good. I keep telling him I no like live like my muddah and my fahdah, I want someting new and exciting. So you Ah Goong quit being professor and he save his money and sell his house. He say he start one school in Hawaii . . . one Chinee language school. [*Lights dim*] I hate this boat, Chew Mung. I hate the ocean. The motion of the boat makes me ill and my feet make it hard for me to go on the deck to get fresh air. I curse you, Chew Mung. I want to go back home. There are only poor people on this boat. There are no servants. Only common people. I will not cook rice, that is servant's work . . . Ah Goong, he did his best to please me. He would buy salted fish and oranges and cook the rice. He would make me eat and not speak of home any more. He did not write any more poetry and he did not seek out people to talk philosophy. These are useless occupations, he said. He worked in the ship kitchen and became a meat cutter. He learned bookkeeping from a man who could make the abacus beads fly. He never talked of starting school again. I kept asking him, I asked him over and over, Chew Mung, our house in Hawaii, how many rooms will it have? How many servants will we have? How many orange trees can we have? He always said we will have enough. Not more, or less. We will have enough. Chew Mung said when we come to Hawaii we must be like Americans and do things in the right way. We must learn English and the new ways. I had no big house, no servants, no orange trees. I stayed in the house and refused to learn English. We lived above the store where he worked . . . I want to move out of here, Chew Mung. You say that poetry and philosophy is worthless, waste time, you say. It is good that you learned meat cutting and bookkeeping. I will only talk Chinese to you. I will only go to the Chinese stores. I will only eat Chinese food. Things American are no good. I do not want my children to become American. Why don't they listen to me? Chew Mung, why don't they listen to me . . . [*Lights brighten*]

ESTHER: Blow out da candles, Ah Po. It good luck, you blow out da candles. Good luck, Ah Po . . . jes' like orange.

DEBBIE: Make one wish first, Ah Po . . . Hurry up before da candles burn down.

[AH PO *looks confused, she doesn't understand what's going on*]

ESTHER: Ah Po, you make one wish, something that you want to make you happy, den you blow out da candles. If you blow out all da candles one time, you lucky and you wish come true.

AH PO: I make a wish . . . I want . . .

DEBBIE: Ah Po, you not supposed to say da wish aloud . . .

AH PO [*looks around quizzically*]: . . . I make wish . . . I wish to be American . . . da first president is George Washington.
[AH PO *takes a deep breath, gets ready to blow*]

Blackout

Curtain

All Brand New
Classical Chinese Theatre

EDITOR'S NOTE

All Brand New Classical Chinese Theatre has a similar theme to that of *Oranges Are Lucky,* but in other respects it offers a sharp contrast. The difficulties of cultural accommodation are presented from the point of view of a character much younger than Ah Po, so it is appropriate that the play's style is aggressively iconoclastic. The clash of values and loyalties is dynamically worked into the play's form, with its weather-vane transitions and parodies of Chinese opera and western soap opera. The initial productions successfully employed hilarious collisions between eastern and western scenic and acting techniques. There is ample external conflict in the plot: between son and mother, son and girl friend, mother and girl friend, mother and roommate, girl friend and roommate. But again the more important conflict is the internal one between Michael's two selves, which is the trampoline for all the devices used to depict his schizophrenia.

ALL BRAND NEW CLASSICAL CHINESE THEATRE *was first produced by Kumu Kahua at the Kennedy Laboratory Theatre for a series of performances beginning on July 21, 1978.*

Cast

MICHAEL 1	*Russell Omori*
MICHAEL 2	*Timothy Sean Hayes*
DAVID	*Kelly Ray*
MOTHER	*Sherrie Kido*
JENNY	*Bunny Hartman*

Directed by John McShane
Assistant Director Rod Martin
Music directed by Kelly Ray
Musicians: Mead Rose and Eden Tomboulian
Lighting by Gerald Kawaoka

All Brand New Classical Chinese Theatre

BY

ARTHUR AW

Characters

(in the order in which they speak)

MICHAEL 2
MICHAEL 1
DAVID
MOTHER
JENNY

SCENE ONE

The living room of a two-bedroom apartment in Kakaako, Honolulu. The doors to the bedrooms are on opposite sides of the stage. There should also be a door leading to the outside world. Allowances in the set should be made for unconventional and not readily visible entrances. A kitchenette is not necessary but it would help. A refrigerator is necessary (nobody likes warm beer). Basic furniture items, at least; nothing should stand out.

[*When curtains open,* MICHAEL 1 *is discovered seated, looking straight into the audience.* MICHAEL 2 *enters and approaches audience. He dons an oriental-looking cap with an attached pig-tail and plays with this throughout. Otherwise,* MICHAEL 2, *like* MICHAEL 1, *should be attired casually and not unusually. The two Michaels are very much alike simply because they are one and the same person.* MICHAEL 1 *kow-tows to the audience three times, each time accompanied by an oriental gong*]

MICHAEL 1: Our humble good evening, honorable ladies and gentlemen. And if this small person is allowed to make a small judgement, you must all be benevolent sponsors and well-wishers of the theatre. Welcome, welcome to our little play. The cast and crew are indeed indebted to your very venerable presence. [*To off stage*] Will everyone please come immediately and . . . please do hurry, we mustn't keep our distinguished patrons waiting . . . [*All members of cast and crew assemble*] Let us convey our respect to this good audience. [*All bow except for* MICHAEL 1] Thank you for being here. We are honored to be able to perform our small play to such important company. [*To cast and crew*] You may all leave the stage now, and let us put on a really good show. [*Cast and crew leave.* MICHAEL 1 *fakes an Ed Sullivan*] A really good show.

MICHAEL 2 [*ignoring* MICHAEL 1]: This small person is humble and proud, greatly humble and very proud to be here before such a . . .

MICHAEL 1: Stuff it, man.

MICHAEL 2 [*ignoring the interruption*]: . . . before such an assembly of valuable supporters of the theatre. This small and humble person . . .

MICHAEL 1: Stuff it where the sun don't shine already!

MICHAEL 2: Hey! Will you let me do this for just one night?

MICHAEL 1: Let you go on bragging about how humble you are? A slight technical problem here. Mike, you see, from the little I know, you understand, this also small person sees some sort of what-do-they-call-it, contradiction, in someone being high and mighty about his humility. But don't let that worry you . . . we have a little play to perform for these patrons of the theatre.

MICHAEL 2: So I may carry on, thank you.

MICHAEL 1: Go on, go on, go right ahead!

MICHAEL 2: Dear patrons, supporters of drama, please forgive the interruptions . . . we do indulge your patience, you who have been so generous with your time and effort to the theatre . . .

MICHAEL 1: Should I pass along the collection plate now or later?

MICHAEL 2: You said I could proceed, carry on. So now who's being contradictory?

MICHAEL 1: I sure wasn't about to let you go on and on and on. You're making a fool of yourself . . . making a fool of us. Just get on with it, and two things: one, let's not be redundant, and two . . .

MICHAEL 1 and MICHAEL 2: . . . let's not be redundant.

MICHAEL 2 [*returning his attention to audience*]: I am Michael Chun. And he is Michael Chun. [*To* MICHAEL 1] Michael, Michael, come meet the audience. Audience, meet Michael— Mike.

MICHAEL 1 [*approaches audience*]: How the hell are you? [*Returns to where he was*]

MICHAEL 2: We are Michael Chun. Singular. We are one and the same person. [*Pauses*] I know what you are thinking. More slick cute stuff. More cheap theatrics. Well, you know what . . . we have an abundance of theatrical devices in store for you. Look here: masks, a very traditional Chinese dramatic invention. Oh yes, we thought it up first like we did gunpowder and spaghetti . . . well, spaghetti we didn't call "spaghetti" exactly. We called it "mein," like chow mein, which is fried mein or . . .

MICHAEL 1: And we discovered America long before Leif Erikson and the rest of the Minnesota Vikings . . . but let's get on with the play.

MICHAEL 2 [*pauses, still holding masks*]: I best explain the masks. [*Holds up one with a sad face*] This means I am sad. [*Holds up one with a smiling face*] This means I'm happy. [*Pauses. The beginning minutes of a Three Stooges trailer could be projected on the lowered screen upstage right*] Sometimes by putting on a mask, the actor could be someone else or show that he is no longer in the mood he was in previously.

MICHAEL 1: Yeah, it saves a lotta work for the actor . . . cuts down the wear and tear of the face. And you know, hey, in our profession, man, we have to keep looking good.

MICHAEL 2: A mask will also reveal the character's inner feelings rather than what he says. Yes, in the Chinese Classical Theatre, the mask serves many purposes.

MICHAEL 1 [*after wearing and then removing an eye mask*]: Who was that man with that mask? [*In a different voice*] I don't know, but he left a silver bullet. Reckon he must be a werewolf killer of some kind.

MICHAEL 2: So there you have it. We shall have all the novelties you expect . . . all the pleasures of the Chinese Classical Theatre and more.

MICHAEL 1: All the concocted crap.

MICHAEL 2: More! Because we have here the All Brand New Chinese Classical Theatre!

[*Fanfare music begins*]

> This is the All Brand New
> And there's so very few
> Chinese Classical Theatre
>
> And we assume you knew
> This is the All Brand New
> Chinese Classical Theatre
>
> Now we even have a song
> For you all to sing along
> And to make it not sound wrong
> We'll bong a li'l on our gong
> Ask the members of our tong
> Ain't it just like in Hong Kong
>
> This is the All Brand New . . .
> Now please wait for the cue
> Chinese Classical Theatre
>
> Give credit where it's due
> That's to the All Brand New
> Chinese Classical Theatre

MICHAEL 2: Yes, we have everything here. Yes, including two of me. Aha! But you may see through it all immediately and interpret these double manifestations of your protagonist— that's me—in profound ways. [*Turns his back to the audience momentarily*] I see, I see, how clever. How ingenious. Two of me, so twice the message across. [*Pauses*] Thanks, Harold Pinter. The subtlety of it all. Split personality. But of course, yes, schizophrenia! [*Pauses*] Hints of Janus. Double nature of Man. [*A spotlight should come on* MICHAEL 2 *on cue in the following line*] The good light . . . [*gesturing towards* MICHAEL 1] versus the dark side of Man. [*Spotlight goes off. Pauses*] And you can tell, a better-looking actor is playing me rather than the me over there. Aha, we all look better to ourselves. But so much for reading into things. [*Pauses*] Actually, you were right the first time, it's all cheap theatrics!

MICHAEL 1: And isn't that what you are, Mike, cheap theatrics?

MICHAEL 2 [*camps*]: Oooh . . . what a terrible thing to call a person.

MICHAEL 1: You are one big phony.

MICHAEL 2: Takes one to know one.

MICHAEL 1: You are an asshole.

MICHAEL 2: My skin is rubber. What you say bounces right back on you.

MICHAEL 1: And why shouldn't it? I'm you, asshole. [*Pauses*] But so great for me . . . talking to myself again. Chewing myself out.

MICHAEL 2: Mike, you have to live with yourself, you know.

MICHAEL 1 [*camping*]: I have to live with myself . . . Hey, I don't want [*indicating himself*] to go around leaving your—my things all over the house. [*Really camping*] Hey, I can't take this, kid. Do what you have to do, but please don't make me live with myself, okay, but hey, keep me away from me. [*Pauses*] Some B-movie, eh?

MICHAEL 2: This isn't a movie.

MICHAEL 1: What? And they promised me star billing.

MICHAEL 2: This is real life, Mike. And you are thirty years old and you have lived thirty years of it. Most of the friends you know who are thirty are married, proud fathers of nice little facsimiles of themselves, and living the good life. Thirty years old? What happened to all that time?

MICHAEL 1: Mostly spent on good times! And good times ain't so bad, you know. Guy can have a lot of fun with good times.

MICHAEL 2: What happened to you? What happened to your aims and ambitions? Your ideas and ideals?

MICHAEL 1: I think I gave them to some worthy cause. [*Pauses*] Goodwill Industries. [*Pauses*] Great for tax deductions. Aims and ambitions, that's easily forty-five dollars tax deductible right there. And that's nothing compared to what I get back for ideas and ideals.

MICHAEL 2: You should listen to yourself.

MICHAEL 1: I thought I was.

MICHAEL 2: Lines from a TV situation comedy—soap opera.

MICHAEL 1 [*camps*]: Mother of Christ, this is it. This is my last chance. At the crossroads of life and no more gas stations ahead. Who am I? What am I doing here? [*Uses* MICHAEL 1 *as a mirror*] I see myself but I don't see myself. It's an identity crisis . . . the sixty-fourth one, I think, but who counts? And my mirror image fogs up on me. I can't tell who I am.

MICHAEL 2: You can't even sound sincere to yourself.

MICHAEL 1: Yes, yes. I must get a hold on myself. But mother says if I do, I will go blind. And get hair on my palm.

MICHAEL 2 [*firmly*]: How long more are you going to stay on that crappy job?

MICHAEL 1: Listen, it pays good. There's security.

MICHAEL 2: It's not what you wanted.

MICHAEL 1: There's not much stress to it, and I save on the valium.

MICHAEL 2: You hate it. And you are keyed-up about it.

MICHAEL 1: That can be resolved. I'll get to accept it as it is.

MICHAEL 2: When?

MICHAEL 1: Soon enough. What I feel, how I feel is only temporary.

MICHAEL 2: It's been temporary for seven years.

MICHAEL 1: It's a living.

MICHAEL 2: Well, it sure isn't much of a life.

MICHAEL 1: What do you expect from me?

MICHAEL 2: Mike, those were worthwhile aims and ambitions, ideas and ideals.

MICHAEL 1: So how come they've begun to sound like some silly kiddy ditty? some dumb alliterations? I sound like a soap opera. Listen to you . . . "it sure isn't much of a life . . . worthwhile aims and ambi . . ." Christ, Mike!

[DAVID, MICHAEL's *roommate, enters from bedroom door, stage right. He notices only* MICHAEL 1, *and watches him deliver the next few lines*]

MICHAEL 1: Christ, Mike. Goddamn. Hell.

DAVID: Running the whole vocabulary again? [*Pauses*] The usual everyday run-of-the-mill self-castration.

MICHAEL 1: You have very loud imageries, Dave.

DAVID: And you lead a very loud life of quiet desperation, Mike. Hate to bring it up in these tense moments, but I work nights, Mike. It's hard to get any sleep in there when one's roommate's running amok in here.

MICHAEL 1: Well, excuse me . . . I'll tiptoe amok.

DAVID: All right, Mike . . . what's wrong? Again?

[MICHAEL's MOTHER *enters from stage right through nonvisible entrance.* DAVID *does not see her, as she too is only in* MICHAEL's *mind*]

MOTHER [*to audience*]: We named him Michael. Michael is such a pretty name. Why do they spoil it, calling him "Mike?" "Mike," yeeecch. It sounds so negative in Chinese.

MICHAEL 1: Dave . . . it's all screwed up. Or have I told you lately?

DAVID: The world situation? International terrorism? Or is it again just life with a capital "L"?

[MOTHER, *meanwhile, is mouthing and repeating the word "Mike." It gradually sounds less and less as it should*]

MICHAEL 1: "Life with a capital 'L.' " We are all coming across like some TV script or pages from a comic book. And even what I just said seems faked.

DAVID: You are positively negative. And I hate to seem like some know-it-all asshole, but hey, Mike, we all got the same problems. Not similarly the same, but, you know.

MICHAEL 1: Okay, I got a low tolerance threshold—tolerate me!

DAVID: Mike, I'm not too hot about my job either, but I don't make a career out of bitching about my job.

MICHAEL 1: I don't know, Dave, I just . . .

MOTHER [*still to audience*]: My son Michael is not a happy boy. And he used to be such a happy baby. Very pretty smile he had. He always woke up smiling. So we woke him up all the time just to see him smile. He would sleep for about fifte minutes. And we'd wake him up and we'd enjoy his smile. And then rocked him back to sleep. Fifteen minutes later we'd wake him up again. And he would smile.

MICHAEL 1: Not just the job . . . my mother, Jenny . . . [JENNY *enters on cue, again only in* MICHAEL'*s mind*] My mother's not too happy with Jenny, you know.

MOTHER: Michael doesn't smile anymore nowadays. It's this evil woman he goes out with. A Caucasian girl. A witch who has my son under her spell.

MICHAEL 1: She's worried we're going to give her half-breed grandchildren. Eurasians, she calls them. Somehow Eurasians are even worse than Caucasians.

MOTHER: I have nothing against Caucasians now, mind you. I am not a prejudiced old woman. Some of my friends consider me very broadminded. Too broadminded, they say. I have talked to many Caucasians. They are the same as you and I. And God knows over here you can't very well avoid them. I even knew a Caucasian Buddhist monk once. And he knew the scriptures of the Lord Buddha well. But he chants with an accent.

MICHAEL 1: Also, there's the matter of mixing religions on top of the interbreeding.

MOTHER: Michael, Michael. I tell him time and time again, *think* about the children you will have . . . mixed! Like some hideous, what is the word, cocktail. Scotch whiskey and rice wine. [*Pauses*] Or like this dog breeder I once knew. He crossed a German Shepherd with a Doberman. He had to drown the whole litter. Those puppies were vicious. Bit off the nipples of their mother! [*Pauses*] But . . . [*indicating* JENNY] *that* will sure teach her some lesson.

MICHAEL 1: If that woman will only give Jenny a chance . . . meet Jenny without keeping her eyes closed. Christ, Dave, you haven't met a Jewish mother until you've met a Chinese mother.

MOTHER: But I'm not a prejudiced woman. I've met many nice Caucasian girls, fine girls—*who stay away from my sons!*

MICHAEL 1: The really amazing thing is that Jenny respects her. I mean, Jenny tells me to watch my temper with that mother of mine.

[JENNY *goes over to* MICHAEL 2, *kisses him.* MOTHER *squirms upon seeing this*]

MOTHER [*to audience*]: I apologize for my son. This shameful public display of affection. And after the thousands of years of Chinese civilization. Nowadays, a mother's hands are tied.

[MOTHER *goes over to* MICHAEL 2, *pries her way between her son and* JENNY, *and then babies and kisses him*]

MICHAEL 1: She goes berserk when Jenny's around, you know. She calls Jenny every filthy word in Chinese while she smiles at Jenny.

MOTHER [*smiling*]: Slut. [MICHAEL 2 *breaks away from her*] Scheming, promiscuous, hairy female snake.

MICHAEL 1: Jenny doesn't understand a word.

MOTHER [*suddenly shouting at top of her lungs*]: Conniving son stealer!

DAVID [*not really hearing* MOTHER *but appropriately*]: Maybe Jenny does have some idea.

MOTHER: Stick to your own race, bitch.

MICHAEL 2: Mother!

MOTHER: Michael, Michael. You are worried about mother and her temper. You are a good son. Not a great son. But a good son. Why can't you see this, this *tramp* here as what she is? Look at her. Big massive elephant. Open your eyes, my elder son, take a good look. She's not Chinese.

MICHAEL 2: I did notice that, Mother.

MOTHER: Philip, your younger brother, knows better. His wife is Chinese, and from a good family too, I must add.

MICHAEL 2: I don't want to hear about Philip, Mother.

MOTHER: Silly Michael, you are always so jealous of your little brother—just because he is already a tycoon in Hong Kong.

MICHAEL 2: Philip isn't a tycoon, Mother. His father-in-law is.

MOTHER: Well, he chooses his father-in-laws well. Philip's wife is the only child, you know. And someday Philip will take over the business.

MICHAEL 2: Mother, doesn't that sound a little wrong to you?

MOTHER: I don't see anything wrong.

[DAVID, *meanwhile, has gone to the refrigerator and has returned with two beers, which he and* MICHAEL 1 *drink*]

MICHAEL 2: That your younger son married a woman for her father's money.

MOTHER: Philip did no such thing. Why, it isn't even his yet.

MICHAEL 2: That wife of his looks like a big pimple.

MOTHER: At least she isn't a red-haired pimple.

MICHAEL 2: All right, Mother, you are making me do this. Does Philip ever write to you?

MOTHER: Tycoons are pretty busy, you know. Philip has a lot of things to do.

MICHAEL 2: Has he ever even asked you if you would like to stay with him or, for that matter, spend a holiday with him and his pimple?

MOTHER: I wouldn't want to stay with in-laws myself.

MICHAEL 2: That isn't the point, Mother. Has he even asked you to?

MOTHER: That woman has taught you to poison my mind about your brother.

MICHAEL 2: Jenny . . . what did she do? Mother, Jenny has always been the one who tells me to watch my temper with you.

MOTHER: Michael! You talk about your mother with this red-haired foreign slut?

MICHAEL 1 [*banging down the beer and taking over for* MICHAEL 2]: I don't want to hear about Jenny anymore, Mother.

MOTHER: I know how you feel, Michael. Whenever I hear anything about her, I get a pain right here [*indicating her stomach*].

MICHAEL 1: Mother . . . ?

DAVID: Hey, Michael . . . calm down.

MOTHER: The same feeling after inadvertently eating something rotten.

[MICHAEL 1 *gets up abruptly and runs across stage and throttles* MOTHER. MICHAEL 2 *restrains him. All* DAVID *sees is* MICHAEL *acting bananas*]

DAVID: In my part of town, mother ranks right up there with, you know, with Church and apple pies.

MICHAEL 1 [*returning*]: Sometimes I'd like to wring your neck.

DAVID: Boy, is that a no-no where I come from.

JENNY [*approaching* MICHAEL *casually*]: Mike, you must really watch that temper of yours. [*Exits*]

DAVID: Whatever happened to traditional Chinese filial piety? What happened to the great oriental reverence for the elders?

MICHAEL 1: Gave that up when we ran out of great oriental older people. Used to have flocks of them . . . wise old people all over the place. Couldn't make it halfway down a block without being really overwhelmed by some ad-libbed words of wisdom.

DAVID: Your mother gets along with me.

MICHAEL 1: Only because I'm not marrying you.

DAVID: We talked, you know. She tells me quite a few things.

MICHAEL 1: She tells quite a few people quite a few things.

MOTHER: Michael, Michael. [MICHAEL 2 *turns toward her*] I remember that nice foreign student from Taiwan. That very nice and very respectful girl. She writes such nice respectful letters.

MICHAEL 2 [*snatching a paper from her*]: Where did you get this? You've been going through my things again. And reading my personal letters, Mother?

MOTHER: It's a mother's duty. And since when does a son have secrets from his mother? I have seen you naked, Michael. There are no secrets from me, your mother.

DAVID [*still at the refrigerator. To* MICHAEL 1]: Try to look at your relationship with your brother from an objective viewpoint, Mike. Look at everything from a distance.

[MICHAEL 1 *meanwhile, has turned toward* MOTHER *and* MICHAEL 2]

MOTHER: The things you say to your mother . . . the things you say to your mother about your brother!

MICHAEL 2: I am trying to be respectful . . . just like Philip, Mother. Don't read my letters.

MICHAEL 1 [*to* MICHAEL 2]: The woman is due some respect, you know.

MOTHER: The letter was just lying there, under all that rubbish in your file cabinet, and you didn't even open it. It is such a nice letter. It would have been a waste not to read it. And you know very well I have always taught you not to waste anything . . . millions starving in China.

MICHAEL 2: Mother, I don't see what this letter from Taiwan has to do with millions starving in China!

MOTHER: Maybe it's because we're speaking in this foreign tongue. Maybe if my elder son hadn't forgotten half his Chinese, we wouldn't have this problem in understanding each other. I'm sure Philip hasn't forgotten his Chinese.

MICHAEL 2: Christ, Mother, Philip stays in Hong Kong! How the Jesus is he going to forget his Chinese there?

MOTHER: Do not use the names of the Lord in vain, Michael.

MICHAEL 2: Huh? You're a Buddhist, Mother?

MOTHER: Just a local expression I picked up.

MICHAEL 2: You didn't used to like the nice foreign student from Taiwan . . . speaks the wrong dialect, remember?

MOTHER: Oh no, Michael, I liked her.

MICHAEL 2: Your very words, Mother: She wants me "for her green card." So that she could stay here as a premanent resident.

MOTHER: That may be so, but I liked her. And I like her more now . . . as they say, absence does make the heart grow fonder.

MICHAEL 2: Another local expression you picked up.

MOTHER: For an old lady, they say I am very good at picking up things.

MICHAEL 2: Yes, I know . . . like letters buried in file cabinets. [*Pauses*] You even told me you hated her guts.

MOTHER: Guts? Why would I hate her intestines? Michael, you are such a child.

MICHAEL 2: You didn't like her. Why don't you admit to things? Why do you have to lie point blank like that?

MOTHER [*hurt*]: I never lie, Michael. I never lie to you, my older son.

MICHAEL 2: Well, you're either lying or you're hiding a lot of things from yourself! Either way, you're driving me up the . . . goddammit.

MOTHER: God, my son did not mean that. Forgive him. Michael, you really shouldn't talk to me, your mother, like that. Why, Philip would never . . .

MICHAEL 2: Philip . . . Philip . . .

[MICHAEL 2 *goes into a complete rage, slams his fist right into* MOTHER *who is completely decked.* MICHAEL 1 *races over, hits* MICHAEL 2 *a couple of times as the latter slips away off stage.* DAVID *races over, seeing only* MICHAEL 1 *hitting his fists on the wall*]

DAVID: You're worse off than I thought, Mike . . . come on! [*Pulling him back*] Damn, Mike, you don't have to put a show on just for me, you know. [*Pauses*] You're okay, now? [*Takes him back to a seat*] Drink up the beer . . . let's get really sloshed, okay? I know a couple of bars that would be just right for tonight.

[MICHAEL 2 *enters and goes over to* MOTHER *and lifts her back to her feet*]

MICHAEL 2: Mother, I'll never do that . . . you know I'll never hurt you.

MOTHER [*feeling her jaw*]: Your words do hurt me, Michael. Sometimes you really hurt your mother.

DAVID: There's one thing you should know, Mike. Your mother once told me that she really loves you more than she does Philip. [MICHAEL 1 *ignores this*] She meant it too . . . she says she loves you more.

MICHAEL 1: David, I'm not in some contest for her affection with Philip. Nice of you to come up with some cliché pop psychology about some sibling rivalry. She could have smothered that brother of mine till he had choked for all I cared.

DAVID: Hey, man, I was just trying to help . . . aw, what the hell, c'mon, Mikey boy, drink up! Haven't you heard? Booze solves all.

[*The phone rings.* DAVID, *who has been sloshing down his beer, answers it*]

MICHAEL 1 [*to* MICHAEL 2]: Don't you go hurting her feelings again. You hit her one more time and I'll . . .

MICHAEL 2: Well, you strangle her one more time and I'll!

MICHAEL 1: In her way, she's only trying to say she worries about you.

MICHAEL 2: In her way, she's trying to meddle.

DAVID [*louder so* MICHAEL *can hear*]: Yes . . . Mrs. Chun, I'll see if he is in. [*Pauses*] What's that?

MICHAEL 2 [*to the* MOTHER *in his mind*]: I'm sick of talking to you on the phone.

DAVID [*still to phone*]: Just an expression, Mrs. Chun.

MICHAEL 1: What now?

DAVID: She wanted to know why in a small apartment like this I don't just know if you're in or not instead of having to see if you are. [*To phone*] He's here.

MICHAEL 2: I'm not.

MOTHER: You are always out when I call. This time I know better.

MICHAEL 1: Tell her I'm taking a nap.

MOTHER: You sure look wide awake to me.

DAVID [*to phone*]: All right, Mrs. Chun, see you in a while then. [*Replaces phone on cradle*] She's coming over.

MICHAEL 1: Why didn't you say I wasn't here?

DAVID: You know she's going to come right over anyhow. [*Pauses*] Besides, she said she was just stopping by on her way to somewhere else.

MICHAEL : Dave, I can't see her now. I don't want to see her.

MOTHER [*to nobody in particular*]: When a mother hears such
    words, she wishes that God didn't give her ears.
MICHAEL 1: All my juices are acting up.
MOTHER: It's the food that Jinny-Johnny-Jenny cooks. [*Sarcasti-
    cally*] And cooks? She cooks like she's boiling laundry.
MICHAEL 1: I'm going out.
DAVID: What do you want me to say to her?
MICHAEL 1: You two always have something to say to each other.
MOTHER: David is such a nice boy.
MICHAEL 1: You know, she really gets along with you. I am sur-
    prised by it . . . really.
DAVID: Thanks a lot.
MICHAEL 1: She doesn't get along with too many other Caucasians
    as far as I know.
MOTHER: David isn't too Caucasian.
DAVID [*responding more to* MICHAEL 1 *than* MOTHER]: I knew I
    was good at something.

[*During the next few lines,* DAVID *goes to the refrigerator for
more beers and then just sits there, sloshing it up*]

MOTHER: As much as I like David, I feel you should have more
    Chinese friends.
MICHAEL 2: You win one, you lose one, Dave.
MICHAEL 1: Why do I need more Chinese friends?
MOTHER: Because you're forgetting your Chinese ways. [*Pauses*]
    You have been very disrespectful to me lately. [*Pauses*] I
    don't have to say where you've been picking up this disre-
    spectful attitude.
MICHAEL 1: But you're going to tell me anyway, right?
MOTHER: It's that Jinny-Johnny-Jenny. She's teaching you all this
    bad manners. [*A gong sounds, and* JENNY *abruptly runs in*]
    And it doesn't seem like it takes too long for her to erase all
    the years of careful teaching I've given you.
JENNY: Mike, pick your nose.
MICHAEL 1 [*immediately*]: Yes, Jenny.
JENNY: Mike, swear at your mother.
MICHAEL 1: Damn you, Mother.

JENNY: Mike, spit at her. [MICHAEL 1 *does so*] Mike, slap her, choke her, deck her . . . piss on her. [MOTHER *retreats from the advancing* MICHAEL 1]

MOTHER: Go away from me, you filthy woman.

[MICHAEL 1 *pans to audience as he is the one who has been charging toward* MOTHER. *A gong sounds and* JENNY *walks off stage*]

MICHAEL 1: Jenny doesn't influence me, Mother.

MOTHER: A Chinese girl would influence you for the better.

MICHAEL 1: Are you quite finished?

MOTHER: A Chinese boy should marry a Chinese girl.

MICHAEL 1 [*mocking her*]: "A Chinese boy should marry a Chinese girl."

MOTHER: Michael, Michael. [*At times to the audience*] Perhaps that is where we went wrong . . . calling you Michael. Some strong Chinese name might have been better. Maybe you wouldn't be so . . . westernized and rude to your only mother.

MICHAEL 1: Will you leave me alone, Mother?

MOTHER: I thought about it way back then, you know. But your father. He said you'll probably do better with some Caucasian name in an English-speaking business world. Boy, did we goof. [*Pauses*] Chiang Kai-shek. Well, not really Chiang. Chun Kai-shek, now that would've been a strong name. Very Chinese.

MICHAEL 1: Guess you ruled out Mao Tse-tung.

MOTHER: Michael, my oldest son. [*To audience*] And Michael is getting on with the years. He is over thirty years old. In ancient China, a lot of people were dead long before they were thirty. So how long is a mother expected to wait before she can cradle her [*emphatically*] Chinese grandchild in her arms? [*To* MICHAEL 1] Michael, Michael, your father and I had always allowed you to do most things your way. And maybe that's where we went wrong. We obviously went wrong somewhere. [*Pauses*] But anyway, bear with your aging mother who probably speaks a little too much.

MICHAEL 1 and MICHAEL 2 [*simultaneously*]: Not you, Mother
. . . never.

MOTHER: Yes, maybe I deserve that. You young people have no
time for us aging-and-probably-dying-very-soon folks nowadays. [*Pauses*] But at least you must agree we have always
allowed you to do as you please.

MICHAEL 1: Funny thing, Mother, I remember you as the mother
and I was the son . . . but, by golly, we don't seem to recall
the same good old days.

MOTHER: You were spoilt. And boy, does it show. We let you have
everything. And now all I am asking you is just one little
thing in return. You had your way because we love you. But
do you love us? Your father may he rest in peace if you will
just do one small thing for us. Marry a Chinese girl. [*Pauses*]
Marry a Chinese girl who will give you a Chinese son. Not one
of those . . . those—oh, Michael, you break a mother's heart.

MICHAEL 1: Mother, I never want to hurt you.

MOTHER [*grabbing the opportunity*]: So marry a Chinese girl.

MICHAEL 1: Tell you what, I'll meet you halfway . . . I'll marry a
Chinese boy. [*Pauses*] Will our ancestors approve?

MOTHER: That is another thing I am very concerned about. Your
sense of humor. Perhaps that's where we went wrong. We
allowed you to have this grotesque sense of humor.

MICHAEL 1: I feel like some broken-down freak . . . the many
times you two went wrong on me. [*Starts camping it up and
acting like a broken wind-up doll*]

MOTHER: You don't have a Chinese sense of humor.

MICHAEL 1: What does that mean? "A Chinese sense of humor."

MICHAEL 2 [*interrupting*]: Din kuay jhec kai oi kor lo?

MICHAEL 1: What?

MICHAEL 2: That's Cantonese for "Why did the chicken have to
cross the road?" It's a biggie in the Wanchai area.

MOTHER: We Chinese are more reserved in what we consider
funny.

MICHAEL 1: Oh God, Ma.

MOTHER: And that's another thing we don't do. Swearing at your mother. They would've cut out your tongue in the old days. You have been very disrespectful to me lately. [*Fingers her throat where she was choked*] And so very vulgar. And violent. [*Pauses*] In ancient China, they wouldn't stand for that. Vulgarity and such violence! They would've stripped you and cut off your . . . lips. [*Pauses*] If I'm not a Chinese mother, I would've simply walked away and never seen you again. But I am a Chinese mother . . . [MICHAEL 2 *places a box in front of* MOTHER. *She gets up on it*] a Chinese mother, and my first responsibility is to my children . . . never . . .

MICHAEL 1 *and* MICHAEL 2 [*together*]: Never!

MOTHER: . . . never to my pride!

MICHAEL 1 *and* MICHAEL 2: Bravo . . . author! author!

[DAVID *walks over and joins them in the applause*]

MICHAEL 2 [*to* MOTHER *and* MICHAEL 1]: Actors, freeze. [MOTHER *and* MICHAEL 1 *stay in position. To* DAVID]: You're not in this scene.

DAVID: I thought I was.

MICHAEL 2: When we had this thing blocked, you were supposed to stay back there drinking beer.

DAVID: You can only gush down that much, you know. I'll forget my lines.

MICHAEL 2: Well, there's an old Chinese Classical Theatrical device just for that. [*Leads* DAVID *back to a seat, whips out a large black cloth, and covers him completely*] Let's get on with it.

MOTHER: You act very strangely . . . you do not act Chinese.

MICHAEL 1: Maybe I'm a bad actor. Maybe I have the wrong script. Mother, is being a Chinese a twenty-four-hours-a-day career? You don't make it an obsession!

[MICHAEL 1 *walks over to* MICHAEL 2, *hand outstretched. During the following lines, the two play it up to the hilt.* MICHAEL 2 *puts his pig-tail hat on* MICHAEL 1*'s head.* MOTHER *watches it all disapprovingly*]

MICHAEL 2: Well, hello there.

MICHAEL 1: And hello there yourself. I'm a full-time Chinese person.

MICHAEL 2: That's a coincidence. Why, I'm a full-time Chinese person too.

MICHAEL 1: Isn't this a warm day . . . especially for us full-time Chinese people. Oh, this here is my mother. She's a very full-time Chinese person.

MICHAEL 2: Well, if it isn't a full-time Chinese mother!

MICHAEL 1: Believe it . . . she's full of it.

MICHAEL 2: There are not many of us full-timers around, you know.

MICHAEL 1: You can say that again. These part-time Chinese people are just not the same.

MOTHER: You can stop that.

MICHAEL 2: I had a full-time Chinese lunch today . . . No, no, as a full-timer, I mustn't lie. I had a very un-Chinese hot dog.

MICHAEL 1: You what?

MICHAEL 2: I had a hot dog.

MOTHER: You don't know how difficult it is for us old people to control our temper when our little children raise their voices at us.

MICHAEL 1: Control your temper? Don't Chinese old people mellow out with age? And with age comes wisdom . . . rah tah ta ta ta . . . and with wisdom comes understanding. [*Sings*] Side by side, and . . . yes. Flashes of [*perhaps some lighting effects here*] brilliance and total realization of what's what. And then very carefully, selecting the right words, an art perfected by the years, not spewing out whatever petty garbage that comes to mind, but in a couple of choice words—pow! the solution to everything. [*Pauses*] You see, Mother, I have my misconceptions too . . . Believe it or not, I have what you may call very Chinese ideas, long planted in me, which are still very, very much there. I do expect a lot from my elders. I always thought you understood me, and knew what was happening . . . somehow . . . just somehow. [*Pauses. Shouts*] Just somehow!

MICHAEL 2: You make longer speeches than she does.

MOTHER: Don't shout at me. I am your mother. My age at least should give me the right to be not subjected to speeches from my immature son.

MICHAEL 1: I'm not going to believe this.

MICHAEL 2: Ignore it and it's not there.

MICHAEL 1: And be like her.

MICHAEL 2: Get out of this rut! Go far away.

MICHAEL 1: Like Philip. Whatever I do, I'll do it.

MICHAEL 2: My Way. I've Gotta Be Me. Reach the unreachable star.

MOTHER: And just one more thing before I go. You and your sense of humor . . . you don't even take yourself seriously. How does a mother know when you really have something to say to her? [*Pauses*] I am not God, you know.

MICHAEL 2: Sheeesh, I thought Chinese mother and God are on a par.

MOTHER: And just one more thing before I go—do not be irreverent.

MICHAEL 2: To you or . . . Him?

MOTHER: And—I may decide not to ever come back!

[*She leaves. Both* MICHAELS *go toward where* DAVID *is. Both place a black cloth over themselves*]

Blackout

SCENE TWO

As lights comes on, MICHAEL 1, MICHAEL 2, *and* DAVID *are in the same positions as they were at the close of Scene One. The only change is that the black cloths have been removed from both* MICHAEL 1 *and* MICHAEL 2.

MICHAEL 2 [*approaches the audience*]: Dear distinguished audience, our theatre tradition goes back for thousands of years.

MICHAEL 1 [*joining him*]: And you know, you pick up a few tricks here and there along the way.

MICHAEL 2: There are many things that the audience has come to expect of a play: all the characters must be properly introduced, explained, fleshed out, so to speak, in order for the audience to relate to the play as a whole. You have to understand . . . know the characters.

MICHAEL 1: Hey, I'm Mike, how are you? What else do you want to know about me?

MICHAEL 2: And it has to be done *conventionally*.

MICHAEL 1: Birthplace: Hong Kong. Moved here with mother . . . you met Mother. And father, who died . . . of Mother . . . and baby brother, Philip, who has since moved back to Hong Kong, married a pimple, and subsequently never been heard from again.

MICHAEL 2: The information about the characters has to be given gradually. The audience wouldn't want it all in a single pile, so to speak.

MICHAEL 1: I don't talk with an accent . . . not much anyway. Hey, I was brought up here. The truth is, what I know of the old country, as Mother calls it, I got from Mother . . . and Father, whenever he got a word in.

MICHAEL 2: Yes, all the relevant facts revealed . . . subtly.

MICHAEL 1: Stay with a roommate, David . . . hey, who can afford to rent an apartment all by himself nowadays. David's cool . . . too damned cool sometimes. Only gets upset when you wake him up. Come to think of it, David doesn't really get himself bothered too much with many things . . . or many people. No girlfriends . . . no boyfriends either, in case that crossed your mind. Dave, hey . . . you do see Dave over there. [DAVID *removes the black cloth*] Sorry about that, folks. Dave's a night-time security guard . . . that means he sleeps days and nights.

MICHAEL 2: The audience would want to know each and every character of the play.

MICHAEL 1: Hey, what the hell do you think I'm doing here? [*Pauses*] Dave somehow gets along with Mother . . . you remember Mother? He is about the only Caucasian Mother's on speaking terms with.

DAVID [*approaches audience too*]: That's because I'm intensely likeable . . . just an awful nice guy. [*He backs away arrogantly*]

MICHAEL 1: Yeah . . . David. [*Pauses*] Not much more there is to David. [DAVID *reacts*]I mean, no big enigma, you know . . . not much motivation or ambition. Likes it all laid back . . . the kinda guy when opportunity knocks, opportunity better break down the door! Well, that's enough about . . . that's all there is to David. [*Slight pause*] And Jenny, my girlfriend . . . the latest in the series.

MICHAEL 2: Oh, c'mon, Mike.

MICHAEL 1: Yeah, come on, Mike . . . guess I'm playing it down a bit. I . . . ah . . . like Jenny. Like her a lot . . . but Mother doesn't like her a lot. Hates her a lot. Jenny is probably the easiest-to-get-along-with girl I know. . . She doesn't speak badly of anything or anybody.

MICHAEL 2: While you're at it . . . tell them [*indicating the audience*] how the play will end. And the rest of us can just leave. So turn off the lights when you're through.

MICHAEL 2 [*louder*]: What else is there? My likes and dislikes. Favorite color: brown; favorite movie star: Farley Granger; favorite singer: Warren Zevon. Other likes and dislikes: me.

[*Sound of a loud gong*]

MICHAEL 2 [*accompanied by strobe light*]: Ladies and Gentlemen, through the medium of the All Brand New Chinese Classical Theatre, we proudly present the super match-up between Super-Oriental Mother and Intensely Likeable White Boy! Yes, folks, on this stage, the big Big Rumble! The big question: How does this Intensely Likeable White Boy manage to soften up, conquer the granite-hard racial hatred and petty prejudices of Super-Oriental Mother? [*Pauses*] Or will he? [*Pauses*] Do not go away, folks, for here they come!

[MICHAEL 1 *backs off to a corner.* DAVID, *who has slipped on a pair of gloves when he had his back turned to the audience, turns around and waves to audience like a prize fighter*]

MICHAEL 2: Entering center ring, on my left, the symbol of white patronizing niceness, the Intensely Likeable White Boy! [*Both* MICHAELs *run toward the audience and urge them to cheer*] Let us cheer him on, good people! [MICHAEL 1 *urges audience to hiss when* MOTHER *comes on*] And now, entering the stage, the Hateful, Spiteful—and at times, quite subtle about it all—deviously Super-Oriental Mother! [MOTHER *enters and grins insincerely*] This is a tense moment. And we must ask the audience to maintain the proper silence required for this very important scene. I do not need to elaborate on how essential this scene is to the framework of the play.

MICHAEL 1: Get on with it.

MICHAEL 2: This is it! [*The strobe stops*] All right, competitors: [*To* DAVID] Shake hands and come out patronizing. [*To* MOTHER] Shake hands and come out belligerent.

[*They both shake hands with their gloves on. Both* MICHAEL 1 *and* MICHAEL 2 *move to opposite corners of the stage leaving* MOTHER *and* DAVID *in center stage, where they box*]

DAVID [*greeting* MOTHER *after stepping back*]: Good to see you, Mrs. Chun. You're looking well.

MOTHER: I've been ill.

DAVID: And looking young.

MOTHER: No, I look old like I should look. We must all look our age. Otherwise it's hypocritical, deceitful, and an outright lie.

DAVID: A very profound statement, Mrs. Chun: people should act their age. If you don't mind my retelling you a joke I heard, this friend of mine saw this old man in really tight-fitting clothes . . . why, his wrinkles showed through.

MOTHER: We must all be what we are.

DAVID: I can't agree with you more, Mrs. Chun.

MOTHER: Because I am right. So many old people try to dress young. They even try to walk young. [*Imitates a young walk*] But they pay for it . . . [*grips her back*] when their old bones and their old muscles tell them in the night . . . [*feigning pain*] "Oooh, you shouldn't have done that." [DAVID *laughs*] So deceptive it is to try to look young . . . and you young people see right through them, don't you?

DAVID: Oh yes, I am sure most young people do.

MOTHER: And you young people laugh at them, don't you?

DAVID: Well, Mrs. Chun . . . it is so impolite of them, but they do.

MICHAEL 1: Oh, that was good. A low blow . . . but that was good.

MICHAEL 2: Shhhh.

DAVID: I see it myself all the time, Mrs. Chun, and sometimes, I must admit, I do have to stifle a smile.

[*Bell sounds*]

MICHAEL 2: End of Round One. [*Pauses*] May we have the points, please. [MICHAEL 1 *prances over and gives* MICHAEL 2 *a piece of paper*] We have it. In Round One: Super-Oriental Mother, nine; Intensely Likeable White Boy, ten!

[*Bell sounds*]

DAVID: This is some warm weather we are having.

MOTHER: I find it chilly.

DAVID: Warm but windy.

MOTHER: My bones feel cold. [*Pauses. Looking toward* MICHAEL 1] And that is because I didn't listen to my mother. [*Pauses*] When I was young, my mother always told me to dry myself thoroughly after a good bath and never sleep with my hair wet. That was one of the few times I didn't listen to my mother. It is true: if you don't dry yourself well, one day you'll pay for it. Arthritis, rheumatism . . . they are nothing to sneeze at. [*Pauses*] Now all my bones ache. I didn't listen to my mother. [*Pauses*] Can't do anything about those bones now. If Michael will only listen to his mother. [*Pauses*] Do you listen to your mother, David?

DAVID: She's dead.

MOTHER: And most mothers should be . . . so they don't have to be hurt so deeply by their thirty-year-old sons. [*She flashes a look at* MICHAEL 2] I only want him to be happy. [*Pauses*] He may think he can be happy . . . but mother knows better. These things never work out . . . interracial marriages! [*She practically spits the last words*]

DAVID: Perhaps these things are different today, Mrs. Chun.

MOTHER: I am not a prejudiced woman, David. I would like to
think that it is so . . . but just thinking it so doesn't make it
so. [*Pauses*] I wish Michael could see this . . . understand
me. But whenever I see him . . . [*She and* DAVID *slow down
gradually and drop boxing pose*] the words come out wrong. I
cannot explain to him what my heart feels. And he gets angry
with me. Me . . . his very own mother, me after all that pain
of giving birth to him. And he was a big baby too. They say
one does not remember pain, but I sure remember those birth
pangs when that big, big son of mine came to being.

[*Bell sounds*]

MICHAEL 2: End Round Two. [*Pauses*] And the points. [MICHAEL
1 *again prances over and hands him a piece of paper*] Yes . . .
and the results of Round Two: Super-Oriental Mother had
most of the words in, but she is penalized. Yes, ladies and
gentlemen, in the judges' decision, she directed her blows to
opponents outside the ring, so, yes, folks, the winner of the
first two rounds, and the winner of this relationship: the
Intensely Likeable, Super-Patronizing White Boy! [DAVID
steps up. MOTHER *leaves stage*] Is there anything you would
like to say to the good people?
DAVID: Well, I don't deserve it . . . just being myself. Michael
has a super mother.
MICHAEL 2: How's that for some patronizing, folks?

[*Lighting returns to normal. The three remain in the same
position for a brief second as the lights go off and then immediately back on again*]

MICHAEL 1: Do you know why my mother gets along with you?
DAVID [*getting a beer from the refrigerator*]: I'm not her son?
MICHAEL 1: You're one hell of a good listener. And she's one hell
of a talker. [*Pauses*] There should be one in every household.
Someone who will sit there and listen. It'll wipe out mental
problems forever. A boon to mankind, for sure.
DAVID [*after sipping his beer*]: A man may make a fool of himself

talking. [*Pauses*] But a man will never make a fool of himself listening.

MICHAEL 1: You're a regular Charlie Chan. [*Slight pause*] Must be the company you keep.

DAVID: Your mother does have her side of the story.

MICHAEL 1: There are many sides to many stories. And you're going to blow your brains out listening to everybody's side of the story. [*Pauses*] You are my friend, Dave . . . hey, I know I have my faults, doesn't everyone? We screw up all the time. But we sort of expect the people we know, the people we care about, to at least stick with us. [*Pauses*] Does that make any sense?

DAVID: I don't know, Mike, I'll go along with you when you're right.

MICHAEL 1: You're saying I'm wrong, Jenny's wrong, and my mother's right?

DAVID: I'm not saying that.

MICHAEL 1: So what the hell are you saying?

DAVID: Hey, this all has nothing to do with me, you know.

MICHAEL 1: It has nothing to do with you, so you don't even have to have an opinion.

DAVID: Don't see what that'll serve.

MICHAEL 1: Dave, all I'm saying, all I'm asking is what the hell do you think you mean by coming out with that my mother has her side of the story?

DAVID: Now you listen. Your mother's my friend and you are my friend, and I don't even see what my opinion would serve . . . and I don't really care to get into it, okay?

MICHAEL 1: You stick by your guns, don't you—when you are wishy-washy. [*Pauses*] I've never seen anyone so committed to being noncommittal. [*Doorbell rings*] It's probably my mother, your friend.

DAVID: Listen, Mike . . . I know what you're going through, okay? What do you say we hit a few bars after she goes?

MICHAEL 1: Why don't you go have a few drinks with your friend? [*Indicating door*] And tell her I'm not here. [*Goes to the refrigerator*] And since the woman's probably gonna check my room anyway . . . [*takes a couple of beers*] I'll be in yours.

[MICHAEL 1 *goes into* DAVID*'s room.* DAVID *answers the door.* JENNY *enters*]

DAVID [*surprised, he says awkwardly*]: Oh hello . . . Jenny.
JENNY [*suspicious*]: Where's Mike?

[JENNY *does not wait for an answer but heads straight for* MICHAEL*'s room.* DAVID *is somewhat annoyed at* JENNY*'s attitude. He goes over to the couch and starts browsing through a magazine*]

JENNY: So where's Mike? [*Slight pause*] What are you reading?
DAVID: Trash.
JENNY: You don't have to be nasty.
DAVID: How am I being nasty? I just answered your question. I'm reading trash, so I said I'm reading trash.
JENNY: I asked you where Mike was.
DAVID: And did you give me a chance to answer that? You ignored me and went straight for Mike's room.
JENNY: I don't know what's with you, but you seemed kinda shocked to see me back there.
DAVID: I was expecting Mrs. Chun.
JENNY: Is that damned bitch coming here?
DAVID: Oh, she's a damned bitch now. Somehow you come across different when Michael's around.
JENNY: I don't see how this is any business of yours . . . but since you want to have things out, you creep, let's get it out.
DAVID: Oh . . . there's more things on your little mind. I didn't think that was conceivable.
JENNY: Don't you get nasty with me!
DAVID: I sure didn't start it. It's quite human to be annoyed when one is called a creep, you know.
JENNY: Well, you better get used to being called a lotta other names, you queer, fruit, homosexual.
DAVID [*stunned*]: What?

JENNY: You're damned palsy-walsy with my boyfriend. [*Pauses*] You go palsy-walsy with someone else.

DAVID: You . . . .you think I'm gay, Jenny?

JENNY: Listen, thirty-year-old guys don't room together unless something funny is going on.

DAVID: So that makes Mike gay too. [*Pauses*] Doesn't it, Jenny? [*Longer pauses*] You're under a strain, Jenny . . . take it easy.

JENNY: Screw that patronizing attitude of yours! You don't like me and I don't give a damn . . . Just don't you get near Mike, you queer . . . but as long as you're going to be around, for a while anyway . . . [*screams*] let's be civil with each other!

DAVID [*noticing that* MICHAEL 1 *is in the room*]: Hey . . . Mikey honey, we have a visitor.

[DAVID *gets up and proceeds to his own room.* JENNY *is somewhat startled to find that* MICHAEL 1 *is around, but even more when she sees him emerge from* DAVID*'s room.* MICHAEL 1 *and* JENNY *stay silent for a long time*]

MICHAEL 1: Hello, Jenny.

JENNY: Mike . . .

MICHAEL 1: What was that all about?

JENNY: Mike . . . Michael . . .

MICHAEL 1: What was that all about, Jenny?

JENNY: Dave's right . . . I'm under a strain.

MICHAEL 1: You think I'm gay?

JENNY: Not you, Mike.

MICHAEL 1: Hey, I was in Dave's room . . . I heard everything.

JENNY: I don't think that, Mike.

MICHAEL 1: You suspect it?

JENNY: That's not important, Mike.

MICHAEL 1: That's not important?

JENNY: I just felt he was being too chummy with you. [*Pauses*] God knows I already have to share you with . . . your mother.

MICHAEL 1: "That damned bitch." [*Pauses*] That's what you said, Jenny.

JENNY: Your mother isn't the easiest person to get along with, you know. What the hell were you doing in that creep's room?

MICHAEL 1: You want to know that, Jenny? [*Pauses*] I was drinking beer. [*Pauses*] I was avoiding "that damned bitch" thinking it was "that damned bitch" when the bell rang. [*Pauses*] Jenny? [*Pauses*] What the shit is happening here?

JENNY: Mike . . . I don't mean anything by that.

MICHAEL 1: What were you saying out here? I've never heard you say anything like that before.

JENNY: It was just David. He doesn't like me, and I can feel it. I was just trying to get back at him for the things he has been saying about me.

MICHAEL 1: Dave hasn't been saying anything . . . that guy never voices his opinion about much.

JENNY: He hints at them . . . and he tries so very hard to be your friend. There's just something about it . . .

MICHAEL 1: Why didn't you really express these things to me before?

JENNY: I was just waiting for the right time!

MICHAEL 1: And it seemed right right now? [*Pauses*] Oh, Jenny, Jenny . . .

JENNY [*pushing herself into* MICHAEL 1*'s arms*]: Mike, let's forget about this, okay?

MICHAEL 1 [*kissing her*]: Jenny . . .

JENNY [*kissing him*]: Mike . . . Mike . . .

MICHAEL 1 [*pushes her down on the couch*]: Jenny . . . what is happening with us? [*Strobe comes on again*] What's happening here? [*They embrace*] Oh, Jenny . . . Jenny.

[MICHAEL 2 *enters, approaches audience. The stage goes suddenly dark. A spotlight immediately falls on* MICHAEL 2]

MICHAEL 2: There are many animals that may soon be extinct if we do not get your help. [*A film of whale slaughtering or of any display of cruelty to animals may be shown here*] Now that we have your attention, it may be a good time to tell you about the situation as it stands. As you watch this play before you, the Japanese and the Russians are killing the very few whales, dolphins, and yes, even tunas left in the ocean. And meanwhile the Canadians, yes, our good neighbors, are killing off baby seals by the thousands. So please take the time to write . . . to your government, your congressmen, your senators, and tell them something has to be done about that. It may also interest you to know that our very government is profiting from all this too . . . granting fishing licenses or permits or whatever they call it to these very same Japanese, Russian, and Canadian fishermen and seal-killers to do it in our territorial waters. Thank you so much, ladies and gentlemen.

[*(Instead of the above, whatever commercial deemed appropriate may be substituted. If a touch of slapstick is workable, perhaps* MICHAEL 2 *should follow or chase the spotlight.) The stage goes dark as* MICHAEL 2 *leaves. Reddish dimmed light silhouettes* MICHAEL 1 *and* JENNY]

MICHAEL 1: Not now, Jenny . . .
JENNY: Michael, I need you . . .
MICHAEL 1: Dave's in the room, you know.
JENNY: Screw that fag.
MICHAEL 1: Dave's not a . . . but so what if he is?
JENNY: You're his roommate.
MICHAEL 1: Why . . . is it contagious?

[*Lights gradually brighten during the following exhanges*]

JENNY: I don't want you staying here . . . with him.
MICHAEL 1 [*pauses*]: Okay . . . I'll move in with you and your family.
JENNY: Don't make a joke of it.
MICHAEL 1: Oh, sorry, you should have read the sign: dangerous sense of humor ahead, approach with caution.
JENNY: They don't know about you . . . yet.
MICHAEL 1: Who?

JENNY [*pauses*]: My family.

MICHAEL 1: You haven't told them?

JENNY: All in good time, Mike.

MICHAEL 1: And all the time I thought I was doing the avoiding.

JENNY: It takes time, Mike.

MICHAEL 1: I was avoiding people who never heard of me.

JENNY: Well . . . I wasn't sure.

MICHAEL 1: You weren't sure . . . about me?

JENNY: I wasn't sure how my family would take it.

MICHAEL 1: I'm beginning to understand. I don't know what's going on around here.

JENNY: You don't have a monopoly on prejudiced parents, you know.

MICHAEL 1: Is that the point? [*Pauses*] Well . . . at least I try to tell my mother.

JENNY: And how's the old creep taking it? Huh?

MICHAEL 1: Hey! All of the sudden you've been calling a lot of people "creep" around here.

JENNY: We all have our tempers, too, Mike.

MICHAEL 1 [*after long pause*]: I don't think you see the point here. [*Pauses*] You haven't exactly been on the level with me. You've been two-faced about all this. You made it seem like you didn't mind my mother . . . and that you liked David . . . or you'd told your parents about us. At least, I thought you did, you know.

JENNY: I was just being civil . . . to your mother. And I never told you I told my parents about us.

MICHAEL : You never told me you never told them either.

[*Doorbell rings*]

JENNY: Why should I? [*Pause. Doorbell rings*]

MICHAEL 1: You weren't sure about us, were you?

JENNY: I love you, Mike . . . at least I think so . . . thought so.

MICHAEL 1: So it's past tense now. You loved me but you weren't sure we were going to make it.

JENNY: Mike, we may still make it.

MICHAEL 1: I'm glad to hear you have doubts.

[MOTHER *opens the door by herself; enters*]

MOTHER: No one answers doorbells around here.

MICHAEL 1: Mother . . . you have a key?

MOTHER: Yes. But did I get it from my elder son? No, I have to get it made all by myself. [*Noticing* JENNY] Oh, Johnny's here.

JENNY: How good to see you, Mrs. Chun.

MOTHER [*emotionlessly*]: How good to see you. [*Pauses. To* MICHAEL 1] "How good to see you." "How are you." "Have a nice day." There are so many expressions here that don't seem to mean anything. In the old country, when we asked a person how they were we would sit down, sip some tea, and listen to how they were. [*Pauses*] But here. They ask you how are you and before you can get a word in, they are halfway down the road. [*Pauses*] And "how good to see you"—what is so good about seeing an old lady like me?

MICHAEL 1: Mother?

MOTHER: You are not looking well, Michael. [*Pauses*] And Johnny . . . you look sickly too.

MICHAEL 1: Mother!

JENNY: It's all right, Mike. I am very fine, Mrs. Chun.

MOTHER: Straight from the donkey's mouth. [*Feigns ignorance of the meaning of the remark*] Isn't that the expression here?

JENNY: There are many expressions here, Mrs. Chun. [*Walks to the door*] Sometimes they don't even have to say it out. [*Raises her middle finger at her*] Have a good day, Mrs. Chun. [*Exits*]

MOTHER [*acting angered*]: Did you see what that vulgar woman just did? [*Looking at* MICHAEL 1] I am not completely ignorant of these signs you young people have. Michael, what are you going to do about this?

MICHAEL 1: I don't care.

MOTHER: What? You are going to allow that tramp to insult your very own mother? That vulgar piece of garbage, that slut?

MICHAEL 1: Call her whatever you want.

MOTHER [*after a pause*]: Something is . . . [*dawning on her*] wrong with you two. I hope. [*Pause*]

MICHAEL 1: Something is wrong with everything.

MOTHER [*happily*]: Is this a dream? I have gone to mother's heaven. My son is finally seeing the tramp for what she is. [MICHAEL 2 *enters and approaches* MICHAEL 1] Now we can find you a decent Chinese girl.

MICHAEL 1: I . . . I don't want to care anymore.

MICHAEL 2: The trick in life is to realize how screwed up you are. And then you have it all solved. Nothing is worth solving.

MOTHER: I know this girl from this Tan family, a very respectable family. You are very fortunate, Michael. You know, in the old days, the Tans and the Chuns were really one and the same family group. And many people frowned on one marrying another with the same last name . . . but of course, in this day and age, we're more broadminded about this.

MICHAEL 1 [*suddenly screaming*]: I'm not caring anymore! [*Rushes into his room*]

MOTHER [*raising her voice a little*]: That's what I said . . . they don't care about it anymore. Nobody makes a big thing out of marrying someone else with the same last name.

DAVID [*entering from his bedroom*]: Why, Mrs. Chun. Hello.

MOTHER: Oh, hello, David.

DAVID: Is something wrong with Michael?

MOTHER: Oh, you know Michael. [*Pause*] Michael has some good news to tell us. [MICHAEL 1 *has already emerged from his room with a small suitcase*] Michael has broken up with that horrible girl.

MICHAEL 1 [*no longer noticing* MOTHER *or* DAVID]: Where the hell am I going?

MICHAEL 2: Anywhere, Mike. Just anywhere.

MICHAEL 1: Just anywhere . . . [*Goes toward the door, stops momentarily*]

MOTHER: Where are you going, Michael?

[MICHAEL 1 *doesn't hear her. He is completely oblivious to both* MOTHER *and* DAVID]

DAVID: Mike?

MOTHER: Well . . . when you return, I will have a nice dinner all prepared.

[MICHAEL 1 *takes one more look around but does not really see anything. Exits abruptly*]

DAVID [*after a pause*]: You think he's all right?
MOTHER: Michael? Yes, he's all right. You know my son . . . full of sense of humor and dramatic flair. Should've been an actor. Oh, that theatrical son of mine.

[*Lights goes off a split second before* MICHAEL 2 *suddenly speaks*]

MICHAEL 2: And now, ladies and gentlemen, the Chinese Classical Theatre, the All Brand New Chinese Classical Theatre, presents the alternate ending! [*Fanfare music*] Nobody wants to leave a theatre depressed. After all, this is a comedy . . . or don't you know already.

[*Lights come on.* JENNY *and* MICHAEL 1 *are facing each other*]

MICHAEL 1: You never told me you never told them either.

[*Doorbell rings*]

JENNY: I'm sorry, Mike. I should have, I know now.

[*Doorbell rings. Pause*]

MICHAEL 1: I guess I can understand why you didn't.
JENNY: I love you, Mike.
MICHAEL 1: And I love you, Jenny. We are going to make it!
JENNY: I am sure we will, Mike.
MICHAEL 1: I'm glad to hear you say it.

[MOTHER *opens the door by herself; enters.* MICHAEL 1 *and* JENNY *are in each other's arms*]

MOTHER: No one answers doorbells around here. I guess everyone is too busy around here.
MICHAEL 1: Hello, Mother.
JENNY: Nice to see you, Mrs. Chun.
MOTHER: Nice to see you too, Johnny . . . Jenny. [*Pauses*] Oh, sometimes mother's eyes can be blind. And a mother's

tongue can be so cruel. [*Pauses*] You two really care for each other, don't you.

[*Violin music comes on*]

MICHAEL 1: Yes we do, Mother.

JENNY: I love your son very much, Mrs. Chun.

DAVID [*entering*]: Did I hear the doorbell? [*Pauses*] Oh, how are you, Mrs. Chun?

MOTHER: Hello, David. [*Slight pause*] David, I've just been en-lightened by the true love of young people. I never really knew it. In my day, marriages were arranged by our parents. Sometimes even before we learned to walk, they were telling us who we were going to be walking with on our wedding ceremony. [*Pause*] But how nice it is . . . true love.

[*Violin music really builds up*]

DAVID: Jenny and Michael do make a nice couple.

[MICHAEL 1 *and* JENNY *separate from embrace.* MICHAEL 1 *faces* MOTHER, *and* JENNY *faces* DAVID]

MOTHER: My son, Michael! I'm so happy you will be happy!

MICHAEL 1: I'm so glad you understand.

MOTHER: She may be a red-haired Caucasian, but she will be *our* red-haired Caucasian.

JENNY: Dave, please forgive me for all those irrational things I've said.

DAVID: I've forgotten them already.

MICHAEL 2: And who says we can't have happy endings around here? [DAVID *gives* JENNY *a hug. Then* MICHAEL 1 *gives* MOTHER *a hug.* MICHAEL 1 *then goes over and hugs* JENNY. DAVID *hugs* MOTHER] And now, here's the big finish.

DAVID: Oh, we must have a big finish.

JENNY: Yes, wouldn't be right without something the audience will remember us by.

MOTHER: Yes. Some famous Chinese theatre director once said that even if all the dialogue in a play runs smoothly, and even if you have a great plot, great character interaction, the audience goes home with what they see last.

MICHAEL 2: So . . . are we ready?

[*They all form a line. Music comes on*]

[*All sing*]

> This is the all brand new
> And there's so very few
> Chinese Classical Theatre
> And we assume you knew
> This is the All Brand New
> Chinese Classical Theatre

MICHAEL 1 [*taking the solo*]

> So we even have a song
> For you all to sing along
> And if it should sound wrong
> We'll just bong bong bong on our gong . . .

MICHAEL 2 [*encouraging the audience*]:

> This is the All Brand New
> And there's so very few
> Chinese Classical Theatre
>
> Yes, the all brand new
> Please wait for the cue
> Chinese Classical Theatre

[MICHAEL 2 *joins the line again, and the group sings and kicks out with the music*]

MICHAEL 2: Softly, softly

[*All sing softly*]

> Yes, the all brand new [*pause*]
> The all brand new

MOTHER: If you hate it, sue!

[*All softer and softer*]

> All brand new
> Chinese Classical Theatre

[*Suddenly loud*]

> All brand new
> This is the
> All brand new
> Chinese Classical Theatre

[*Actors can ad-lib lines, cheering*]

> All brand new, all brand new
> Chinese Classical Theatre

[*Softly again*]

> All brand new
> All brand new

Blackout

[*Off*]

> Chinese Classical Theatre
> All brand new
> All brand new
> Chinese Classical Theatre

[*Voices substituted by a tape recording which speeds up, then breaks*]

Curtain

In The Alley

EDITOR'S NOTE

In the Alley is possibly the best short play ever written in Hawaii on the dynamics of racial conflict. Sakamoto loosens up his structure and creates a believable picture of group frustrations with an aimlessness and repetitiveness early on: boasting of past exploits and future plans, swilling of beer, arm wrestling, sparring. Most are rituals of male bravado, mild outlets which only feed a need for stronger ones. Haoles are the main scapegoats for feelings of alienation, but several of the group have confused attitudes: for instance, Manny has dreams of being successful on the mainland and is contemptuous of the crude hostility of Bear to haoles; Cabral is thinking of joining a haole-dominated military as an alternative to his home life. What unifies the gang and precipitates violent action is not just the fact that a haole passes by, but that he is making out with a local girl. The comic male competitiveness of the men turns to a more deep-seated sexual competitiveness with an outsider. It is interesting that in an earlier draft Joe stayed behind and carried JoJo off to get help. The present ending, worked out for the original production, is much less sentimental.

IN THE ALLEY *was first produced by the UH Theatre group at Farrington Hall, University of Hawaii, for a series of performances beginning October 20, 1961.*

Cast

MANNY	*Robert Heen*
JOJO	*Albert Hee*
BEAR	*Robert Fong*
CHAMP	*Arthur Caldiera*
CABRAL	*Chip Douglas*
JOE	*Arthur Parson*
GIRL	*Valerie Char*
SAILORS	*Marc Schlachter, Richard Noordyk, James Britt*
GIRLS	*Sperry Millikin, Tinker Taylor*
NEIGHBORS	*Cindy Devereaux, Leonora Ching, Carol Kouchi*

Directed by Edward Langhans

Revival production by Kumu Kahua at Kennedy Lab Theatre for a series of performances beginning May 10, 1974.

Cast

MANNY	*Peter Stone*
JOJO	*Ed Baxa*
BEAR	*Stefan Yoshiota*
CHAMP	*Jim Bell*
CABRAL	*Arthur Yorita*
GIRL	*Leslie Anderson*
JOE	*Chip Arnold*
HAOLES	*Warren Helm, Leo Jones*

Directed by Dando Kluever
Lighting by Dian Kobayashi Lopez and Darryl Kaneshiro

In the Alley

BY

EDWARD SAKAMOTO

Characters

(in the order in which they speak)

JOJO. *A local youth about twelve or thirteen years old. He is very unlike Manny—always smiling, good natured, eager to please. He is skinny and small, wears a colored T-shirt and bell bottom trousers, and goes barefoot.*

MANNY. *JoJo's older brother; about twenty-one years old; sharp, dark features. He is silent, sensitive, and rarely smiles. He is barefoot and wears a pair of old blue jeans and a T-shirt.*

BEAR. *Dark, about eighteen or nineteen years old. He is stockily built, thick-necked, has a blunt nose and hair fuzz growing under his lower lip. He has an overall fierce, animal-like appearance. Wears rubber slippers.*

CHAMP. *His friends call him "Champ" because he is an amateur boxer. He has a muscular physique, and he shows it off by wearing a tight V-necked T-shirt. A cosmopolitan, he is fairly handsome. Has plaster over one eye which is cut. Goes barefoot.*

CABRAL. *Local Portuguese boy who is the same age as Bear. Wears a bright, new aloha shirt and a pair of baggy pants. Barefoot.*

JOE. *Haole in casual ivy league clothes, rolled-up shirt sleeves. He is a sailor on short leave. Has crewcut and overall clean-cut appearance.*

GIRL. *A not too pretty and not too young local woman. She is dressed quite gaudily.*

THREE HAOLES. *Friends of Joe who are a little drunk but it is hardly noticeable.*

A Honolulu city side-alley, one end of which leads to an unseen maze of tenement houses, while the other leads to an open street. Broken wooden crates and overflowing garbage cans litter the area. The set lighting should indicate night.

[*At curtain rise,* MANNY *and* JOJO *are discovered seated on crates onstage*]

JOJO: Eh, Manny, how come Pa pick on you all da time?

MANNY: Because he hate my guts and I hate his guts. Aaaa, but no make difference to me. I ain't going stay around hia anyway.

JOJO: Why? Wea you going?

MANNY: I like go up da mainland. I can get one job dere.

JOJO: I can go, too, Manny? I can go wid you?

MANNY: You too young yet. Afta high school you can come up. Maybe we can team up and do someting good, eh, JoJo?

JOJO: Yeah, man. I no feel so good at home wid Pa always squawking, drinking, swearing. I wish I can go wid you right away. Wat we going do together on da mainland?

MANNY: I dono. Open up one garage maybe. You know, get so many cars nowdays, we can make plenty money fixing om up.

JOJO: Terrific idea, man.

MANNY: But befo I go to da mainland, I like smash da old man and pay him back fo all da trouble he cause me.

JOJO: No blame Pa too much. I bet he feel bad enough already. Maybe if he no drink so much . . . [*Slight pause*] When you going leave? Not right away, eh?

MANNY: Naw. I gotta get some money first. Get plenty jobs fo busboys nowdays. I figure I can get enough money in about two months. Tomorrow I going look fo one job.

JOJO: Tomorrow? Oh, I almost foget—tomorrow Ma's birthday.

MANNY: Wat? You shua?

JOJO: Yeah. I was going tell you, but I wen foget 'til now.

MANNY: Why you neva tell me mo early so I could save some money?

JOJO: I sorry . . . but I get tirty-eight cents. You no mo nutting?

MANNY [*searching his pocket*]: I get about tree bucks. But wat can we buy fo her wid only tree bucks?

JOJO: And tirty-eight cents.

MANNY: And tirty-eight cents.

JOJO: I was tinking, you know, everytime Ma gotta open da cans wid da hand-kine opener, eh? Humbug, eh? Why we no buy her da crank kine? Dey get one small magnet on da top to lift up da cover when come off. Real nice.

MANNY: How much cost, though?

JOJO: Was only about two buck someting, I tink.

MANNY: Okay. Hia da tree bucks. Tomorrow go buy her da can opener. And no foget give me back da change.

JOJO: Yahoo! I no foget. No worry. Oh, Ma going be real happy. Too bad we no can buy her da real expensive kine, eh? One electric can opener. You just have to press down one lever and da can open by itself.

MANNY: Yeah. How much cost?

JOJO: Twenty someting bucks.

MANNY: Someday we can buy her dat kine stuff. When we get da money.

JOJO: When we come millionaires, eh, Manny?

MANNY: Yeah. When we come millionaires.

JOJO: How long you tink going take us fo be millionaires?

MANNY: About one hundred years.

JOJO: Dat long? Ass too long, Manny. Ten years maybe, eh?

MANNY: Yeah, maybe ten years.

JOJO: Den we can buy one big white house just like da kine da haoles get.

MANNY [*getting excited also*]: One two-story house wid tree bathrooms. One fo you, me, and da old lady.

JOJO: Wat about Pa? Gotta get one fo Pa too.

MANNY: Naw.

JOJO: Come on, Manny, one fo Pa too.

MANNY: Okay. One fo da old man too.

JOJO: I like one big yard, too, Manny. One big, big yard wid nice green grass, so I can lie down and sleep o play football wid my

friends. We go get one dog, too, okay? One German police
dog. One nice big German police dog. I go call him "Rocky".
MANNY: Easy. You can get all dat. You can get anyting you like.
JOJO: Wat about one swimming pool like da haoles get?
MANNY: Fo wat? You can go Waikiki swim.
JOJO: Yeah, but I like one swimming pool like da haoles too.
MANNY: Okay. You no going get someting fo da old lady?
JOJO: Oh yeah. We go get Ma one nice big white stove. Good
idea, eh? And one new washing machine. And . . .
MANNY: We gotta get her some new clothes, too, right?
JOJO: Yeah. Da real expensive kine. [*Slight pause*] Wat you like,
Manny?
MANNY: Me? I like one racer, da small kine fo race in da Indiapolis
500. Aaaa, I not fussy. I like everyting money can buy.
JOJO: When we going be rich, Manny? I no can wait already.
MANNY: No worry. Someday. Someday.

[BEAR *enters and lazily shuffles over to the boys*]

BEAR: Eh, Manny, babe.
MANNY: Hi, Bear.
BEAR: Eeh, JoJo, you skinny baga.
JOJO [*jumps up, hits fighting stance. Jokingly*]: Wat! Wat! Wat
you call me? You like fight, o wat?
MANNY [*smiling*]: Beat om up, JoJo.

[JOJO *approaches* BEAR, *who quickly grabs the youngster and
applies the bear hug*]

JOJO: Aa-a-a! I give up! I give up!

[BEAR *lets go and* JOJO *tries a bear hug on his rotund friend.*
JOJO *grunts loudly as he squeezes* BEAR, *who just laughs at*
JOJO's *futile efforts. Soon* JOJO *gives up, exhausted. In the end
both get a good laugh out of it and sit down near* MANNY]

MANNY [*to* BEAR]: Wea Cabral and Champ? Dey not coming, o
wat? And wea da bia?
BEAR: Dey said dey was coming. Cabral said he was going bring da

bia. I tired tonight. And tonight fo hot. So damn hot and sticky. [*Fans himself with his hand*]

MANNY: Why you tink I ask fo da bia? I like one ice-cold one right now . . . Why you so tired? Wat you did today?

BEAR: I was down da beach wid some of da boys. Almost had one fight today.

MANNY: Who and who?

BEAR: Had dese bunch of haoles, service guys, trying to cause trouble, da bagas.

MANNY: Wat dey wen do?

BEAR: You know Lei and Margie, eh? [MANNY *nods*] Dese damn haoles wen whistle and make some wisecracks at da girls. Dey tink dey so terrific. Dey go say, "Honey, you look tired. You need a stiff injection. How about it?" Den one odda baga wen say, "Wanna earn a fast ten bucks?" You know wat he was meaning, eh? Make us blow up. We almost tangle wid dem. All dey looking fo is one wahine to sleep wid. Da damn sharkbaits give da girls V.D. and whose hard luck? Us guys, man! Den da girls give us da disease and us da suckers. Stinking haoles betta not fool around wid our girls. Da over-sexed bagas!

MANNY: Da haoles always making trouble.

BEAR: Dey figure dey so hot. If one haole get smart wid me, I pity him. [*Pounds fist into palm of hand menacingly*]

JOJO: But not all da haoles like dat, eh? Get plenty good haoles, I bet.

BEAR: Yeah. Da haole wahines cute, man. Just one night wid one of dem. Eat om up, man!

[CABRAL *and* CHAMP *enter, each toting a carton of beer*]

CHAMP: Howzit!

CABRAL: Hiya, bums!

BEAR: About time, you bagas, I almost die of thirst.

CHAMP: No make me laugh, you get enough beer in you to last you da rest of da year.

MANNY: Cabral, dat one new shirt you wearing?

CABRAL: Yeah, slicka one, eh?

BEAR: No tell me you wen buy om, you miser.

CABRAL: No be stupid. I wen lift om from one store. Real easy.

BEAR: How?

CABRAL: I not going tell you my professional secrets.

BEAR: Wat you mean professional secret? Come on, I like learn someting new every day. Share your knowledge of stealing, I your good friend, eh? Last week when you was hungry I gave you one bowl poi, eh, rememba?

CABRAL: Big deal. I had sore stomach afta dat.

BEAR: Chee! Not my fault you get weak stomach. Rememba da time . . .

CABRAL: Okay, okay. Enough already. Champ, tell om how I wen scoop dis shirt.

CHAMP: Me and Cabral wen walk in dis clothing store. Was kinda busy dat time, Cabral was wearing only one T-shirt and so he wen pick one shirt off da rack, put om on, wait a little while, and den walk out. Nobody notice nutting.

CABRAL: Pretty smooth, eh? Timing and guts. Ass all you need.

MANNY: You guys wen buy da beer?

BEAR: You tink dese misers going buy anyting?

CABRAL: Fo wat waste money?

BEAR: You see!

CABRAL: We went in dis store dat sell liquor. Champ go talk wid da owner in one far away corner, and I just go pick up one six-pack and walk out when nobody looking.

[BEAR *steals bottle from the six-pack as* CABRAL *goes by, knocks cap off lid of can*]

CHAMP: We did da same ting at one odda store.

BEAR [*drinks, grimaces*]: Ugh-h-h. Why you no steal da cold kine at least?

CABRAL: Hell, be grateful fo wat you get.

CHAMP: You like one, JoJo? [*Offers beer to* JOJO]

MANNY: He too young. I no like he drink yet, no good fo him.

BEAR: Chee, just like one fada worrying about his kid.

CHAMP: Not like my old man. Stinking bastard, everytime he drunk and running around wid some broad.

CABRAL: Wat you moaning about? You do da same ting.

CHAMP: So wat? I still young so I get excuse fo doing wat I do.

BEAR: My old man only good fo da toilet bowl. Good-fo-nutting jackass.

MANNY: Da hell wid all of om. Gimme one bia.

[CABRAL *responds to the request. All gulp down their beer*]

BEAR: Eh, Champ, why you get dat plaster ova your eye? Your girl wen hit you when you try kiss her, eh?

CHAMP: No get funny. You know I wen box last night.

BEAR: Oh yeah. Last night was amateur night, eh? You knock out da guy?

CABRAL: Da odda guy wen flatten him out in da third round.

BEAR: No! Bull lie! [*Laughs*] I wish I was dere. Shame, man, shame.

MANNY: Wat kine guy he was?

CABRAL: One haole from da Army.

BEAR: No lie! Oh, mo worse. You wash up if one haole can wipe you out. Hang up your jocks, Champ. Pau, finish already.

CHAMP: Shut up, you dono why I lost. You know why I lost?

BEAR: Why? Why?

CHAMP: Well, shut up and I tell you. [*Stands up to demonstrate*] I had dis haole on the run, see. I give om two left jabs, den one terrific uppercut, one right to da body, and I get om on da ropes, see. Den he start running away. So I step on his feet, give om one elbow in da face and one rabbit punch. Den I all ready fo give my killer right and you know wat he wen do?

BEAR: Wat?

CHAMP: Dat damn haole wen hit me one low blow. Suppose to be one foul.

BEAR: If one foul, how come da ref neva call om?

CHAMP: Wise up, stupid, damn ref was one haole too. Favoritism, favoritism—ass why I lost.

MANNY: Ass why hard.

BEAR: Ass why hard when you good fo nutting.

CHAMP: I see you like one boxing match tonight. [*Rises*] Come on, I take you on. [*Sets himself in boxer's stance*]

BEAR: Shua, shua, I challenge you. [*Leans bottle on can*] Arm wrestle, arm wrestle. [*Lies down center stage, raises arm up at elbow*]

CHAMP: Okay. Anyting. I wipe you out like dat. [*Snaps fingers*]

BEAR: Show me, show me, you weakling. Eh, Cabral, you da judge. Make shua dis baga no cheat.

CHAMP: Watch dis stinka, he going try use his whole fat body fo win.

MANNY: Wait. I sit on Bear, den. JoJo, sit on Champ.

BEAR: Cheee, no fair. I got sore back.

CHAMP: Shut up, crybaby.

CABRAL: In dis corner, dat animal known as da Bear, da one and only flabby piece of piggy from Kalihi. And in dis corner, dat guy we know as Champ, dat muscular, handsome Hercules.

BEAR: Eh, eh, favoritism already.

CABRAL: Shut up, Bear, ass da truth. Okay, you bums, get ready, set . . . [BEAR *jumps the start and begins to force* CHAMP's *arm down*] Cheating, cheating, I neva say go.

BEAR [*stops*]: Wat you waiting fo?

CABRAL [*says quickly*] Go!

[BEAR *is caught off-guard and mouths inaudible words to* CABRAL, *who, along with* MANNY *and* JOJO, *is laughing at* BEAR's *handicapped start. The two battle for quite a while until* CHAMP *finally pins* BEAR *down.* BEAR *rolls over on his back, arms outstretched, mouth wide open*]

BEAR: Bia! Bia! [JOJO *pours the drink down his throat*] Hey, da taste good. Ono!

CABRAL: Bear, you betta hang up your BBD's.

BEAR: I tired tonight. I wen work hard today. I was busy lifting heavy boxes, ass why I no mo strength. [*Massages arm*]

[CABRAL *and* MANNY *open up beers for all and pass them around*]

CHAMP: Excuses, always excuses.

BEAR: So wat. At least I no let one haole beat me.

CHAMP: I told you he wen foul me.

BEAR: Excuses, always excuses.

CABRAL: Ass true, da haoles real dirty. At least I ain't one no good haole. I one good Portagee.

[*They all laugh and drink some more*]

MANNY: Bear, tell dem wat wen happen at da beach today.

BEAR: I was down da beach today and . . .

CHAMP: I tawt you was busy lifting heavy boxes.

BEAR: I no can go down afta work? Chee, this baga no give up yet.

CABRAL: So wat was so interesting at da beach?

BEAR: Some service guys wen get smart wid Lei and Margie. Dey go whistle and make dirty kine suggestions. One baga wen say, "Want a hot dog, honey? You supply the bun and I'll bring the wiener."

CHAMP: Ass all? You act da same way wid da haole girls. In fact, you mo dirty and sickening.

BEAR [*trying to ignore* CHAMP's *remark*]: I was going rap da haole in da face, and da guys was ready to back me up when one cop wen pass by. Jam everyting up. I was all set fo one good fight and . . .

CHAMP: Too bad da cop came, eh? I bet da haole could chop you down real easy.

BEAR: Chee, you love da haoles, o wat?

CHAMP: No get stupid.

CABRAL: So wat you guys did afta da cop went away? You neva tangle wid dem aftawards?

BEAR: Nah. Da haoles chicken. Dey run away befo we can fight.

JOJO: Why you guys hate da haoles? Get one good haole in my room . . . real nice guy. Him da president of our class. Nobody hate him. Me, I like him.

BEAR: You too young, JoJo, you no undastand. Dis haole in your room just catching you sucker. You find out about dem when you get mo old. Manny, you no tell your brother nutting, o wat?

MANNY: Wat you like I tell om?

BEAR: Tell om about da no good haoles.

MANNY [*in bored manner*]: JoJo, da haoles no good, no be friends wid dem.

JOJO: But I know kinda plenty good haoles in school.

BEAR: You get one stubborn brada, Manny.

CHAMP: Dey no good, JoJo. On da outside maybe dey look good, but inside dey dirty. Dey hit you below da belt in everyting.

CABRAL: Dey like act bossy . . . order you around . . . do dis, do dat. And wat you tink dey doing . . . just sitting on dea fat rears watching you work your sweat out. Dey let you do all da dirty work, just like my boss. Someday I going broke his mouth.

BEAR: Dey steal your girl, but dey no let you even look at dea girls.

MANNY: And you know how dey treat popolos.

CHAMP: Yeah. Someday, da popes going wipe out all da haoles.

BEAR: You know wat mo betta? Make all da haoles sterile, den dey finish. No mo haoles, no mo trouble.

JOJO: I still tink da haoles okay.

CABRAL [*to* JOJO]: I neva see one funny-kine kid like you.

JOJO: But Manny, if we going to da mainland, we gotta mix around wid da haoles, eh? We gotta be friends wid dem fo make good business in da garage, eh?

CABRAL: Manny, you going to da mainland?

MANNY: Yeah.

BEAR [*lies face down, facing* MANNY, *on elbows*]: Why you neva tell us?

MANNY: Wat fo? Anyway, I only made up my mind tonight.

CHAMP: How come so fast? Wat wen happen?

MANNY: I wen fight wid my old man.

CABRAL: Jesus, you always tangling wid him, eh?

BEAR: Ass nutting. Be like me. When my old man get smart wid me, I whack om one in da face. He no fool wid me now, I just show him dis. [*Holds clenched fist in front of them*]

CHAMP [*to* MANNY]: Why you wen fight fo?

MANNY: He was pushing around da old lady, yelling, swearing, making her cry. Just get me so mad I told om to stop. Den he start pushing me around. JoJo like try help me, so da old man slap him in da face. I was so damn mad, I kick om in da stomach. Da bastard was crying fo air when I wen walk out.

CABRAL: I told you guys about my old lady, eh? If my old man get tough wid her and hit her, she run quick get da butcher knife and wave om in da air. Da old man come scared, man. He know she mean business. Da butcher knife is da real equalizer.

CHAMP: Good your old lady get guts like dat.

BEAR: But, Manny, if you going to da mainland you no can get dates on Saturday nights.

MANNY: Why?

BEAR: Chee, you know you kinda dark, eh, and if da haole girls tink you one pope, dey not going out wid you.

MANNY: No get stupid. I took out some haole girls already.

BEAR: Yeah, but ass da stupid-kine haole wahines. Down hia get plenty suntan-kine guys and da wahines tink you one of dem sun-lovers who toasted on da outside but still white on da inside.

MANNY: You nuts!

BEAR: I not kidding. Sammie told me when he was on da mainland, da haole girls neva like go out wid him.

CHAMP: I no blame dem. He so damn ugly.

CABRAL: No lie, Bear, somebody told me he saw Sammie in L.A. walking around wid one haole wahine. [*Shoving* BEAR*'s head with his foot*]

BEAR: Shua, shua, but she was one whore. Sammie wen get so disgusted he wen start looking fo whores.

CHAMP: Wassa matta, ass the only kine he like. I know Sammie.

MANNY [*to* BEAR]: So I get me one whore every Saturday night o else I go out only wid Aunt Jemimah. Now you happy?

BEAR: No get mad. You hate da world, o wat?

MANNY: Yeah, I sick of everyting. I gotta get off dis rock.

CABRAL: Me too. I figure I going join da army.

BEAR: Dey no like 4-F bagas like you.

CABRAL: Wat you mean, man, they going make me one general. [*Stands up and salutes*] General Cabral. Terrific, eh?

CHAMP: Mo betta I go to da mainland too. Be one pro boxer and knock out all da weaklings.

BEAR: No make me laugh. Dey going be carrying you away in da stretcher every night.

CHAMP [*starts pulling* BEAR *to stage right by his legs*]: You really looking fo trouble tonight, eh? Come on den.

JOJO: Somebody coming.

[*They all crouch low near the rubbish cans, looking off stage and waiting. Soon a local girl and* JOE *appear hand in hand. The couple do not notice the gang. They stop, embrace, and kiss*]

JOE: Now, that was something. [*Slight pause*] By the way, what're you doing tomorrow night?

GIRL: Why you so nosy for?

JOE: Ha! Honey, you don't have to put on an act with me. How 'bout making the rounds again?

GIRL: Maybe I going be busy tomorrow.

JOE [*moves with her to center*]: Ah, come on, now. I'm a lonesome soul lost in the land of paradise. Give a guy a break. How 'bout it?

GIRL [*after a short while*]: Okay.

JOE [*smiling triumphantly*]: Where do we go from here?

GIRL: I gotta go home.

JOE: Already?

GIRL: Late, you know, and I live kinda far away.

JOE: Your folks waiting for you?

GIRL: No be silly. I living with only my mother and she no care when I come home.

JOE: Is she the understanding type?

GIRL: Maybe. Why?

JOE: Oh, I, ah . . . just asked.

GIRL: She not going be home tonight.

JOE: No kidding?

GIRL: You like come my house little while?

JOE: Great. But, ah, how 'bout . . .

[*She obliges.* MANNY *signals the others and they all creep up on the unsuspecting couple*]

BEAR: Eh, haole, wat you tink you doing?

JOE: Huh?

[JOE *tries to move upstage but is blocked. He looks around at the faces of the boys and then realizes he is carefully being surrounded*]

BEAR [*belligerently*]: You no going answer me? I said, wat you
    tink you doing?

JOE: Well, just having a little fun—if it's any of your business.

CABRAL: Cocky bastard, eh?

MANNY: He tink he so hot.

CHAMP: Wat you expect from one haole?

JOE: Real tough guys, huh?

CHAMP: Tough enough. You like test us out, o wat?

JOE [*smiles weakly*]: I didn't mean nothing. I was just kidding.
    Forget it.

CABRAL: Wea you pick her up—on Hotel Street?

GIRL: Eh, watch dat crack, eh. Wat you tink me?

CHAMP: One little old slut.

GIRL [*moves a step toward* CHAMP]: No call me one slut, you
    punk.

BEAR [*laughing*]: You betta watch out, Champ, o she going beat
    you up. And no call her one slut; chee, you no mo manners, o
    wat? She not one slut, she one bitch.

GIRL: Look, ugly, why don't you mind your own business and shut
    your mout. [*Crosses to* BEAR]

BEAR [*rises and retreats*]: Chee, da rough wahine. You figure
    you can beat me up, o wat? You like fight? [*Jabs at her
    lightly*]

MANNY: Bear, why you no pick on somebody your own size?

BEAR: Wat you mean? She just my size.

[*He puts his arms around the girl, who quickly stamps on his
foot.* BEAR *dances around holding his foot, but then moves
toward the* GIRL *with an outstretched arm*]

BEAR: You dirty . . .

JOE [*stops* BEAR]: Hold it, pal. Don't lose your head.

CABRAL: Yeah, Bear, no bruise her up, he still gotta use her yet.

MANNY [*moving between* JOE *and* BEAR]: Wat you going do to
    her aftawards? Jump her when you reach one bed?

BEAR: And give da disease to her.

JOE: You sure have some wild ideas. I can see the natives are rest-
    less tonight.

CHAMP: Making fun of us, eh?

JOE: No, no, don't take it the wrong way. I'm not looking for trouble. Hey, listen. My name's Joe.

CABRAL: We wen ask fo your name? Wat da hell we care wat your name?

BEAR: Eh, bitch, wat your name? [GIRL *remains silent*] Wassa matta, we not good enough fo you? Da haoles betta den us local guys, o wat? You figure you going get good fun wid him, rolling around in da bed?

JOE: Hey, she's a nice kid. Watch what you say to her.

BEAR: You ordering me around? Who you tink you?

CABRAL: He like act bossy, eh.

JOE: Now don't get mad. Listen, I just got into port a couple of days ago, and I'll be leaving in a few days so . . .

CHAMP: One sailor boy, eh? I hia you guys get one girl in every port.

JOE [*trying to be friendly*]: That's the scuttlebutt; but don't believe it, there's not a bit of truth in it.

MANNY: You tink you one real lover, eh? One real Casanova.

JOE: I bet I could learn a lot from you guys.

CABRAL: Getting mo and mo cocky! You tink you so terrific, eh? You really looking fo trouble, eh?

JOE: No, don't get me wrong. I don't hate you guys. I want to be your friend.

JOJO [*moves between* CABRAL *and* CHAMP, *toward* JOE]: I be your friend.

MANNY: Shut up, JoJo.

JOJO: No be like that, Manny, we go be friends wid him. He look like one good guy.

JOE: Thanks, kid. See, he's got the right idea. Shake, pal. [*Offers his hand to* JOJO]

MANNY [*pushes* JOJO *aside, moves to* JOE *and shoves him to the right*]: No bodda us, JoJo, go home.

JOJO: I like stay, I no like go home.

MANNY: Den shut up.

CABRAL: Dis bastard figure he get muscles, o wat, rolling up his sleeve like dat?

[CHAMP *circles around* JOE, *who circles with him and moves more right.* GIRL *sneaks to right of* BEAR]

CHAMP: Yeah. [*To* JOE] You tink you get big body, o wat? [*Flexes his arm*] When you get biceps like dis, you can roll up your sleeve.

BEAR: Us local guys no roll up our sleeves fo show-off like dat.

JOE: I see what you mean. Against local customs, huh? Thanks for telling me. [*To* CHAMP] You sure have a powerful build. I wish I had a muscular body like you.

BEAR: Jealous baga. I bet he wish he was handsome like me too.

MANNY: Shut up, Bear, no joke.

BEAR: Wat you mean joke? I not joking. I serious.

JOE: Well, it's getting pretty late, we have to go. Nice meeting you guys.

CABRAL: Maybe we betta teach him one lesson first, eh, Manny?

MANNY: Yeah.

JOJO: No fight. Bambai we get in trouble.

GIRL: You punks betta watch out. Some of his friends stay down da street. If you make trouble, I going call dem.

BEAR: Eh, bitch, if you no shut up, I going punch your mouth. You like get raped, o wat?

JOE: We'd better go.

[JOE *and* GIRL *move toward exit, but* MANNY *stops them and pushes* JOE *back*]

MANNY: Wea you tink you going, haole?

JOJO [*pleading*]: Let om go, Manny, please.

[MANNY *pushes* JOJO *away.* GIRL *suddenly darts off stage*]

CHAMP: Eh, she running away.

MANNY [*to* JOJO]: Now you see wat you did. Go follow her and see if she getting his friends and come back quick tell us.

JOJO [*hesitantly*]: Yeah, but . . .

MANNY: No stall. Hurry up.

JOJO: No do nutting, okay? [*Exits*]

BEAR: Now, haole, you going get your medicine.

JOE: Hey, this is stupid. I'm not looking for a fight.

CABRAL: Damn yellow bastard.

CHAMP: Let me get my cut first.

[*They pile into* JOE, *punching and kicking until he slumps to the ground unconscious*]

BEAR: Weak baga.

CHAMP: We go befo somebody come.

CABRAL: Yeah, we had our fun fo da night.

MANNY: I gotta wait fo JoJo.

BEAR: You gotta wait? You crazy, o wat? Wat if da cops come?

CABRAL [*pulls* MANNY]: Come on, Manny, come on.

MANNY: Wat about JoJo?

CHAMP: JoJo not dumb. When he see wat happen he going dig fo home.

CABRAL: Yeah, ass right, Manny, no worry, nutting going happen to him. [CABRAL *and* CHAMP *exit*]

BEAR: JoJo can take care of himself.

[MANNY *looks back one more time, finally gives in, and goes off stage with the others. There is a slight pause while* JOE *slowly regains consciousness*]

JOJO' [*off stage*]: Manny, I dono wea she went.

[JOJO *enters, now breathing hard from what seems to have been a long run. He sees* JOE *on the ground, walks slowly to him, and then bends down to help him*]

JOJO: You okay? I sorry about this. [JOE *tries to get up, so* JOJO *makes him lean back against a garbage can*] Sometimes dey dono wat dey doing. Dey gotta fight every time, ass why no good. Hard luck you wen come dis way. If you neva come, dey go fight wid somebody else. Me, I no like dat kine stuff. I like be friend wid everybody . . . Maybe I can get some medicine fo you.

JOE [*with faint smile and muttering voice*]: I had my medicine already, pal.

[*Offstage there is the sound of loud talking. Suddenly a girl's voice says, "There's one of them. Look, he trying to steal something." Several haoles enter with the* GIRL. *They move swiftly toward* JOJO, *who, realizing the danger, starts to exit. They catch him, however, and begin pounding him to the ground. They continue to hit him until* JOE *finally stops them*]

JOE: He's just a kid. What's the matter with you guys? Didn't you see he was trying to help me?

FIRST HAOLE: She was the one that pointed him out. It's dark in here. We couldn't see if he was a kid or not.

SECOND HAOLE: How is he?

THIRD HAOLE: Aw, the kid's all right. We didn't hit him that hard.

FIRST HAOLE: Well, let's scram before the cops come.

SECOND HAOLE: Come on, Joe. [*Tries to help* JOE *off stage*]

JOE: Let me go. I'm staying.

THIRD HAOLE: You out of your mind? You stay here and you'll have big trouble—up to here. [*Levels hand at his neck*]

SECOND HAOLE: Don't be a sucker, Joe.

FIRST HAOLE: Let's get the hell outta here, man. Somebody must've called the cops by now. [*Begins to pace around and looks up the alley*]

JOE: I gotta take care of the kid.

THIRD HAOLE: Look, you don't owe the kid nothing. What do you want—a good conduct medal or something?

SECOND HAOLE: If you gotta think of somebody, think of us, we're your buddies. If they catch us, we'll all get the ax.

[*Siren sounds softly*]

FIRST HAOLE: Dammit, I hear it, you guys—the cops.

[GIRL *exits*]

THIRD HAOLE: Shake a leg, Joe.

FIRST HAOLE: Hurry it up, man. The cops, I tell ya.

SECOND HAOLE: Come on, Joe, come on.

[THIRD HAOLE *is almost pushing* JOE *off, while the other two pull him out of the alley.* JOJO *is still lying on the ground as the siren gets louder and louder*]

Curtain

Paradise Tours

EDITOR'S NOTE

Paradise Tours exposes the Hawaii marketed in tourist traps as something less than Paradise, something closer to Hell. The first production was done very simply: five red chairs representing the bus interior, backed by a red curtain, against which the matching aloha attire stood out all the more significantly.

Though it never gets too heavy, the play brings to mind earlier ones such as Baraka's *Dutchman* and Sartre's *No Exit,* and its structure similarly suggests a closed cycle.

The stereotypes in this surreal cartoon-land include not only the gullible haole tourists but also the opportunistic local who signs over his land, language, and heritage. There is little conflict because everyone has sold out. In this world of "doggie lives and doggie jokes," Hawaiian place names and pidgin are subject to wild punning, and local customs seem pumped out to prompt canned laughter. The Devil himself is revealed as a sit-com henpecked husband in disguise.

Here Hell is neither self nor other people. It's Hawaiian scenery —through glass.

PARADISE TOURS *was first produced by Kumu Kahua at Kennedy Laboratory Theatre for a series of performances beginning November 18, 1976.*

Cast

RUFUS	*Tim Hayes*
AGATHA	*Colleen Cosgrove*
BERTHA	*Leslie Freundschuh*
BUCK	*Ralph Hirayama*
BOSS	*Howard Noh*

Directed by Barbara S. Hartman

Paradise Tours

BY

ROBERT J. MORRIS

Characters

(in the order in which they speak)

DRIVER, *a Hawaiian whose life of beer and cigars has given him something of a gut and whose philosophy is one of "Ain't no big thing." He has a mustache, partial goatee, long hair, and wears whatever parts of a bus driver's uniform suit him for the day.*

RUFUS, *Bertha's husband. A true milque toast if ever there was one. He is slightly paunchy and pasty, and lisps slightly in subjection to his wife and her friend.*

AGATHA, *Henry's wife. She belongs to the Edith Bunker school of nasal twangers and is the dominant force in her marriage, if not in the bus. You would hate to meet up with her in a dark alley.*

BERTHA, *Rufus' wife. She belongs to the Marianne Lorne school of good-natured, bumbling incompetents.* BERTHA *is a little dingy but harmless. She likes to think of herself as being just a tiny bit racy.*

BOSS, *really Henry, Agatha's husband. He likes to play the role of a rake, but in the presence of his wife he becomes submissive. He is an actor's actor.*

The scene is a bus. There are four chairs, side by side for the four passengers, and a chair down left of them for the driver.

There is a sign, "Paradise Tours," hanging in front of the driver's seat from above. A stuffed cockatoo sits on a perch near the driver's seat.

[*The* DRIVER *enters near the bus and spies* RUFUS *on the extreme opposite side of the stage reading a newspaper*]

DRIVER: Eh, bra . . .

[RUFUS *glances up tentatively from his paper, not quite sure whether or not the* DRIVER *is speaking to him; goes back to reading*]

Eh, bra . . .

[RUFUS *points to himself as if to ask, "You mean me?" The* DRIVER *gestures with a jerk of his head for* RUFUS *to come across the stage to him.* RUFUS *puts down his paper and crosses to the* DRIVER *still very unsure of himself*]

Eh, bra, you get one tour ticket already?

RUFUS [*recognizing the* DRIVER, *after squinting closely at him*]: Oh, it's you. You've put on weight. [*Glances furtively. Whispers loudly*] We're not supposed to be seen together. You know that.
DRIVER: Hey, you like help me out?
RUFUS: I don't know. The Boss said . . .
DRIVER: You just gotta stand here.
RUFUS: Stand here?
DRIVER: Till your wife comes. Here. Put this on.

[*The* DRIVER *helps* RUFUS *take off his aloha shirt, which matches his shorts, and put on a T-shirt the* DRIVER *has handy. Emblazoned on the front of the T-shirt are the words "Beach Bum Hotel" in letters large enough for the audience to read. The T-shirt is way too small for* RUFUS, *and it really exaggerates his paunch*]

DRIVER: You just stand back by the bus and say, "Free bus to the Hotel Beach Bum," as the tourists come by. It's a trick.

RUFUS: What's in it for me?

DRIVER: Free bus ride.

RUFUS: If you say so.

DRIVER: The Boss says so. "Free bus to the Hotel Beach Bum." Practice it, over and over.

RUFUS: Free bus to the Hotel Beach Bum. Free bus to the Hotel Beach Bum. Free bus to the Hotel Beach Bum. [*Continues practicing in a low mutter*]

DRIVER: Oh-oh, here they come. Get ready. [*Stands by the bus to welcome* AGATHA *and* BERTHA *aboard*]

RUFUS: Free bus to the Hotel Beach Bum.

DRIVER: Tickets please, ladies. Boarding now.

[AGATHA *and* BERTHA *enter with the usual tourist trappings and with sack lunches. The aloha wear of* BERTHA, AGATHA, *and* RUFUS *all match each other*]

AGATHA: Alooooha! There you are, young man, our tickets. Oh, Bertha, a local Hawaiian bus driver. Look!

BERTHA [*slightly naughty*]: I think real Hawaiian boys are sooo good looking, Agatha.

RUFUS [*loudly*]: Free bus to the Hotel Beach Bum.

DRIVER: Actually, I'm Vietnamese-Hawaiian, ma'am. My name is Thieu. Timothy Thieu. But most of my friends just call be Buck.

BERTHA: Nice to meet you, Buck.

AGATHA [*cleverly catching on*]: Oh, I get it. You're Tim . . . [*Nudges* BERTHA]

BERTHA: Oh, ah . . . Tim . . . Buck . . . Thieu. [*Laughs*]

DRIVER: Thieu. Yes, ma'am. We'll be departing now, ladies.

RUFUS [*loudly*]: Free bum to the Hotel Beach Bus.

BERTHA: Why, Rufus, what are you doing back there? [*Suspiciously*] I didn't know you were coming with us. You're supposed to be with Henry.

RUFUS: Oh, hello, dear. Just doing what the Boss ordered. Bust your bum at the Hotel Free Beach.

AGATHA: Rufus, you look silly in that get-up. How come Henry isn't with you?

DRIVER [*interrupting*]: All aboard, folks.

RUFUS: Free your bust at the Hotel Beach Bum.

> [*All enter the bus and take their seats. The ladies and* RUFUS *begin looking around like typical tourists. The* DRIVER *makes bus sounds with his lips and tongue, mimes driving, and they begin the tour*]

AGATHA: Oh, Hawaiya!

BERTHA: I'm just fine, dear. How are you?

AGATHA: Is that your cockatoo, Driver?

DRIVER: Yes, ma'am. I call her Flipper.

BERTHA: Flipper the Bird?

DRIVER: Yes, ma'am. But she's just another turkey.

AGATHA: Don't tell me we're the only ones on this tour, Driver. They told us at the travel agency that all Paradise tours were very crowded.

RUFUS: Beach your bum at the Hotel Free Bust.

DRIVER: Most are, ma'am. But since this is your first time, you get to see it all alone.

BERTHA: How nice. I hope you'll go slow so we can take pictures.

DRIVER: I'll try, ma'am, but sometimes I just get carried away and start speeding. Sometimes it almost seems like we get from one place to another before you know it. We're leaving Honolulu now and heading toward the North Shore.

AGATHA: You know, Bertha, I'm learning a lot of new Hawaiian words. It helps you talk to the beach boys.

BERTHA: Like what, dear?

AGATHA: Like "mahalo," for instance. "Mahalo" means "garbage." It's printed on all the garbage cans around here.

BERTHA: That's funny. I thought it meant "butts."

AGATHA: And the names of the streets here are so interesting. You know that little back street by our hotel?

BERTHA: Hotel Street?

AGATHA: The other one.

BERTHA: You mean Kaupai Street?

DRIVER: Do you folks understand pidgin?

BERTHA: Could you teach us?

DRIVER: Well, I am permitted to give you one short lesson if you want it. Just repeat after me. Eh . . .

AGATHA, BERTHA, RUFUS [*in unison*]: Eh . . .

DRIVER: Eh, bra . . .? Eh, bra, wea da chicks?

AGATHA, BERTHA, RUFUS: Eh, bra, wea da chicks?

BERTHA: Eh, bra, wea da chicks? What does that mean, Buck?

RUFUS: Free bra to the Hotel Beach Chicks.

AGATHA: Oh, Bertha, I've heard it lots of times around the hotel. Every time we walk onto the beach in our bikinis . . .

DRIVER: Lots of haoles live on that street, ma'am.

RUFUS: Free your chick at the Hotel Beach Bra.

AGATHA: Driver, I'd like to rest my head.

DRIVER: Me too, lady.

AGATHA: Is there a pillow on this bus?

DRIVER: Only pilaus, ma'am.

BERTHA: Pilaus?

DRIVER: Yes, ma'am. Feather pilaus.

BERTHA: Oh, pillows! Isn't that quaint, Agatha. The natives call them pilaus. Buck, you're pulling our leg.

DRIVER [*naughtily*]: That's what she said.

AGATHA: Come again?

DRIVER: That's what she said . . .

RUFUS: Free pilaus at the Haole Beach Bum.

DRIVER: An old local joke, ma'am. We're coming up on Waimea Bay now, folks. And this is the little community of Pupukea.

AGATHA: Sounds slightly obscene, Driver.

RUFUS: Free pupus at the Hotel Beach Chicks.

DRIVER: It would, ma'am. I mean, to the pure, all things . . .

AGATHA : Oh, look at all the natives, Bertha! Driver, where are all the little grass shacks of Kahala-Kukui?

DRIVER: No mo da kine, lady. I mean, dey all go to da Polynesian Cultcha Centa—I mean—oh, forgive me, I'm slipping again.

BERTHA: Do we get to see that place?

DRIVER: For an extra five bucks we can drive through. We and the Hotel Beach Bum got a deal with them.

AGATHA: What do you mean, "a deal"?

DRIVER: We're in cahoots, ma'am.

BERTHA: Cahoots? Are you sure? I don't see the sugarmill.

AGATHA: According to my map, we're in Hauula.

BERTHA: You know, Agatha, all these local natives here are just as happy as we are.

RUFUS: Free chicks at the Hotel Beach Bust.

AGATHA: Say, Buck, this bus is awfully hot. We paid for air conditioning.

BERTHA: That's right. And why are all these windows sealed shut?

AGATHA: Yes, and how come we can't open them to take pictures and get some fresh air?

DRIVER [*nervously changing the subject*]: Coming around the windward side on the right, folks. This is the Valley of Love and Delight.

AGATHA: Sounds slightly obscene to me.

DRIVER: It would, ma'am.

AGATHA: About these windows . . .

DRIVER [*yields grudgingly*]: It's a hermetic bus, lady.

AGATHA: That's strange. I didn't know buses had any sex at all.

DRIVER: That's what she said.

BERTHA: Well, it's getting hotter.

AGATHA: But I do feel a breeze. Driver, where is that breeze coming from?

[DRIVER *licks his index finger and holds it up to test the wind; grins at the audience deadpan*]

DRIVER: From off stage, ma'am.

AGATHA: Well, let me tell you, I had to pull some real strings to get these tickets.

DRIVER: Yes, ma'am, just like you always do.

BERTHA: Buck, do you know Agatha?

DRIVER: Not biblically, ma'am.

AGATHA: What do you mean by that wisecrack?

DRIVER: In a way, I sort of know you both. You know, of course, that all this is being recorded.

AGATHA: Recorded? Here in the bus?

DRIVER: Yes, ma'am. In stereo. We type it out for you and give
   you a transcript.

BERTHA: You type in stereo, Buck?

DRIVER: Yes, ma'am. You might call it stereotype. There's the
   famous lookout up ahead, folks.

BERTHA: Oh, it's the Pally, Agatha.

RUFUS: Free your pally at the Hotel Beach Bum.

AGATHA: Just what do you mean, ''just like I always do?''

DRIVER: Just buffalo your way through, ma'am, just like you
   always do.

BERTHA: Buffalo her way through?

DRIVER: Yes, ma'am, and let the chips fall where they may.

AGATHA: Well, who are you anyway? Another token local?

DRIVER: Just Buck, ma'am. That's all Scratch calls me.

BERTHA: Scratch?

AGATHA: That sounds slightly obscene.

DRIVER: It would, ma'am. Scratch is the Boss.

RUFUS: Free scratch at the Hotel Beach Chicks.

DRIVER: Well, that's Honolulu ahead, and the business district.
   My, how time flies when you're . . .

AGATHA: My husband Henry, and Rufus here, are here partly on
   business.

DRIVER: We'll be seeing Henry shortly, ma'am.

AGATHA: How do you know that?

DRIVER: We always see him when he's here on business. We knew
   yesterday that you were coming today.

AGATHA: Where is he now?

DRIVER: In make-up.

BERTHA: I don't think I like this, Agatha.

AGATHA: Well, Buck, we are free, white, and twenty-one, and
   women like us certainly would not be treated like this back
   home in the U.S. of A.

DRIVER: Where are you ladies from, as if I didn't know?

BERTHA: Montana.

DRIVER: Oh, I've been to Montana. Butt, Montana.

RUFUS: Free butt to the Hotel Beach Bum.

AGATHA: That's *Butte,* Montana, Buck. *Butte.*

DRIVER: But ma'am, it's spelled "butt"! B-U-T-T-E.

BERTHA: Agatha's right, Butte. It's Buck, Montana.

DRIVER: Are you sure, ma'am?

AGATHA: That's right, Buck. It's Butte.

BERTHA: I thought it meant "mahalo."

RUFUS: Free beach at the Hotel Bus Butt.

DRIVER: I don't know, ma'am—I've seen some butts that were beauts.

RUFUS: Beach your free at the Hotel Bum Bust.

AGATHA: Have you been to Butte recently, Buck?

DRIVER: Years ago, ma'am, passing through in the Army.

BERTHA: Did you like it?

DRIVER: Ma'am, I spent two weeks there one night.

BERTHA [*noticing out the window*]: Say, isn't this the same place we started this tour earlier?

DRIVER: Yes, ma'am. Well, we're leaving Honolulu now and heading toward the North Shore . . .

AGATHA: What? Are we going around again?

DRIVER: That's what *she* said.

AGATHA: I want off! I demand off! Can't you get me off?

DRIVER: I doubt anyone could, ma'am.

AGATHA: No, no, no! We have a luau tonight, just like last night.

BERTHA [*grimacing*]: By the way, what was that fish we ate at the luau last night?

AGATHA: Mahu-mahu, dear, mahu-mahu.

BERTHA: I thought it tasted a little queer.

DRIVER: Coming up on Waimea Bay, folks, and Pupukea.

BERTHA: I'm going to eat my lunch. [*Begins to eat*]

AGATHA [*huffy, to* DRIVER]: Now just a minute, boy, my husband could buy this whole . . .

DRIVER: Ma'am, ma'am! You folks are such special guests, and I am so pleased to inform you that you, Agatha, have been awarded the first prize in our weekly *Okole Maluna* contest.

RUFUS: Free bus to the Okole Beach Bum.

AGATHA: First prize? [*Cautiously, somewhat mollified*] Well . . . you say it's a weekly contest?

DRIVER: Yes, ma'am. Very.

AGATHA: Well, what is it, this first prize?

DRIVER: One all-expense-paid week in Kalihi.

AGATHA: I never won anything before in my life.

DRIVER: And you, Bertha, have won second prize, compliments of the Boss.

BERTHA: Ooooo, I can't wait. What is it? What is it?

AGATHA: Stop being so greedy, Bertha. My heavens. Who is this Boss, anyway?

DRIVER: We'll be meeting him at Makapuu.

BERTHA: What's the second prize?

DRIVER: Two weeks in Kalihi.

RUFUS: Kalihi okole at the Hotel Beach Bust.

AGATHA: So when do we start? When do we get off this bus?

DRIVER: Actually, you don't, ma'am. This is really all we do—just keep going around and around. This week in Kalihi is in the bus, parked in front of a crack seed store.

BERTHA: But where do we get off?

DRIVER: You wouldn't know, ma'am.

AGATHA: But I have an appointment with my hairdresser.

DRIVER: It won't matter to you after a while.

BERTHA [*daubing herself*]: It's getting hotter and hotter in this bus.

AGATHA: Well, you never did sweat much for a fat girl, Bertha.

BERTHA: What an awful thing to say!

DRIVER: I agree, ma'am. I think you should tell her you're sorry.

AGATHA: I'm sorry, dear . . .

BERTHA: That's better, Agatha.

AGATHA: . . . that you don't sweat much for a fat girl.

BERTHA: It is getting hotter.

DRIVER: Yes, ma'am. Every seventh pass around, we go out the long way to Kaena Point and you get a box lunch of cold poi and squid on a bed of frozen, day-old malasadas, while we drive the Point Road at fifty miles an hour. We take all our meals on the bus. We just go [*like a scratched record in both action and voice*] around and around and around and around and around and around and . . .

AGATHA [*finally making herself say it*]: Then this can't be . . .

DRIVER: No, ma'am, it's not Paradise. We use the name on a time-sharing basis just for PR purposes. Please take your seat.

[AGATHA *obeys*]

BERTHA: Well, Agatha, see what you've got me into this time.

DRIVER: I'm being promoted myself. Becoming a Master Driver five days from now. Also getting more and more into incendiaries, pyrotechnics, and combustibles. You see, we fasten them up front there to the front of the bus for instant firing. Really clears the road in a jam.

BERTHA: Is that the bumper?

DRIVER: No, ma'am. It's the grinder.

AGATHA: Since when is a bumper a grinder?

DRIVER: Since they started serving mahu-mahu on Hotel Street.

RUFUS: Since feather haoles became pilaus.

AGATHA: That's redundant.

BERTHA: You say you're getting promoted?

DRIVER: Yes, ma'am. I'm finally getting horned.

AGATHA: That sounds slightly obscene.

BERTHA: You sound slightly obscene, Agatha. Be quiet.

[AGATHA *has a look of total astonishment on her face*]

DRIVER: Yes, ma'am, but that will be part of another play with a different cast.

AGATHA [*recovering*]: Another play?

DRIVER: Yes, ma'am.

BERTHA: Do you have any female parts?

DRIVER: No, ma'am. Only the bus is hermetic.

RUFUS: Squeeze your bust at the Hotel Beach Bum.

AGATHA: But young man, if this isn't Paradise, then it must be . . .

DRIVER: Correct, ma'am.

AGATHA [*almost in worship and fear*]: Then are you—him?

DRIVER [*laughing*]: Oh, no, ma'am. Just one of his humble servants. Actually, the Boss brought me here originally for the *exact same reasons* that you two are here.

AGATHA: And what would those be, young man?

DRIVER: I can't tell you now, ma'am. You wouldn't understand. You have to figure it out for yourself.

BERTHA: Then are we condemned to going around and around this island in this bus forever?

DRIVER: We prefer to call it a hold-over engagement.

AGATHA: Are we—dead?

DRIVER: Yes, ma'am.

BERTHA: And this is our punishment?

DRIVER: Yes, ma'am. In addition, you will be listening to the same jokes and eating the same luau food every day from now on. After the first month, we start you listening to three hours every day of "Aloha Oe," and then gradually work up to twelve.

AGATHA [*resumes her seat*]: What about my husband?

DRIVER: Regarding them, I have some bad news and some good news. Which do you want first?

AGATHA: The bad news.

DRIVER: You would, ma'am.

BERTHA: The bad news, Buck.

DRIVER: The bad news is that from now on, your husband will only be allowed to consort with "good-lookin' haole chicks" from Waimanalo. Oops, there I go again! Sorry.

AGATHA: Old Henry would call that good news. Where is he, Rufus?

RUFUS: Free Beach to the Hotel . . .

AGATHA: Oh shut up, Rufus!

DRIVER: It depends on how you look at it, I guess.

AGATHA: This is more than slightly obscene, Buck.

DRIVER: Yes, ma'am.

BERTHA: What's the good news?

DRIVER: All the "good-lookin' haole chicks" from Waimanalo eat nothing but kim chee.

BERTHA: Kim chee? What's kim chee?

[DRIVER *takes a bottle of kim chee from under his seat and passes it back to* BERTHA]

DRIVER: This stuff, ma'am.

AGATHA: So what if they only eat kim chee?

[BERTHA *passes the opened bottle to* AGATHA; *they both smell it and grimace*]

DRIVER: All the buses are closed like this one.

AGATHA [*returning the bottle to the* DRIVER]: I see what you mean. Good heavens! Oh. Sorry, Buck.

DRIVER: This here is in fact Waimanalo, where they have the chicks and the blues.

BERTHA: I don't see your Henry.

DRIVER: That's the lighthouse cliff at Makapuu.

AGATHA: But Buck, if *we* have to go around and around forever in this bus, then so do you.

DRIVER [*after a long pause*]: Yes, ma'am . . .

BERTHA: That's my line, Agatha.

AGATHA: Even if you are a Master Driver.

BERTHA: Those are pretty steep cliffs.

DRIVER: Yes, ma'am. That highest point is Suicide Cliff.

BERTHA: It makes me dizzy.

AGATHA: Dizz*ier*, dear.

DRIVER: This is the only time we will ever come this way on the trips, and the only time we will ever open the bus. We only open it once for every passenger.

BERTHA: Are you going to open it for us?

DRIVER: If you wish, ma'am. Then you will have five minutes to decide.

AGATHA: To decide? To decide what?

BERTHA [*panicking*]: To jump! That's what you're saying, isn't it? [*Runs forward and grabs the* DRIVER] To jump off Suicide Cliff?! Ooooo! [*Falls to her knees and pleads*]

DRIVER: Ma'am, ma'am, please don't make a scene. Oh-oh, I see the Boss down the road. I'm stopping the bus here. [*Makes more bus sounds as the bus comes to a stop*]

BERTHA: Ooooo, I wish I could get my hands on that travel agent.

DRIVER: Oh, he's one of our people, ma'am. Wiry little Pake, right?

AGATHA: That's redundant.

DRIVER: You're catching on, ma'am.

BERTHA: Well, at least we know one thief in Paradise. Why have we stopped?

DRIVER: You folks seem to misunderstand me. I'm not suggesting that you jump. That would be absurd. You're already dead, right? We just want you to make a choice.

AGATHA: What choice?

DRIVER: On the one hand, you may resume your seats on the bus and go around and around and around and around and around and around . . .

AGATHA [*slapping him on the back again*]: And on the other hand?

DRIVER: Thanks, ma'am, I needed that. On the other hand, you may stay here forever at Makapuu as tour guides yourselves.

[*During* AGATHA's *next line,* RUFUS *and* BERTHA *join her and stand up in the bus. They stand close together in matching aloha wear to form a solid tableau*]

AGATHA: You mean . . . [*puzzling it out slowly*] look at all their straw hats and aloha shirts and koa seeds and matching dresses forever?

BERTHA: That's worse than looking at Agatha's home movies.

AGATHA: Forever?

DRIVER: Yes, ma'am.

BERTHA: I'm scared.

AGATHA: Are you saying it's better to be a servant in hell than a tour director at Sea Life Park?

DRIVER: Not me, ma'am. Milton.

AGATHA: John Milton?

DRIVER: Milton Fukumoto, your travel agent.

AGATHA: I'm scared too, Bertha.

DRIVER: You're learning, ladies. The Boss is coming over our way.

AGATHA: But Milton—you know, the travel agent—he said that when we paid our dues, we would get the best things in life in Paradise.

DRIVER: Oh, yes, ma'am, I keep forgetting. I'm just not being a very good host. I'm sorry. Just a moment. [*Reaches under his*

*seat and pulls out two bottles of beer and a couple of cigars
and hands them to the passengers*] There you are.

AGATHA: What are these?

DRIVER: The best things in life, ma'am. Even if you are dead.

AGATHA: Beer and a cheap cigar?

DRIVER [*firing up a lighter and lighting their cigars for them*]:
What else is there?

AGATHA: At least you brought a case of ice, didn't you?

DRIVER: Oh-oh, here's the Boss.

AGATHA: We want a minute to think about this.

DRIVER: Just a minute is all. I have an appointment at my hairdresser.

AGATHA: Come on, Bertha, let's huddle. You stay put, Rufus.
You're in this somehow.

[*The ladies retire to the rear of the bus, somewhere far
upstage. The* BOSS *enters. He is horned and a most handsome
person. He wears a large black cape and a Lone Ranger mask
over his eyes. He hands the* DRIVER *a beer and cigar, and has
one of each for himself*]

BOSS: Eh, bra, wea da chicks? [*Does a flashy fire trick as the stage
lights flash red*]

DRIVER: Eh, howzit, Boss?

BOSS: Eh, Rufus, howzit?

RUFUS: Freeze your beach at the Hotel Bum Bust.

DRIVER: He kinda mix-up.

BOSS: I know. I've been listening to your conversation.

DRIVER: Boy, am I glad to be getting that promotion, sir.

BOSS: Five more days, eh?

DRIVER: Yessirree. I can't wait. I'm slipping sometimes.

BOSS: I know. I heard you. Sometimes it's a little bit of heaven, if
you'll pardon the expression.

DRIVER: Right on, Boss. Eh, you tink dey like stay wid da bus?

BOSS: They always do, don't they? [*Indicates audience*] *They*
would.

DRIVER: I guess you're right. Here come the ladies.

[AGATHA *and* BERTHA *return downstage, puffing on their cigars*]

BOSS [*nervously, covering his face with his cape away from view of the ladies*]: Well, time to be going . . .

AGATHA and BERTHA: Hi, Boss!

AGATHA: We've decided, Buck. We'll stay with the bus.

DRIVER: You would, ma'am.

BOSS: Ahem. Yes, well, told you so, Buck. Well, nice seeing you all. Take care, Buck, and . . . [*Starts to exit rapidly, still covering himself*]

DRIVER: Easy, sir.

AGATHA [*getting tough*]: Just a minute there, "Boss." [AGATHA *grabs the* BOSS, *swings him around by the shoulders, and rips the mask off his face*] I'd know your voice anywhere. What are you doing in that get-up, Henry?!

BOSS: Er, ah . . . hello, dear. Howzit?

DRIVER [*aside*]: Meet Mr. and Mrs. Agatha Brown.

AGATHA [*grabbing him by the ear*]: Don't you "Howzit" me, Henry! Have you been listening to us?

BOSS: Yes, dear.

AGATHA: Where?

BOSS: In the wings. [*Pause*] What are you doing smoking a cigar?

AGATHA [*blowing smoke in his face*]: You're going to that luau with me tonight, Henry, and you are going to eat every bean and pea on your plate. Now take that silly costume off. Where did you get it anyway?

BOSS: In wardrobe. [*Takes his cape and mask off to reveal aloha wear that matches that of all the others*] You can't make out till you make up.

BERTHA [*trying her wings*]: That sounds slightly obscene.

AGATHA: Shut up, Bertha.

DRIVER: I'm afraid there's no luau, ma'am.

AGATHA: What do you mean there's no luau?

BOSS [*fishing for words*]: He's right, dear. This, ah . . . this Paradise Tour is, ah, for real . . . actually.

DRIVER: Actually, ma'am, all it amounts to is that you just go on much like when you were all alive.

AGATHA: How's that?

DRIVER: Living your same little doggie lives with all these same little doggie jokes. Just like always. That's it.

RUFUS: Hey, chicks, wea da bras?

AGATHA: But so do you, Buck! Your same doggie life!

DRIVER [*nods admittingly*]: Yes, ma'am.

BOSS [*after long pause, clears his throat*]: Yes, well . . . ahem . . . no need to be glum, after all . . . [*throws another flashy fire trick as the stage lights flash red*]

AGATHA: Shut up, Henry. No smoking in the theater.

BOSS [*humbly*]: Yes, dear.

AGATHA: "Wea da chicks" indeed. That's a lot of hooey.

DRIVER: Welcome to the club, ma'am.

AGATHA: You too, Buck.

DRIVER: Eh, Boss, you know da chicks? You like check om out?

AGATHA: He would indeed. Sit down, Henry.

DRIVER: Well, back on the road again, folks. All sit, please. [*Makes bus sounds as they take their seats*] Coming up on Koko Head and Hanauma Bay.

BERTHA: Buck, how much longer did you say before you get horned?

DRIVER: Five days.

BOSS: And I'm giving him a bonus [*to* AGATHA] if it's all right with you, dear.

BERTHA: Is it a raise?

DRIVER: No, ma'am, better. As the Boss put it, a little bit of heaven. I get to talk pidgin again—*all the time.*

AGATHA: What about us?

DRIVER: You get to talk turkey, ma'am.

AGATHA [*loud and emphatic*]: Turkey?!

BERTHA [*snapping to attention*]: Yes, dear, what is it?

BOSS [*indicating the bird*]: And the cockatoo?

DRIVER [*with Italian accent*]: Watcha you language.

BOSS [*imitating Paul Lynde*]: Oh, that's tacky!

RUFUS: Free bus to the Hotel Cockatoo.

DRIVER: Coming up now on Hawaii Kai and the haole pilaus . . .

AGATHA [*to the* BOSS]: So this is what you were doing when you flew out to all those conventions and business trips.

BOSS: It's hell to pay, dear.

DRIVER [*checking his watch*]: Hey, folks, it's getting late. Time for the climax.

AGATHA [*wagging her finger at the* DRIVER *as if to say, "I gotcha"*]: That's what *he* said.

DRIVER: That sounds slightly obscene, ma'am.

AGATHA: It is, believe me.

DRIVER [*like a scratched record*]: That's what she that's what she that's what she that's what she that's what she . . . [AGATHA *raps him on the back again.* DRIVER *winks at* AGATHA] Eh, thanks, Boss.

AGATHA [*winking back*]: Eh, bra, wea da chicks?

RUFUS: Bust your boss at the Hotel Bum Beach.

AGATHA [*flashing a shaka sign, reclining bossily, and puffing her cigar*]: Let's get this show on the road. Sing, Henry!

[BOSS *begins to lead them all in a chorus of "Aloha Oe," as he conducts and gesticulates broadly. They sing loud and brassy*]

Curtain

The Travels of Heikiki

EDITOR'S NOTE

The Travels of Heikiki has a deliberate naiveté which recalls the techniques used in some of the best Hawaiian plays for children. The original production of the play was performed extensively in secondary schools, and it perhaps works best for both children and adults when its exotic qualities are minimally suggested in production rather than literally embodied. For here there is a shotgun wedding of motifs from Hawaiian legend and echoes of Homer's *Odyssey,* and the static tableaux of "serious" pageant plays are pulverised by pidgin and plastic water pistols. There are other anachronisms—Oreo cookies, Primo beer, Purina Dog Chow, puka shell necklaces—that suggest the tacky encroachment of the new on the old. But the warmth of Hawaiian family relationships are charmingly captured in the scenes between mother and child and Heikiki and his tutu grandma.

THE TRAVELS OF HEIKIKI *was first produced by Kumu Kahua at Kennedy Laboratory Theatre for a series of performances beginning September 30, 1976, by the following company of actors and actresses:*

Carol Honda
Lester Mau
David Furumoto
Lynne Nakamura
John McShane
Ralph Hirayama

Directed by Keith Jenkins
Assisted by Paula Rodgers
Lighting by Theresa Wong and Gerald Kawaoka

The Travels of Heikiki

BY
CHARLES R. KATES

Characters
(in the order in which they speak)

MOTHER
SON
TARO
PINEAPPLE
TI LEAF
SUGARCANE
NATURE
HEIKIKI
TUTU GRANDMA
MENEHUNE 1
MENEHUNE 2
LOCAL BOY 1
LOCAL BOY 2
TITA OF WAIPAHU
RAIN GODDESS
FILIPINO
DOG-MAN
CLOUD, MAGIC FLOWER, FOUR DOG-MEN

SCENE ONE

A four-foot platform is located up-stage center with steps on each side of the platform. Up-stage center of this platform is a two-foot platform. Located down-stage right is a small bed.

[*The lights go up on the bed as* MOTHER *and* SON *enter*]

MOTHER: Come now, moopuna, time fo you go moe moe.

SON: I no like go sleep now, mama. I like watch T.V.

MOTHER: No. You have to go to bed now. Stay getting late.

SON: Okay, but first tell me one story, okay? Please, please.

MOTHER: Okay, but you betta go sleep when I pau da story now.

SON: I promise . . . cross my heart and hope to die.

MOTHER: You no have to do dat, just do as I say. Wat you like hia?

SON: I like hia one Hawaiian story. Please, please.

MOTHER: Let me see . . . I'll tell you about da low god and da local boy called Heikiki, who wen go on one trip looking fo experience, and Heikiki's tutu papa, and da Rain Goddess of Waimanalo.

SON: Mama, wat is dat—"low god?"

MOTHER: Wait a minute and I'll tell you da story. Da low gods were da gods of rain, rivers, rocks, ti leaf, and all minor tings in da world. Dey lived on da top of Mauna Loa, and dea dey look after all dea own kine stuff in da islands. Looking ova all da low gods are da bigga gods who watch everybody. [*Lights dim slowly on the* MOTHER *and* SON *and go up on the platform*] One day on da top of Mauna Loa, all da clouds were gathering, waiting fo da Rain Goddess to appear. [*People playing parts of clouds enter and walk slowly around the platform.*] As she came, she looked around and finally wen find da magic flowa she love, and dea she rain on top da flowa and da village wea da flowa lived.

[*Lights on* MOTHER *and* SON *dim.* RAIN GODDESS *enters and steps onto platform, looking around. She is wearing a blue sarong draped over her shoulder and a white veil over her head. She has a water gun. Enter below the platform a person dressed as a flower, who stops and kneels below the* RAIN GODDESS. *The* RAIN GODDESS *squirts her water gun*]

MOTHER: But she neva know sneaking behind da rock was da wild Dog-Man of Kaneohe. [*Enter a person dressed like a rock, and behind him the* DOG-MAN *of Kaneohe. He is dressed in a lava-lava, a fur cape, and a dog mask*] When da Dog-Man wen spock da flowa, he wen quick take om and wen run away. Da clouds wen get all panic, and da Rain Goddess wen scream, and dey all wen follow afta da Dog-Man. [*All this is portrayed on stage*] Fo you see, da Rain Goddess love da flowa so much dat she had to follow weaeva it went. [*Lights dim and slowly go up again on the platform where* PINEAPPLE *appears, wearing a dark green sarong draped across his shoulder*] Meanwhile, standing alone, was da low god Pineapple. He was a god wid no experience and so he could not ripen and grow in abundance. But one day . . .

[TARO *enters*]

TARO: Aloha, Pineapple. Howzit.

PINEAPPLE: Aloha, Taro.

TARO: What's da matta? You look funny-kine. How come you stay hia by yourself? You not going to da party?

PINEAPPLE: I dono . . . I no feel so hot.

TARO: Well, I spock you lata den. I gotta go bring all da taro plants fo da party. It's been a good season fo us low gods, yeah? [*Crosses over platform and down the steps on right. Exits*]

PINEAPPLE [*standing alone*]: Yeah, good fo all da odda low gods . . . but not fo me. I stay still green . . . all da odda gods stay ripe and get plenty of dea own kine plants, but fo me dea is hardly anyting. I feel so sad and lonely. I dono wat fo do.

[PINEAPPLE *sits down on the smaller platform and starts to listen to the music in the background. From left steps of platform enter* SUGARCANE *and* TI LEAF. *They are both laughing and enjoying themselves. Draped over* SUGARCANE*'s shoulder is a white sarong, and over* TI LEAF*'s shoulder, a maroon sarong with some ti leaves*]

TI LEAF: Howzit, Pineapple. How come you look so sad? What's da matta? Lost your wahine?

SUGARCANE: You no can see, o wat? He still stay green . . . he still one virgin. [*Laughs*]

TI LEAF: Dat's okay, Pineapple. One of dese days you going become ripe like us. Yeah, Sugarcane? [*Looks at her and winks. They both start to laugh*]

SUGARCANE: Yeah, wat you need is experience . . . like us guys.

PINEAPPLE [*looks at them*]: Yeah, you guys can talk because you guys stay ripe and everybody know you and your plants. But nobody dono me and dey no even kea.

SUGARCANE: Eh, if you feel dat way, why you no call one of da bigga gods and ask dem fo go help you den?

TI LEAF: Yeah, Pineapple, why you no do dat? Ass da best way. Use your akamai. You not dat dumb, o wat?

PINEAPPLE: Yeah . . . [*excitedly*] das one good idea. Eh, tanks, you guys. I spock you lata at da party, okay?

SUGARCANE and TI LEAF: Yeah, shua. Aloha. [*Exeunt right*]

PINEAPPLE: Aloha. [*Pauses. Walks toward front of platform. As he speaks, music fades out*] O you bigga gods . . . mo bigga den us guys, I ask you fo your kokua. I very unhappy and dono wat to do. I call on you fo show me wat to do. Da peopo no kea fo me, and da Pineapple no grow plenty ova hia. I stay still green and no mo any experience . . . I ask fo help. [*Pauses and looks around*] Eh, you stay listening, o wat?

[*Loud thunder. Music starts as the light fades to a soft blue. Then slowly* NATURE *enters from steps on right of the small platform. She is wearing a brown sarong draped over her shoulder and a gold feather cape*]

NATURE: Pineapple, I have been sent to give you guidance. I have been sent by the god of all things.

PINEAPPLE [*looks up*]: Gee tanks . . . but quick, tell me wat I gotta do.

NATURE: First I must tell you that the Rain Goddess is in need of help. She has been stolen from the small village called Waimanalo by the Dog-Man of Kaneohe.

PINEAPPLE: Why you no go and look fo her?

NATURE: We are not allowed to interfere with what goes on with you lower gods. It's not in our contract. We may give advice and guidance, though. So you have been elected to go on this adventure and save the Rain Goddess from the wild Dog-Man of Kaneohe.

PINEAPPLE: But wat dis gotta do wid my problem, and how can I help when I dono wea Kaneohe stay?

NATURE: That is why you must go down from here and get help from the people of the village, who, by the way, are in need of help themselves. Because of the loss of the Rain Goddess, they are being destroyed by the drought. Their young men are lost also, trying to find the Rain Goddess. But there is one young man left. His name is Heikiki. He has been forbidden by his grandmother to leave the village alone, because she does not want to lose him. Her husband is lost somewhere. You must convince her to allow him to travel with you. It is for his sake and yours that you both make this trip.

PINEAPPLE: But is dis going help me?

NATURE: Yes, it will. Only through experience will you be able to mature in life.

[*Thunder.* NATURE *slowly crosses down steps on left, and the music fades. Normal lighting returns*]

PINEAPPLE: O bigga gods . . . tanks fo all your kokua. I going make shua I vote fo you on da next election. Mahalo.

[TARO *enters and walks up steps on right*]

TARO: Eh, Pineapple, we stay waiting fo you. You going come, o wat?

PINEAPPLE: Yeah, I stay coming. [*Walks with* TARO *down steps on right. Lights dim slowly*]

SCENE TWO

[*In front of the platform area down center stage are* HEIKIKI *and his* TUTU GRANDMA. HEIKIKI *is wearing cut-off jeans with an aloha shirt. His* TUTU GRANDMA *is wearing a colorful muu-muu. The lights slowly go up on them*]

HEIKIKI: Come on, Tutu Grandma. Let me go and find Tutu Grandpa. Come on, okay?

TUTU GRANDMA [*fans herself with a Japanese fan*]: So hot dis place. I tink I going die. [*Looks at* HEIKIKI] No. I told you how many time you no can go . . . you deaf, o wat. Ho, da hardhead dis kid . . . no can listen when I say no. I stay so hot and you stay boddaing me.

HEIKIKI: Gee . . . I getting old already. Everybody laugh at me.

TUTU GRANDMA: Wat you mean, everybody? You da only kane left in dis village.

HEIKIKI: Dat's why. All da wahines stay laughing because I da only one stay hia. Make shame, you know.

TUTU GRANDMA: Who wen say dat? I punch dat wahine in her big maka eye . . . den dat tita not going say nutting. Go fishing o someting . . . no bodda me already.

HEIKIKI [*insisting*]: Come on, Tutu. Let me go.

TUTU GRANDMA [*getting mad*]: I said *no,* and dat's final now. No bodda me. I already lost one kane, your Tutu Papa. I not going lose you. [*Looks at him*] Keep it up and I going slap your head.

HEIKIKI: Shit.

TUTU GRANDMA: Wat you wen say?

HEIKIKI: I neva say nutting, Tutu.

TUTU GRANDMA: You betta not say nutting. Go, get outa my sight . . . I tired. [HEIKIKI *runs off stage right. Enter* PINE-APPLE *from stage left*] Who's dat stay coming? Aloha. Come, come . . . let me get you someting fo eat and drink.

PINEAPPLE: Aloha. Aole pilikia . . . no, tank you.

TUTU GRANDMA: You shua? I get plenty fo eat. My moopuna can go make fo you. No shame, you know. [*Shouts*] Heikiki . . . hui, come quick.

HEIKIKI [*enters from stage left*]: Yeah, Tutu, wat you like? [*Sees* PINEAPPLE] Aloha.

PINEAPPLE: Aloha.

TUTU GRANDMA: Go get him someting fo eat . . . Go quick, I said. [HEIKIKI *runs off*] Come sit down by me.

PINEAPPLE: No tank you, I no need anyting fo eat.

TUTU GRANDMA: Nah . . . look, how skinny you stay . . . and green too. Must be da heat . . . I tink mo betta you eat. Come, come sit down. I not going bite you. [*As he sits*] So wat I can do fo you?

PINEAPPLE: I need your kokua. I need your kane fo help me.

TUTU GRANDMA: I dono if I can help you o wat, because my husband stay lost and nobody know wea he stay. All da odda kane no stay too . . . da only one is my moopuna, Heikiki. Ass all stay left.

PINEAPPLE: Ass who I like fo help me.

TUTU GRANDMA: But I no undastand. Help you do wat? Ass wat I like know. [*Stands and looks down at him*] Who you anyways? You one of da evil bagas dat stay stealing all da men, and you came fo take da only kane left in da village, my moopuna, Heikiki. [*Runs a little away from him and shouts*] Heikiki, quick go get my big sticq so I can smash dis baga one!

PINEAPPLE [*stands*]: No, no. I not one evil guy. I one pineapple god.

TUTU GRANDMA: Auwe . . . Wat's dat—"pineapple?" I neva heard of dat befo, wea you find dat?

PINEAPPLE: Dat's wat I stay trying to tell you. Nobody know wat dat is, and so I need to find one mo betta place to grow in, so dat someday everybody going know me as da one who wen come fo help da village find all da kanes and fo bring back da Rain Goddess. But I gotta have your moopuna fo help me too.

TUTU GRANDMA: Wat he going do? He dono nutting. He neva go

school. He only young boy yet, and I scared lose him fo nutting.

PINEAPPLE: I give you one case pineapple den.

TUTU GRANDMA: I dono wat dat is and you going give me dat.

PINEAPPLE: Okay, den one case of Primo bia.

TUTU GRANDMA: Ass mo like it . . . but I not stupid, you know. I like one case a week until he come back home.

PINEAPPLE: A week? You crazy, o wat?

TUTU GRANDMA: Eh, you like him go, o wat?

PINEAPPLE: Okay.

TUTU GRANDMA [*turns and sees* HEIKIKI *standing looking at them. Walks toward him*] Moopuna, you wen hia? [*He nods*] You like go, o wat?

HEIKIKI: Yeah, Tutu, please. Dat way I can go find our Tutu Papa fo you, so dat you not going be lonely no mo.

TUTU GRANDMA: Aa, you such a good boy. Okay, I let you go, but wait one minute. [*Walks off stage quickly and comes back with a bag*] Hia, take dis wid you. Dat's wat you Tutu Papa wen give me when he wen shopping at Afat Supa Market, befo he wen get lost and neva come back home again. [*Starts to cry*] I going be really worried fo you. My hair going turn mo gray.

HEIKIKI: Aa, come on, Tutu Grandma . . . no make like dat. Shame, you know. Da pineapple stay looking. No cry . . . pau now.

TUTU GRANDMA: Hia, you no tell me wat fo do . . . you like one slap in da head, o wat? Go den, befo I start crying again. [*Kisses* HEIKIKI, *who starts to walk away slowly with* PINEAPPLE. *They cross to stage left*] And you—wateva you are—you betta bring back my moopuna safe, o I going make shua you one squash guava instead of wateva you are. [*Shouts*] You wen hia me?

PINEAPPLE: Yeah.

HEIKIKI: No worry, Tutu. Aloha.

TUTU GRANDMA: Aloha. [*Waves*] And no foget da Primo bia now.

PINEAPPLE: No worry. I going send somebody fo bring it to you every week.

TUTU GRANDMA: You betta, o else you going get it.

HEIKIKI: Enough already, Tutu Grandma, o we going stay hia all day listening to you talk.

TUTU GRANDMA: Go. I not stopping you guys. [*Shouts at them as they go*] Go. Just make shua he not going foget . . . das all.

[*Blackout*]

SCENE THREE

[*Lighting should suggest a dark forest.* HEIKIKI *and* PINEAP-PLE *enter from downstage left. They look around and walk up center stage*]

PINEAPPLE: It shua stay dark ova hia.

HEIKIKI: Yeah, you can say dat again.

PINEAPPLE: It shua stay dark ova hia.

HEIKIKI: Foget it . . . Dis is da forest of da menehunes.

PINEAPPLE: Wat's dat?

HEIKIKI: Dat's da kine small man. Dey mo short den us, and dey catch you and beat da shit outa you. So you betta look out.

PINEAPPLE [*hears a sound*]: Eh, did you hia dat?

HEIKIKI: Wat's dat?

PINEAPPLE: Dea. [*Points downstage right*]Look ova dea, coming toward us . . . wat's dat?

[MENEHUNE 1 *enters, wearing a lava-lava. He is a six-foot tall haole*]

MENEHUNE 1: Who dares to enter my forest without my permission?

HEIKIKI [*to* PINEAPPLE]: Wat's dat—''permission?''

PINEAPPLE: I dono . . . you betta ask him befo he start getting mad.

HEIKIKI [*walks ova to the* MENEHUNE]: Eh, wat's dat "permission" you stay talking about?

MENEHUNE 1 [*looks down at him*]: Who are you who dare to speak to me in that tone of voice?

HEIKIKI [*looks at* PINEAPPLE]: Wat's dat—"tone of voice?"

PINEAPPLE: No look at me.

HEIKIKI: Eh, my name Heikiki and dis my friend Pineapple. He one god, you know . . . so you betta watch out how you talk about permission wid da tone of voice.

MENEHUNE 1: I am the menehune of the forest and . . .

HEIKIKI: What's dat you said you was?

MENEHUNE 1: I said I am the menehune of this forest. Can't you understand English?

HEIKIKI: How can you be one menehune? You one haole . . . and who wen hia of a tall menehune anyway?

MENEHUNE 1: Did you see a menehune before?

HEIKIKI: No.

MENEHUNE 1: Then how do you know what a menehune looks like if you have never seen one before?

PINEAPPLE: I tink he right, you know.

HEIKIKI: Whose side you stay on?

MENEHUNE 1 [*walks toward them*]: So now I will eat your friend and beat you up later. [*Laughs and goes for* PINEAPPLE, *who tries to run but gets caught*]

PINEAPPLE: Heikiki, Heikiki, help, help!

HEIKIKI: Hey, wait bra, no do dat . . . bambai you get sick eating Pineapple. Hia, I get someting mo betta den him. [*Reaches into his bag and brings out a package of Oreo cookies*] See, get da kine white stuff inside dat real one! [*Gives it to the* MENEHUNE, *who drops* PINEAPPLE]

MENEHUNE 1: Let me have that. [*Eats some*] Um-um, good. I like it . . . I like it! [*Sees* HEIKIKI *bring out something*] What is it that you have in your hand?

HEIKIKI: Ass one puka-shell necklace my Tutu Grandmada wen make. You can have om if you let us go. Hia, try om on. [*Gives it to the* MENEHUNE, *who tries it on*] You look shaka, bra!

PINEAPPLE [*runs over to* HEIKIKI]: Yeah, you look like one of da bigga gods!

MENEHUNE 1: Do you really think so? Yes, I guess you're right . . . All right, I'll let you pass through unharmed.

HEIKIKI: Tanks, bra. Hey, I give you one odda one if you tell me wea dey wen take da Rain Goddess from Waimanalo, and if you wen see one old man pass thru hia.

MENEHUNE 1: Well, I don't know. But if you give me another one of these . . . what do you call them?

HEIKIKI: Puka shells.

MENEHUNE 1: Yes, that's it, puka shells, I will tell you of someone who might be able to.

PINEAPPLE: Who's dat?

HEIKIKI: Yeah, tell us.

MENEHUNE 1: There's a tita in Waipahu who might know. But beware of her powers. She can change men into pigs.

PINEAPPLE: Yeah, I wen hia of her.

HEIKIKI: Dat's okay. I no scared of her . . . just tell me wea she stay.

MENEHUNE 1: She lives on the other side of this forest. You must leave now before my brother gets back. He's not as nice as I am.

HEIKIKI and PINEAPPLE [*as* HEIKIKI *gives the* MENEHUNE *the puka shell*]: Aloha. [*Exeunt downstage right*]

[MENEHUNE 2 *enters from upstage left. He is smaller and has a dark complexion*]

MENEHUNE 2: Aloha, bra.

MENEHUNE 1: Greeting, brother . . . look what I have here. They're puka shells. I got them from two strangers who passed through the forest. Do you like them?

MENEHUNE 2: You dumb, o wat? I just wen get om on sale at Holiday Mart fo two dala. How come you neva just take om from om and beat da shit outa om. . . Make shame, now everybody going talk about us. [*Looks at him questioningly*] You shua you my brada? You really lolo and you wen grad from school.

MENEHUNE 1: Ass not my fault if I wen only graduate from the University.
MENEHUNE 2: No, but you no have to act like om.

Blackout

SCENE FOUR

[*An outline of the front part of a hale has appeared stage right. It is just about daybreak. Two local boys enter from downstage left. They are wearing lava-lavas and no shirts. In the background a voice is heard singing*]

LOCAL BOY 1: Hui . . . I thirsty, bra.
LOCAL BOY 2: Yeah, and I tired too.

[*They both cross over to centerstage*]

LOCAL BOY 1: I wish I can get someting fo kaukau.
LOCAL BOY 2: Hey, you hia dat? [*They both pause*] Somebody stay singing.
LOCAL BOY 1: Yeah, stay coming from da hale ova dea.
LOCAL BOY 2: We go take a look.

[*They both stop by the side of the hale and shout*]

LOCAL BOY 1: Aloha.
LOCAL BOY 2: Anybody stay inside dea? [*Waipahu* TITA *comes out of the hale, wearing a sexy sarong with floral print*]
TITA: Aloha. [*Looks at them top to bottom*] Uu, you good-looking kanes. [*They look down shyly*] Aa, no shame . . . come inside. I was just making some poi and I make da best poi hia in Waipahu. Come, hele mai, no be shame wid me. [*Laughs*] Uu, you really cute boys. I tink I going like you guys . . . come, come.

[*The boys go in. Pause. At the same instant, two screams are heard coming from the hale.* TITA *comes out laughing*]

TITA: Dat wen fix da bagas. I teach om fo act like pua'as. [*Laughs*] Now they stay like one. [*Laughs*] Come outside you bagas. [*The boys come out on all fours wearing pig masks and sobbing*] Like fo eat my poi hia? [*Laughs*] Go, get outa my sight.

[*The boys exit, and* TITA *goes back into the hale singing.* HEIKIKI *enters upstage with* PINEAPPLE *behind him*]

HEIKIKI: I stay really tired, bra. [*Stops centerstage*] Look, ova dea get one hale and can hia somebody singing. [*Looks at* PINEAPPLE] Dat gotta be da Tita from Waipahu.

PINEAPPLE: Yeah . . . but no foget da Menehune said she can make you change into a wild pua'a, you know.

HEIKIKI: Yeah, I know. But wat I going do den? Eh, you one god, you suppose to know what fo do.

PINEAPPLE: Let me tink first.

HEIKIKI: While you stay tinking, I going take a look. [*Goes over to the hale*] Aloha.

TITA [*comes out and sees* HEIKIKI]: O, wat dis . . . uu, you is one really good-, good-looking Hawaiian. You must be hungry . . . come inside, I get some real ono poi I just wen pau make.

HEIKIKI: Yea, just wait one minute, I be right back. [*Goes over to* PINEAPPLE, *who is still thinking*] Well, she like me go eat some of her da kine poi . . . what I going do? She one real pokey-looking wahine.

PINEAPPLE: It gotta be in da poi dat make you change into one wild pua'a. So hia, eat dis, pineapple. Dat going make da poi sour. Quick, befo she starts wondering wat you doing ova hia. [*Gives* HEIKIKI *the pineapple to eat*]

HEIKIKI [*coming back to the hale*]: Aloha, I stay come back.

TITA [*inside the hale*]: Hele mai, come inside da door, no lock. [HEIKIKI *enters the hale. After a moment, a scream is heard, but this time the* TITA *comes running out*] Auwe, you must be one of da gods, please no kill me. I one good tita. I promise not to make any more trouble again. I going be nice to all da kanes. I do wateva you like me fo do.

HEIKIKI: Well, I dono . . . Okay, but you gotta turn all da guys dat stay pua'as back to kanes again and tell me someting.

TITA: Yeah, yeah, I promise fo do dat, but wat kine god you, you neva wen change into a wild pua'a.

HEIKIKI: I not one god, but my friend is. He da one who wen help me. Eh, Pineapple, come ova hia. [PINEAPPLE *goes over*] Dis is Pineapple and I is Heikiki. We stay looking fo da Rain Goddess from Waimanalo and my Tutu Grandpapa. So if you can da kine tell us . . .

TITA: You one slick baga . . . so dat's how come you wen get away from me. Well, since you kinda akamai . . . I going tell you. I dono about your kine grandpapa, but I know who get da Rain Goddess. It's da Dog-Man of Kaneohe. He one real pilau man. He stay keeping her fo wata because he one lazy guy dis guy.

HEIKIKI: Wea I can go find da stinka?

TITA: You gotta go back ova dea, pass through da Pali. Ass okay, 'cause dey wen make one hole ova dea, so mo easy fo you fo pass.

HEIKIKI: Going take us long time fo get ova dea.

TITA: Aks Pineapple, he one god. He get da powa fo go.

PINEAPPLE: Eh, dat's right. I wen foget about dat.

HEIKIKI: Quick, let's go den, befo get dark.

TITA: Wait, Heikiki, no go yet. [*Smiles*] Come inside fo little bit. We go make quicky-quicky. Den I give you someting dat can help you wid da Dog-Man of Kaneohe.

HEIKIKI: Wat's dat, "quicky-quicky," Pineapple?

PINEAPPLE: Must be someting you mix like poi.

HEIKIKI: Oo, I betta go find out fo experience.

PINEAPPLE: Yeah, go ahead. I wait fo you.

[TITA *and* HEIKIKI *go into the hale. Lights dim fo a while, then go up again.* HEIKIKI *comes out*]

PINEAPPLE: Chee, you wen take one long time. [*Sees* HEIKIKI *smiling*] How come you stay smiling like dat?

HEIKIKI: O, fo nutting.

PINEAPPLE: Well?

HEIKIKI: Well wat?

PINEAPPLE: No act wid me, dat was quicky-quicky dat you wen make wid Tita from Waipahu.

HEIKIKI: Just like you wen say.
PINEAPPLE: You mean just like making poi?
HEIKIKI: Yeah. Except you must do da pounding.
PINEAPPLE: So—?
HEIKIKI: So wat?
PINEAPPLE: So wea da stuff?
HEIKIKI: Oo, I wen leave om wid her fo keep.
PINEAPPLE: Oo.

Blackout

SCENE FIVE

[*Lighting suggests a forest with deep shadows. The sound of dogs can be heard in the background.* HEIKIKI *and* PINEAPPLE *enter. They walk toward center stage. As they proceed, four* DOG-MEN *come out slowly from each side of the stage surrounding the two. They have on lava-lavas and dog masks*]

HEIKIKI [*looks around and sees them coming slowly toward them*]:
    Pineapple, quick, use your kine powa.
PINEAPPLE: Wat powa?
HEIKIKI: I dono, any one kine powa, as long as it can work, dat's
    da main ting . . . Quick, do wateva you can do!
PINEAPPLE: I no can do nutting except give om pineapples.
HEIKIKI: Do anyting . . . dey stay coming closa. Hurry up, you!
PINEAPPLE: I no mo da stuff dat da Tita from Waipahu wen give
    you . . . Hurry, hurry!
HEIKIKI [*struggles with his bag as the* DOG-MEN *draw nearer*]: Dea,
    I got da kine, Alpo Dog Food.
PINEAPPLE: Quick, give om to dem.

[HEIKIKI *gives it to the* DOG-MEN, *who take it and run away barking at each other*]

HEIKIKI: Shit, dat was one close one, bra.
PINEAPPLE: You can say dat again.
HEIKIKI: Shit, dat was one close one, bra.

PINEAPPLE: Foget it. Look ova dea . . . ass da Rain Goddess. She stay all tied up.

[*They run upstage right, exit, and re-enter with the* RAIN GODDESS *who is wearing a light blue sarong and over her head, a white veil. She also has a water gun which she squirts when she speaks*]

HEIKIKI: Eh, you stay okay?

RAIN GODDESS: Yes . . . Thank you so very much. [*Looks at them*] Who are you?

HEIKIKI: Heikiki is da kine, me, and dat's Pineapple. He one god, too, you know.

RAIN GODDESS: No, I didn't. [*Looking at* PINEAPPLE] You must be one of the lower gods. Well, I am so glad to see you both, but I am sorry that you have gone through all this trouble for nothing. For you see, the Dog-Man of Kaneohe has the magic flower that I am drawn to. That's how he was able to take me away from Waimanalo. [*Sobs and squirts water gun*]

PINEAPPLE: And wea da flowa stay now?

RAIN GODDESS: He still has it on him. He went out to get his dinner. He should be coming back soon. Oh, what are we to do? [*Sobs and squirts*]

HEIKIKI: No cry . . . we going help you, no worry. I tell you wat. I get one sneaky idea inside my head. You go back to Waimanalo and no worry, 'cause we going take da flowa from da guy when he come back fo kaukau his meal.

RAIN GODDESS: Are you sure?

HEIKIKI: Eh, I said no worry . . . So you betta hele on back now.

[RAIN GODDESS *smiles and exits*]

PINEAPPLE: Eh, you talk big, but how we go get da baga? Wat if he eat us instead?

HEIKIKI: Wid da stuff da Tita from Waipahu wen give me, no worry, bra. We gotta go hide now befo he come and spock us hia.

[*Enter the* DOG-MAN *wearing a lava-lava, fur cape, and dog mask and carrying a screaming old* FILIPINO MAN *on his back*]

FILIPINO MAN [*with a heavy accent*]: You betta let me go o I going call da policeman on you. You sonnama gun!

DOG-MAN: Shut up before I eat you right here instead of over there.

FILIPINO MAN: Ay soos . . . dis guy is crazy, o someting? I told my brada dis is one crazy place fo crazy people—dis guy tink he one dog.

DOG-MAN: Shut up, you old bony man.

FILIPINO MAN: Put me down, I said. [*The* DOG-MAN *does as he says. Then the* FILIPINO MAN *starts to jump around the* DOG-MAN *as if to fight*] Okay, you like fight wid me, we fight. I going cut your head right off. [*The* DOG-MAN *grabs hold of his left leg and starts to bite on it*] Aaah! Wat you doing wid my leg? Let go of my leg.

DOG-MAN: I'm trying to eat you, stupid. Stay still.

HEIKIKI [*leaping out*]: Eh, leave dat poor bony man alone, you ugly baga!

DOG-MAN: Who you?

HEIKIKI: Wat you kea who I is?

DOG-MAN: I don't, that's why I am going to eat you instead of him.

[DOG-MAN *lets go of the* FILIPINO MAN, *who runs off stage. He starts to go for* HEIKIKI, *who pulls out a box of Purina Dog Chow and stops the* DOG-MAN]

DOG-MAN: Give me, give me.

HEIKIKI: No way, bra. [*Shakes the box*] Not until you give me da magic flowa!

DOG-MAN [*looking at box*]: Okay, okay, okay!

[DOG-MAN *gives the flower to* HEIKIKI, *grabs the box, and runs off to the side of the stage and eats ravenously*]

PINEAPPLE: Quick! Heikiki, let's get outa hia befo he pau eat and go fo us fo dessert.

HEIKIKI: Yeah, we betta go quick!

Blackout

SCENE SIX

[HEIKIKI *'s village. Lights go on and* TUTU GRANDMA *is discovered pacing back and forth*]

TUTU GRANDMA [*with a Japanese fan*]: Hui, stay so hot and my poor moopuna neva come back yet. I stay getting so much gray hair on dis head of mine, worrying fo him and my poor Tutu Papa. All da odda kane wen come back to da village afta my moopuna and da wat-you-ma-call-it wen save om from da Tita of Waipahu . . . But my moopuna neva come back. Nobody know wea he stay . . . just like my poor Tutu Papa. [*Sobs*]

HEIKIKI [*off stage*]: Tutu . . . Tutu . . . I stay home!

TUTU GRANDMA: Heikiki . . . Heikiki! [*He runs into her arms*] Oh, my moopuna . . . [*Looks about*] Wea is da kine?

HEIKIKI: You mean da kine Pineapple? He went back to weaeva. And da Rain Goddess wen come back too. See . . . look, da clouds stay getting dark. [*Lights change to blue*] Going start to rain, we betta go inside da hale, Tutu.

[*They take a few steps and stop*]

TUTU GRANDMA: You neva wen find your Tutu Papa? [*Looks at him and cries*] Ass okay, as long as I still get you, I stay happy.

HEIKIKI: Come, Tutu. No worry. Lata on I going find Tutu Papa fo you . . . Come, we go inside now. [*Thunder*]

Blackout

SCENE SEVEN

[*Lights come up on the large platform. Soft background music is heard. Discovered center are* TARO *and* SUGARCANE]

TARO: Eh, you wen spock da Pineapple yet?

SUGARCANE: Yeah, I wen hia wat wen happen to him. Da baga wen change too.

TARO: Dea he stay coming now . . . Aloha, Pineapple.

PINEAPPLE [*entering with a light green sarong*]: Aloha, Taro.
Aloha, Sugar. Howzit?

SUGARCANE: Eh, you looking good, bra. You must have had one
real good experience, yeah?

PINEAPPLE: Yeah, you can say dat.

TARO: Eh, we betta go . . . almost time fo da bigga gods fo come
down to da party. You going come wid us, Pineapple?

PINEAPPLE: Yeah, bambai.

SUGARCANE: I wen hia you going on one odda trip wid da guy,
Heikiki. Ass right, o wat?

PINEAPPLE: Maybe . . . I spock you guys lata.

[TARO *and* SUGARCANE *exit.* PINEAPPLE *walks toward the edge
of the platform and calls out*]

PINEAPPLE: Heikiki, Heikiki. [HEIKIKI *re-enters. Lights dim on*
PINEAPPLE. *He looks up and waves*] Spock you lata. Aloha.

HEIKIKI: Aloha.

[*Lights dim on both of them and cross-fade on the* MOTHER
and SON]

MOTHER: Now time fo you go and sleep.

SON: Not now, you neva tell me wat wen happen to da Tutu Papa.

MOTHER: Ass fo bambai. I tell you dat one lata. Now, good night.

Blackout

Curtain

Twelf Nite O Wateva!

EDITOR'S NOTE

Shakespeare's *Twelfth Night* is the major ingredient in Benton's play, a dramatic stew that almost melts the melting pot. In it Illyria, with its apocryphal sea coast, quite appropriately becomes the Hawaiian Islands, and aristocrats and their servants become déclassé alii and their hangers-on. The result is a surreal fairy tale in which pain and external conflicts are minor elements.

In the original production of the play, the acting space consisted of tapa mats surrounded by potted plants, which suggested the lush but strangely formal landscape of Hawaiian myth. The costuming suggested the nineteenth century but not without incongruous contemporary touches—jeans, a bicycle, Lahaina pearls, zoris, and orange lava-lavas.

Pidgin pervades *Twelf Nite* more than the other plays in this volume and, together with the romantic plot and its classical resonances, keeps the play aloft. The most pretentious and studied characters tend to use the lightest pidgin; the unpretentious and spontaneous characters, the heaviest and most free-wheeling. Benton's tactic of quoting almost verbatim from Shakespeare and then deflating the mood with a burp of pidgin or a four-letter word stresses the more farcical aspects of the original model. Some of the more unusual pidgin expressions were contributed by the multiracial company during rehearsals.

TWELF NITE O WATEVA! *was first produced by Kumu Kahua in collabo-*
ration with Leeward Community College at the Kennedy Lab Theatre for
a series of performances beginning on December 26, 1974.

Cast

PRINCE AMALU	*James Grant Benton*
ATTENDANT	*Lisa Pascua*
LAHELA	*Ann Philip*
FISHERMAN	*James Bell, Jr.*
KUKANA	*Carol Honda*
COUNT OPU-NUI	*Ed Kaahea*
SIR ANDREW WAHA	*Mel Gionson*
LOPE	*Rap Reiplinger*
PRINCESS MAHEALANI	*Pamela Viera*
MALOLIO	*Ron Nakahara*
KOA	*Keith Jenkins*
LOKA	*Dennis Nakano*
KOHALA	*James Bell, Jr.*
FIRST OFFICER	*Joan Gossett*
SECOND OFFICER	*Scott Cabral*
PRIEST	*Lester Mau*
MUSICIANS	*David Choy, Daniel Choy,*
	Ted Lau, Sal Ramento,
	Haunani Apoliona, Mary Griffiths

Devised and directed by Terence Knapp
Lighting design by Ed James
Lighting by Scott McDonald
Assistant to the Director, Joan Gossett

Twelf Nite o Wateva!

BY

JAMES GRANT BENTON

Characters

(in the order in which they speak)

PRINCE AMALU

KAWIKA

ALIKA

LAHELA

FISHERMAN

KUKANA

COUNT OPU-NUI

SIR ANDREW WAHA

VALENTINE

LOPE, *a clown*

MAHEALANI

MALOLIO

KOA, *a sea captain*

LOKA

KOHALA, *a gardener*

FIRST OFFICER

SECOND OFFICER

KAHUNA

CHIEFS, SERVANTS, ATTENDANTS

ACT ONE
SCENE I

[*Enter* PRINCE AMALU, KAWIKA, *and other chiefs*]

AMALU: If music going be da food of love, go play on, gimme mo
den extra, so dat appetite going get sick and go make. Oooh,
dat vamp again. It had one dying beat, and wen come ova my
ear like da sweet sound dat breathes on one bank of pakalana,
stealing and giving odor. Nuff, pau already. Da baga not as
sweet as was befo. Ho, spirit of love, you so alive and fresh dat
if you was da frolicking Pacific, I would drink you all. Auwe!
So full of different forms is love dat, by himself, he is one
unending purple dream.

KAWIKA: Prince Amalu, you going hunt, o wat?

AMALU: Wat, Kawika?

KAWIKA: Da deer.

AMALU: Of course, me too, da noblest dear dat I have. Oooh,
when my eyes firs wen spock Mahealani, I tawt she made da
air one big pestilence. Dat instant I wen turn into one dear,
and my desires, like savage pig dogs since den, started chasing
me. [*Enter* ALIKA] Eh, bra, any news, o wat?

ALIKA: Eh, you know wat, Prince, dey neva let me in; but her Portagee maid wen give me dis answer. She said dat Princess
Mahealani no going show her face to anybody fo seven years.
She going walk around her chambers once a day and cry fo her
brada's dead love, dat she going try preserve wid her fresh
tears.

AMALU: Ho, shucks, she wid one fine heart going give all her aloha
to one brada dat already said aloha! If she going keep dis up,
she fo shua going lose all da love dat she got in her. Auwe!

Wat a waste! All dat fo one dead brada. Alika, take me away and bury me in one bed of pikake, 'cause love tawts are rich when covered wid flowers.

[*Exeunt*]

SCENE II

[*Enter* LAHELA *and* FISHERMAN]

LAHELA: Eh, brada, wea we stay?

FISHERMAN: Chee, lady, dis Oahu!

LAHELA: You know, I dono wat I going do hia, and mo worse, I tink my brada he stay home on Maui. Either dat o he wen go drown when our ship wen wreck! Eh, you shua you neva spock om in da wata too?

FISHERMAN: Eh, look tita, jus be happy no was you dat wen make. But, you know, if I wen see right, I tink I saw om tie himself to da mainmast wid some limu dat was floating around in da area. Chee, ass pretty smart!

LAHELA: Oooh, ass heavy, maybe he stay still alive! Eh, by da way, pal, you know dis island, o wat?

FISHERMAN: Shua! Dis wea I wen born and grow up. Wat you tink me, one haole?

LAHELA: Eh, cool head! And ah, who run da joint?

FISHERMAN: One alii named Prince Amalu.

LAHELA: Amalu! Eh, my fada tol me about om.

FISHERMAN: Yeah, but he no stay da same. Right now he in love wid da Princess Mahealani, whose fada wen make las year and den her brada and so she no like see any men. So because of dat, Amalu, he all jam up.

LAHELA: Eh, bra, you can fix me up wid her, o wat?

FISHERMAN: Eh, hotcha, she not like dat.

LAHELA: Nooo, I neva tink dat! I not queaa. Anyway, I was tinking about looking like one man and go hohana fo da Prince Amalu. Dis way, I can find out about my brada and be working at da same times. Wat you tinks?

FISHERMAN: Okay, but . . . ho, lady . . . you need help!

LAHELA: I know, but les go . . . and, ah . . . mahalo, bra.

[*Exeunt*]

SCENE III

[*Enter* OPU-NUI *and* KUKANA]

KUKANA: Eh, manong, jus because you Mahealani's uncle, dat no mean nutting to me. Mahealani was telling me da odda day dat she no dig your ill hours, you and dat odda nut Andrew. You bagas stay up all night and drink dat mean okolehao. Dat shit drive you blind, you know.

OPU-NUI: Yeah, but me and Andrew, we get some good fun. Eh, plus he can talk about tree or four different languages widout one book; plus he get plenny kala! Anyway, hia's to my niece and her healt.

KUKANA: So wea's your odda half today? Probably drunk and laid out in da taro patch already.

OPU-NUI: Who, Andrew? No, no. You get him figured all wrong already. Why, anybody who talk stink about Andrew should be hung on da fish lines to dry ova a ton of cow-pie! O, dat was pretty good, Andrew would love dat one. Eh, but look who stay coming. Eh, bra!

[*Enter* ANDREW]

ANDREW: Bless you, Opu-nui, how are you? Hui, and how you stay, my little pork adobo? Ooo, spicy.

KUKANA: Spicy? Pork adobo? Auwe! I no undastand dis kine talk. Bye. [*Exits*]

OPU-NUI: Chee . . . wea all da smarts dat I tol her you had. Jus like your brain is one stone until you drink some booze to soften om up . . . den you can tink, ah? Hia, have one cup okolehao.

ANDREW: Tank you, Opu. [*Drinks*] Ahh. Suck om up to soften it up! My friend, I tink I going back to Manila soon. Your niece

no can be seen, o if she be, it's four to one she no like see me.
Prince Amalu is always afta her.

OPU-NUI: Eh, no ack. I tol you she no like Amalu. She no like his
rank, she no like his land, and talk about stones fo brains
. . . auwe! Chee, no get rash, bra, you get plenty time.

ANDREW: I stay one mont longer. I am a fellow of da strangest
mind in da world.

OPU-NUI: Eh, brada, come on, cheer up. No use go get all bum-
med out. Eh, Andrew, you good at cheap talk, o wat?

ANDREW: As good as any man in Hawaii, whosoeva he be, but yet
I no like to challenge one ol man.

OPU-NUI: Wat is your bes move when you do one Tahitian dance?

ANDREW: Ay soos, I can cut up one dance floor.

OPU-NUI: Yeah, and my hatchet can do da same.

ANDREW: Plus I get one flashy back-step hula stronger den any
man in Hawaii.

OPU-NUI: Right! And wea you hiding all dese good stuff? Behind
one curtain? . . . wea it going turn to dust? . . . like you
head? How come you no go church dancing da Tahitian and
come home wid your flashy back-step hula? Even when I walk
I vamp. When I do my Tahitian, den I sweat. Man, wat you
trying do? No good hide all dat talent. From da look of your
legs, I tawt it was made by Haleloki.

ANDREW: My legs are strong, and dey look even betta afta tree
days in da sun. Opu, let's go get drunk and make some noise.

OPU-NUI: Sound good to me. No mo nutting else fo do.

[*Exeunt*]

SCENE IV

[*Enter* LAHELA *and* VALENTINE]

VALENTINE: You moving pretty fas, Honeyboy, you been hia tree
days and already you're no stranger . . . you know wat I
mean.

LAHELA: Tanks, eh. Da Prince coming now.

[*Enter* AMALU]

AMALU: Eh, Honeyboy, wea you stay? O, dea you stay. Well, since you know I love Princess Mahealani, I get one job fo you. I like you go to her house and tell om you not going move cause your feet going grow in da ground until dey hia you speak.

LAHELA: Okay, brada, I'll do dat, but she lost in her tears ova her brada's death and she not going hia me talk.

AMALU: Eh, jus make plenny noise and tell om you going keep making noise until dey listen to wat you have to say.

LAHELA: Okay. [*Starts to leave, then stops*] But wat I going tell her?

AMALU: Oh, den tell her dat my love fo her is higher den da high tension wire. Jus lay one good rap on her head and tell her dat my love fo her is deeper den Hanauma Bay.

LAHELA: Nah, she no going believe me, and mo worse, I no believe you.

AMALU: Nah, come on, you gotta believe me. Anyway, wahines like to hia dat good talk . . . you know, all dat romantic stuffs. I mean, tell her she mo beautiful den da sunset down Makaha side o someting like dat. Now go and do dis fo me, and if you succeed, you going share my fortunes too. [*Exits*]

LAHELA: I going do my bes to fix you up wid your lady, but man, dis is heavy. I going lay da rap on her, but I wish he would tap my high tension wire. [*Exits*]

SCENE V

[*Enter* LOPE *and* KUKANA]

KUKANA: Eh, no ack, wea you was hiding? And no give me any lip either! Wait till Princess Mahealani see you . . . she going lepo your head and hang you from dat coconut tree!

LOPE: I no care . . . let her hang me. He dat is well hung get plenny to be proud of!

KUKANA: Dat's a pretty cheap answer . . . seems like you jus trying to convince your own self. Well hung . . . oh, I doubt it.

LOPE: Well, ah . . . God geev om wisdom dat have it, and dose dat are fools, let dem use dea talents! Whootah!

KUKANA: Okay, get silly, 'cause you going get hanged fo being gone so long.

LOPE: Eh, a good hanging always prevents one bad marriage!

KUKANA: Eh, sheep dip, you betta cool head, cause hia comes Princess Mahealani. You going to see wat I was talking about . . . and make it good! [*Exits*]

LOPE: I will! You keep fogetting dat I one sharp baga. Rememba, betta a witty fool den a foolish wit! [*Enter* PRINCESS MAHEALANI *with* MALOLIO *and* ATTENDANTS] Ah, God bless dee, lady.

MAHEALANI: Auwe! Take dat fool fo one walk.

LOPE: Okay, you heard her, take her fo one walk.

MAHEALANI: Eh, I no mo time fo your dry jokes. Anyway, I tink you growing dishonest. I know you padding your time you know.

LOPE: Dea's nutting wrong wid me dat one drink and good counsel no can fix. Besides, geev da dry fool one drink, den da fool is not dry! And das why I say take da lady fo one walk.

MAHEALANI: Lope, I tol him fo take you away.

LOPE: You going make one big mistake. Wassamatta, you tink I get one psychedelic brain, o wat? Give me some rope and I'll show you who has da colorful mind.

MAHEALANI: Shoot! Prove it den.

LOPE: Okay, but no get huhu at me when I tell you wat you no like hia . . . okay?

MAHEALANI: Okay, okay, okay. Come on, I no mo anyting important fo do so I might as well get bored wid your colors.

LOPE: Ah . . . my good Princess Mahealani, how come you always stay crying?

MAHEALANI: Good fool, because my brada wen make.

LOPE: I tink his soul stay in hell, lady.

MAHEALANI: I know his soul stay in heaven, fool!

LOPE: Den you one fool to mourn fo your brada's soul fo being in heaven. All right, take away da fool.

MAHEALANI: Wat you tink about dat, Malolio?

MALOLIO: I tink dat I marvel dat you take delight in one barren
  rascal. I saw om make facetious wid one regular fool dat had
  no mo brain den one piece of black coral. Look at him, he no
  can tink already. Unless you laugh and minister occasion to
  him, he get stuck throat.
MAHEALANI: O, you sick wid self-love, Malolio. And besides, you
  trying to make one crab into one lobsta. I mean, even do' he
  allowed to ack nuts as do' talking was going out of style, all he
  stay doing is trying to help.

[*Enter* KUKANA]

KUKANA: Princess Mahealani, get one young man at da gate who
  said he like to talk to you and nobody else.
MAHEALANI: I bet das one of Prince Amalu's men . . . Ho, dat
  fishhead, all he do is bodda peopo.
KUKANA: I dono wea he is from, but he is young and he is looking
  fine. Whootah!
MAHEALANI: You know I no like see anybody, how come you tol
  him to wait?
KUKANA: Not me! Your uncle Count Opu-nui tol him fo stay.
MAHEALANI: Well, tell him fo go away. All he going talk about is
  da high tension wire and how Prince Amalu's love is deeper
  den Hanauma Bay. [*Exit* KUKANA] Malolio, go help her too.
  If he did come from Amalu's place, tell him I sick o I not
  home o someting . . . Hurry, go!

[*Exit* MALOLIO]

LOPE: Wat?

[*Enter* OPU-NUI]

MAHEALANI: And look who's coming half drunk out of his mind.
  Eh, Uncle, who stay at da door?
OPU-NUI: Which one? . . . Oh, dat one, no need get all hot at
  me, yeah, da front door . . . ah, one young gentoman. *(Hic.)*
MAHEALANI: Wea he come from?
OPU-NUI: I dono, but I know he like talk to you. *(Hic.)*
MAHEALANI: Chee, wat's wid dis pilute?

LOPE: He jus like one drowned man, a fool, and one madman. Firs he drink mo den he can handle which makes him one fool, da second go make him man plus nuts, and da tird drowns him.

MAHEALANI: Yeah, shua looks dat way, and Lope, go look afta him 'cause I tink he get tird-degree drunkedness.

LOPE: Okay, da fool will look afta da madman! [*Exits, following after* OPU-NUI]

[*Enter* MALOLIO]

MALOLIO: Madam, da fellow swears he going talk to you. I tol him you was sick, and he said he know and deafore comes to talk wid you. I tol om you was sleeping, and he seems to have fork-knowledge fo dat too and deafore comes to speak wid you. Wat I going tell him, lady? I mean, dis baga no going move!

MAHEALANI: Jus tell om I no going talk to him.

MALOLIO: I tol him dat. And he says he going stand by your door like one coconut tree and be da supporter to one coral reef, but he going talk to you.

MAHEALANI: Wat kine guy is dis?

MALOLIO: One of very ill manners. He going talk to you whether you like it o not!

MAHEALANI: Ho, shucks! Awright, tell him come, and tell Kukana I like see her firs. [*Exit* MALOLIO. *Enter* KUKANA] Kukana, bring me one cloth fo cover my face. Looks like we gotta hia wat fishface has to say again.

[*Enter* LAHELA]

LAHELA: Howzit. Eh, who's da big lady of da house?

MAHEALANI: Eh, jus talk to me, I'll answer fo her. Wat you like?

LAHELA: Eh, you know I no like you get mad at me, but I was tol only to talk to da Princess Mahealani herself and nobody else. Besides, I get one choice speech dat took me some long fo write om, and I know da Princess would like hia dis.

MAHEALANI: Eh, I tink dis joka need some help!

LAHELA: I know I need help, but dis speech is da real ting! Are you da lady of da house?

MAHEALANI: If I no going be one liar, I gotta admit she is me.

LAHELA: Okay, if wat you say is true, dat she is you, you usurping yourself lady, 'cause wat is yours fo bestow . . . is not yours fo reserve. Ah, but ass none of my business. So I will tell you da speech, making you look good, den I will show you da aloha in dis message.

MAHEALANI: Ah, come on, jus tell me da message, eh?

LAHELA: Slow down . . . took me long time fo write dis speech, and besides, dis is real poetry, you know.

MAHEALANI: Ass all I need to hia—one nodda poet! I heard dat you was acking sassy at my gates; and let me tell you, sweetie, we was mo curious to see you acking silly den to hia you message. If you nuts . . . get outa hia; if you get someting fo say . . . make it snappy!

KUKANA: Hia's your paddle . . . da canoe is waiting outside!

LAHELA: Wait! I wen come in peace, and I suppose to talk to you in private. [KUKANA *exits*] Good lady, let me see your map—I mean, your face.

MAHEALANI: Look hia, you not suppose to negotiate wid my map —I mean, face. I tink you trying get da mile fo da inch. But no get excited, I draw da curtain and show you da picture. [*Unveils*] Hia . . . look . . . isn't it well done?

LAHELA: Oh, excellently done . . . if God did om all. And if he did, you going be one fool not to leave da world widout one copy.

MAHEALANI: Don't worry 'bout dat, because I going make one list and hang om out to all da peopo. I going inventory my map and body. Like fo instance, ah, item: two leeps, wid nice red color; item: two brown eyes wid lids to dem; item: one neck, one chin, one pair of . . .; and so on. But you no was sent hia fo praise me?

LAHELA: I was but I tink too many peopo already come wid my message. But anyway, Prince Amalu loves you mo den you can tink.

MAHEALANI: Oh, yeah? . . . How he stay love me?

LAHELA: Wid adorations and good kine tears, wid good kine groans dat make da love tunder, and wid Pele's love of fire o, ah, sighs of Pele's fire . . . o, ah . . . fire sighs of Pele?

MAHEALANI: Prince Amalu know dat I no can love him! Ah, come

on, look, I know Prince Amalu is one virtuous and noble guy
who get plenny land, and he young and almost good-looking,
and, I mean, he is one numba one good Joe. But I tink we
failing fo communicate, because he already supposed to know
dat I no can love him, fo da uku millionth time! Holy Moses
. . . he no learn, o wat! Hia, take dis and make it already
. . . Keep your kala! I tired talk to you.

LAHELA: Eh, lady, I no like take handouts . . . Kala stay above my
fortune and my state is well. I is one gentoman. Plus, lady, I
tink you pretty mean fo not love my masta . . . spock you
lata. Haimakamaka. [*Exits*]

MAHEALANI: "I stay above my fortune and my state is well. I is one
gentoman." Hmmm, I'll say he is! Whootah! I must admit
he does look pretty good. Hmmm, eh, Malolio. Eh, Malolio,
you mullet, come hia!

MALOLIO: Hia, madam, at your cervix.

MAHEALANI: Eh, Malolio, go and run afta Prince Amalu's messenger, and give him dis ring dat he wen leave behind. Tell him
dat I no like om. Plus tell him dat if he come dis way tomorrow, I going explain to him why, okay? Now hurry up and
hele on as fas as you can go.

MALOLIO: Madam, I will. [*Exits*]

MAHEALANI: I dono how dis going turn out, but I hope Malolio
catch him so he come back tomorrow. Whoa, I betta cool
head wid my emotions! But he did look good. Whootah!
[*Exits*]

ACT TWO

SCENE I

[*Enter* LOKA *and* KOA]

KOA: Brada, why you no stay longer? O at least let me go wid you?

LOKA: No, bra, I no can. I gotta go by myself. I haftu do all kine
stuff dat might take time and trouble, and I no like bodda you.

KOA: Den why no tell me wea you going?

LOKA: Because I dono wea I going. Look, I wasn't even going tell you anyting, but since you no stop aksing me all dese questions, I guess I going have to tell you wat I up to. My real name is Loka, and maybe you know of me from my fada who was Loka of Lanai. But, you see, I neva tell you when you wen save me dat I had one sista, who I tink she wen drown. But I not shua, so I have to go and look fo her.

KOA: Auwe! I neva know.

LOKA: Yeah, she was one beautiful wahine, and many peopo said dat she looked like me. I mean, everybody had good tings to say about her. So anyway, I going look fo her, 'cause right now, dat's all I can tink about.

KOA: Chee, I sorry I wen aks.

LOKA: Nah, das all right, I neva like bodda you wid my family problems, das all.

KOA: I tell you wat, why no let me be your servant and den help you look fo your sista?

LOKA: I wish I could take you, but dis is someting dat I gotta do by myself. Tanks anyway, but meanwhile I tink I going look fo work in Prince Amalu's court. I spock you lata, bra.

KOA: Up to you, brada.

[*Exeunt*]

SCENE II

[*Enter* LAHELA *and* MALOLIO]

MALOLIO: Eh bra, you no was wid da Princess Mahealani jus now?

LAHELA: Yup, dat was me . . . wat you like?

MALOLIO: Hia, she return dis ring to you. You could have saved me some pains if you wen take om away yourself. She multiplies . . . adds? . . . multiplies dat you should tell your prince dat she no like see him. Minus one mo ting, dat you neva be so dumb to come in his affairs again, unless it be to report your prince's taking of dis. Hia, take it!

LAHELA: She took da ring of me?! Aaah, I no like om.

MALOLIO: Come on, we know you wen trow it at her, and her will is dat it should be returned. If dis is wort bending ova fo, dea it is, in your eye; if not, findas keepas, losas weepas! [*Exits*]

LAHELA: I neva leave no ring wid her. I wonda wat she mean? Oooh, no. I wonda if my outside appearance wen charm her eyes. She was giving me da eye, and her eye caused her fo lose her tongue, because she was speaking in starts radda distractedly. Aah, fo shua she is in love wid me, and ass why she tol dat sassy messenger fo call me back. Ooo, da sly! I mean I know Prince Amalu neva give me no ring . . . I must be da man. If it be so, poor lady, she would be betta to love one dream. Ho, ass why so hard! You know, as women, it's our frailty dat is da cause—not we—fo dat's wat we made of, and such we be! Ass not fair! . . . Oh, I wonda how dis going turn out? My masta, Prince Amalu, love her deeply; and me, poor baga, tink much of him; meanwhile she, making one error, seems to love me. Eh, she would be betta to love one dream. [*Exits*]

SCENE III

[*Enter* OPU-NUI, ANDREW, *and* LOPE]

OPU-NUI: Music . . . music, come Lope, sing us one song! Hia's one papaya fo your efforts.

ANDREW: Come on! I will give you two fighting chickens. Jus give us one song.

LOPE: You like one love song o one song of good life?

OPU-NUI: One love song . . . one love song!

ANDREW: One love song, I no care fo good life!

LOPE [*sings*]:

> O mistress mine, wea you stay roaming?
> O, stay and hia! Your true love stay coming,
> Dat can sing both high and low.
> Trip no further, pretty sweeting;
> Journey's end in one lovers' meeting,
> Every wise man's son does know.

Wat is love? It's no hia-afta,
Present mirt is present laughta;
What's to come is still unshua;
In delay dea lies no plenny,
Den come kiss me, sweet and twenny.
Youth's a stuff will not endua.

ANDREW: One mellifluous voice, as I am one true manong.

OPU-NUI: One contagious breadth!

ANDREW: One very sweet and contagious voice.

OPU-NUI: To hia by da nose is like sniffing junk. But we gotta make da sky dance and sing fo us! You know, we make believe dis one luau! Shall we do dat, brada?

ANDREW: If you love me, les do it!

[*Enter* KUKANA]

KUKANA: Aa, aaa, aaaaaa! Wat is all dis moaning about?! If my princess was to hia dis, fo shua she would call Malolio and tell om to trow you guys outa hia.

OPU-NUI: Mahealani plays games . . . we is politicians. And Malolio is nutting but hot air. Nonsense . . . everyting is nonsense.

LOPE: Chee . . . you would make one nifty fool. Hmmm, I betta come work on time o rewrite my script. Hmmm.

ANDREW: Ay soos, he would do well if he be disposed.

[*They go on singing*]

KUKANA: Fo da love of God, shut up!

[*Enter* MALOLIO]

MALOLIO: You bagas crazy, o wat? You no mo brains, manners, o honesty except but to babble like women who pound poi at dis time of da night? Dis is not one Waikiki, wea you can scream and yell widout even tinking twice about it. I mean, you no mo respect peopo, place, o time, o wat?

OPU-NUI: Eh, we did keep time, so go goggle some peanut butter.

MALOLIO: Count Opu, looks like I gotta get obsnocktious wid you. My lady wen tell me to tell you dat, even do' she is your niece, dat no mean she allied to your disorders. However, if you can split yourself from all your ugly habits, den you are welcome to stay hia. If you no can, den she no can; and so she'll bid you aloha!

OPU-NUI [*still singing*]: "Farewell . . . dear heart, since I mus go . . ."

KUKANA: Nah, Opu slow down. Mo betta listen.

LOPE [*sings*]: "His eyes do show his days are almost done . . ."

MALOLIO: No ack!

OPU-NUI [*sings*]: "But I will neva make . . ."

LOPE [*sings*]: "Count Opu dea you lie . . ."

MALOLIO: Dis because of you, you know.

OPU-NUI [*sings*]: "Shall I tell him fo go"

LOPE [*sings*]: "And wat if you do . . ."

OPU-NUI [*sings*]: "Shall I tell om fo go widout one delay?"

LOPE [*sings*]: "O, no, no, no, no, you no dare!"

OPU-NUI: Oh. You stay out of tune, sir. You lie. Malolio, ass all you do, o wat? Go around and check up on peopo. I mean, our R.O.T.C. days are ova. Hia, come have a pound of Li Hing Mui! Bia, mo Primo, Kukana!

MALOLIO: Miss Kukana, you tita, if tink anyting of my lady, dis uncivil rule no would happen. But no try sway me wid your Li Hing Mui, 'cause I have my own stash! Princess Mahealani going know about dis. [*Exits*]

KUKANA: Eh, punk, no get swift!

ANDREW: It's one good deed to drink and get drunk, den to challenge him at da beach; den go break da challenge, and make him look like one nosy fool.

OPU-NUI: Yeah, brada, do it, do it! I'll go write you one challenge and den go tell him wid my own mout.

KUKANA: Nah, be cool, Opu, you gotta have some patience. Since dat yout, Honeyboy, wen come dis aftanoon, da princess all itchy. As fo dis banana, I'll fix his wagon.

OPU-NUI: Grease us, grease us. Wat you going do?

KUKANA: Well, I know dat he is one Puritan.

ANDREW: I tell you, if I know dat, I'll beat him like fish fo
   bagong.

OPU-NUI: Wat, fo being one Puritan? How come?

ANDREW: I have no fragrant reason fo it, but I have reason wid
   much fragrance!

KUKANA: Da devil of one Puritan dat he is, and everyting he say
   to peopo he wen read from one book; and when he do his
   work around da house and you look at him, he tinking,
   "Dese guys love me and wat I do." So because we got his ack
   wired, dis is how my revenge going fo work.

OPU-NUI: And den? And den?

KUKANA: Well, I tink I'll drop one letta in his way about love and
   how he get nice skin color, he get good posture and sexy eyes,
   and we go make him feel real special. Den I'll go sign da letta
   of love wid my lady's hand, and den da rest is easy . . . we
   watch him go like crazy!

OPU-NUI: Ooooo, das tuff! I smell one grease.

ANDREW: Da baga is in my nose too.

OPU-NUI: So in odda words, he going tink by da lettas you slide to
   him dat dey came from my niece, and dat she stay in love
   wid him.

KUKANA: Yes, you might say dat.

ANDREW: Oh, mabuhay fo days!

KUKANA: You betta believe it, brada! I know dis stuff going work
   on him. Anyway, I going plant you two and Lope wea he
   going find da letta, and you watch how he going bite da
   hook. But, fo tonight, les go sleep and dream on dis event.

[*Exeunt*]

SCENE IV

[*Enter* AMALU, KAWIKA, LOPE, LAHELA, *and* ATTENDANTS]

AMALU: Eh, geev me some good kine music. Eh, Honeyboy, sing
   me a piece of song, dat ol kamaaina song we wen hear las
   night. Dat baga wen make me feel good, wen make me foget

about my beloved Mahealani. Eh, come on, les have one verse.

KAWIKA: Eh, but Prince, he dat should sing it no even stay hia.

AMALU: Wat?

KAWIKA: Lope da clown, Prince, dat dodo-kai guy dat da Lady Maile's fada took much delight in. I tink he stay around hia some place.

AMALU: Shoot, go look fo him and meanwhile play me da tune, one of you. [KAWIKA *exits*] Come hia, boy. You know, if you should eva fall in love, da sweet pains of it, rememba me, because all true lovers stay jus like me, dea manners and emotions stay all kapakahi, except fo da stubborn image of da one dey in love wid. Anyway, you like dis tune, o wat?

LAHELA: Like da beauty of Waimea, it geevs one echo to da heart where love stay evalasting.

AMALU: Chee, you talk pretty good, eh? Eh, lemme aks you someting. You know, by da looks of your face, it looks a bit like someone you love. Dis true, o wat?

LAHELA: A little bit.

AMALU: Wat kine wahine is dis?

LAHELA: Stay of your complexion.

AMALU: Auwe, foget it den. How ol is she?

LAHELA: Around your years, bra.

AMALU: She too ol den. Eh, always let da wahine take one older den herself; dis is so dat she can adapt to her husband's affections, radda den odda way . . . you know wat I mean? Fo lemme tell you, no matter how solid you tink you stay, our loves and affection are mo loose and crazy den wahines'. Yeah, even I gotta admit, wahines dey pretty solid.

LAHELA: Yeah, and ass why hard! Dey make even when dey grow to perfection!

[*Enter* KAWIKA *and* LOPE]

AMALU: Eh, brada, wea you was? . . . Come on, bra, sing us da song we wen hear las night. Listen, Honeyboy, it is one old and simple mele. Da weavers and poi-pounding wahines use to chant dis in da real ol style. It's one silly song dat talks about da innocence of love.

LOPE: Okay, bra, you ready?

AMALU: Eesalay!

LOPE [*sings* "Living on Easy"]:

> I'm living on easy
> With a bottle of whisky
> Ain't got no money
> To suit my honey. [*Repeats*]

> To suit my honey
> Ain't got no money
> Ain't got no money
> To suit my honey.

> Street car go clang-a-lang-lang
> Little jeep go beep-a-beep-beep
> Mongoose go goose-a-goose-goose.

> I'm living on easy
> With a bottle of whisky
> Ain't got no money
> To suit my honey.

AMALU: Hanahou! Hia, take dis fo your trouble.

LOPE: No mo trouble, sir. I take plenny pleasure in singing, sir!

AMALU: Den lemme pay fo your pleasure.

LOPE: Okay, bra, many tanks to you, sir. Mahalo and aloha.

   [*Exeunt* KAWIKA, LOPE, *and* ATTENDANTS]

AMALU: Eh, Honeyboy, once mo, go hele on to dat cruel love of
   mine. Tell her dat all my love fo her stay mo noble den da
   world. I mean, she no can miss!

LAHELA: But wat if she no can love you, sir?

AMALU: Eh, bra, I going refuse to be answered so!

LAHELA: Sorry, brada, but you must. Okay, make believe you get
   one lady, and fo shua I bet get one dat love your ass wid a
   great pang of heart as you get fo Mahealani. If you no can love
   her, you going tell her so. Must she not be answered, o wat?

AMALU: Bra, but dea is no wahine whose breast can widstand da beating of so strong one passion as my heart does give; no wahine's heart so big to hold so much; dey jus no mo da capacity like me. Dea love is like one pupu platter, and mine is like one luau! Eh, no compare me between dat love a wahine bear me and how I can love Mahealani.

LAHELA: Yeah, but I know, I know . . .

AMALU: Wat you know?

LAHELA: I know too well dat wahines love jus as much as kanes, fo dey are as true of heart as we. My fada had one daughter love a kane as it might perhaps be, were I a wahine, I would love your lordship.

AMALU: And wat is her history?

LAHELA: One big blank, my lord. She neva say who she love. But let concealment, like one worm in da bud, feed on her bronze cheeks. She wen pine in tawt, and sick to da stomach, she wen sit like Patience on da beach, smiling at grief. Was dis love indeed? Eh, we kanes may say mo, swear mo, but indeed, all talk and mostly no action, fo we still plenny in our vows but little in our love.

AMALU: And did your sista die of her love?

LAHELA: My good brada, I stay all da daughters of my fada's house and all da bradas too, and yet I no can answer dat. My good lord, shall I to dis lady now?

AMALU: Yeah, dat's da theme. Hia, give her dis jewel and wiki-wiki. Tell her I neva going geev up. Imua!

[*Exeunt*]

SCENE V

[*Enter* OPU-NUI, KOHALA, *and* ANDREW]

OPU-NUI: Hui, hui, let's go, Kohala!

KOHALA: No worry, bra. If I wen lose one bit of dis sport, I'll dive into a pit full of sharks!

OPU-NUI: Yeah, it shua would be nice to see dat baga make one ass out of himself.

KOHALA: I would jump fo joy. One time he wen squeal to Mahea-lani about me picking her mangoes! Ho, dat baga made me mad.

OPU-NUI: Well, dis time we'll make him da mango and pick at him. Shall we not, Sir Andrew?

ANDREW: We will make mango bread out of him and watch da dope rise, and den get ready fo slicing.

[*Enter* KUKANA]

KUKANA: Eh, you guys, quick, hide behind da bushes, Malolio stay coming! He was in da sun practicing good behavior wid his shadow. Eh, try watch om, because I know dis letta going make one absolute fool of him. Quick, go hide! You stay right dea, because hia comes da fish dat mus be caught.

[*Enter* MALOLIO]

MALOLIO: Dis is fortune; everyting is fortune. Kukana wen tell me once . . . she kinda like me. Mo worse, I heard her once say dat if she going love somebody, it going be someone like me —medium, dark, and handsome. Besides, she get mo respect fo me den anybody else. I wonda how I should tink.

OPU-NUI: Eesalay [*makes shaka sign*], one real dodo-kai.

KOHALA: Shut dat trap, Opu! Let him tink, he even might sprain his brain.

ANDREW: I would love to beat da brains into him.

OPU-NUI: Shut dat trap, Andrew!

MALOLIO: I like be Prince Malolio.

OPU-NUI: Auwe!

ANDREW: I give him one half slap.

OPU-NUI: No good. Half slap stops right hia.

MALOLIO: I no can see why not. Da Princess Makanai wen marry da butcha of Tamashiro market.

ANDREW: I should beat him, da butcha is may brada.

KOHALA: Shut up, I said. Now he's really hooked! Look, now his imagination made him tink he big.

MALOLIO: Tree months been married to her, sitting on my lanai.

OPU-NUI: O fo one slingshot to hit om in da eye!

MALOLIO: I stay calling my servants around me fo do dis and go do dat, in my hand-painted lavalava; plus, mo worse, I jus came from my bed, wea I wen leave Mahealani sleeping.

OPU-NUI: Oooh, he going get licking!

KOHALA: Peace, peace, brada.

MALOLIO: And den to have one humor of da mind and telling dem, ''I know my stand, so I hope you know wea you sit''; den to send fo dat leech dey call Opu-nui.

OPU-NUI: Shaa! Time fo trow blows!

KOHALA: Jus cool head! Sshhh!

MALOLIO: Seven of my peopo, wid one obedient start, go get da baga. I frown wid my face, and maybe wind up my watch, o play wid my—some rich jewel. Dey bring Opu in; bows ova dea to me . . .

OPU-NUI: Should I kill om now, o wat?

MALOLIO: . . . I stretch my hand to him like dis, den geev him one sly smile wid one curled upper lip . . .

OPU-NUI: Den I punch your mout!

MALOLIO: . . . and tell om, ''Brada Opu, because my fortunes wen cast me on your niece, try unload da wax from your ears.''

OPU-NUI: Wat! Wat!

MALOLIO: ''You gotta stop being one pilute!''

OPU-NUI: Beat it, punk.

KOHALA: Cool head, don't blow it yet!

MALOLIO: ''Besides, you waste da treasure of your time attracting flies wid one dumb haole, one bukbuk . . .''

ANDREW: Ay soos, dat's me!

MALOLIO: '' . . . one Sir Andy Waha.''

ANDREW: I knew was me because he always rain on my parade.

MALOLIO: Try wait, wat is dis? [*Takes up the letter*]

KOHALA: Now it's our turn!

MALOLIO: Wop my jaws, dis my lady's writing. Dese are her c's, her u's, and her t's, and ass how she make her great p's. I know dis hers, because only her handwriting look like one bucket of nergeous worms.

ANDREW: Her c's, her u's, and her s's? Pluck up do'.

MALOLIO [*reads*]:

> I going command wea I going adore,
> But silence, like one love knife,
> Wid bloodless stroke my heart going sore,
> M.O.A.I. stay sway my life.

KOHALA: Hui, dat riddle stay all jam up!

OPU-NUI: Eh, Kukana, ass tuff!

MALOLIO: "M.O.A.I. stay sway my life." Aah, forced to take one nodda look.

KOHALA: Wow, ass one plate full of poison.

OPU-NUI: Yeah! Jus like one retarded cockroach crawling around looking fo one crack!

MALOLIO: "I going command wea I going adore." She can command me, I already work fo her. Dis gotta be da real ting. Hmm, but wat about last alphabet? If I could make om look like someting in my name! "M.O.A.I."

OPU-NUI: Dea he goes, off to neva-neva land!

MALOLIO: "M"—Malolio. "M," das how my name starts!

KOHALA: I tol you he was going work it out. Dat baga is excellent in wrong directions.

MALOLIO: "M." But den da next letta no figure right. "A" supposed to be next but "O" is dea.

KOHALA: And "O" going end, I hope.

OPU-NUI: Yeah, o I'll club him and make him cry "Oh."

MALOLIO: Den "I" comes behind.

ANDREW: And if you had one eye behind you, you'd see mo action behind you den fortunes befo you.

MALOLIO: "M.O.A.I." Dis meaning no stay da same; and yet, if I wen bend da letta, da baga would bow to me, because every one of dose lettas stay in my name. Ooo prose, gotta conscioustrate. [*Reads*] "If dis should fall into one hand, circle. In my stars, I am above dee, but no go be afraid of greatness. Some get greatness trown on some of dem. Da Fates open dea hands; let dye blood and spirit kiss om; and to get used to yourself to wat you going like be, trow way dat outa skin and appear fresh! Go be opposite wid your kinsmen, fo shua wid servants. Let your tongue tang arguments of da state, and put yourself above da rest. She dat advises dee of course sighs fo dee. Rememba who wen commend your yellow stockings and also wen wish to see you eva cross gartered. Keia, rememba, hele on, and you got it made if dat's wat you like desire to be. If you no like, den let me see you always as one servant, da friend of servants, and not worthy to touch fortune's fingers. Aloha. She dat would alter services wid dee. Da Fortunate Unhappy." Whootah! Primo bia fo days! Dis baga is open. I going be proud, I going read smart books, I going baffle Count Opu-nui, I going remake myself; I mean, I going be one champion boy. I no tink I fooling myself, because every reasoning points to dis, dat my lady love me! She wen say my yellow stockings was shaka, she wen praise my legs dat was cross gartered, and if she infests myself to her love, she going drive me right into her . . . liking. Tanks, eh, stars, I happy. I going be strange but good looking in my yellow stockings and cross garter. Praise da Lord and my stars. But try wait, one nodda message. [*Reads*] "You no can choose but gotta know who I am. If you no can stand my love, show me in your smiling map. Your smiles make you look good. So anyway, wheneva you spock me, keep smiling sweetheart." Tanks again, eh, God. Watch dis crease. I going do everyting dat you like me do. [*Exits*]

KOHALA: Ho, man, I wouldn't give my part in dis trick fo all da money in da islands. Eh, tita, too mucken fuch!

OPU-NUI: Eh, you like put your feet on my neck, o wat?

ANDREW: Plus mine too. Ay soos, I going home make pork adobo fo you.

OPU-NUI: You know, you wen put such one dream in his head dat when da image leaves him, dat baga going be all nuts!

KUKANA: Nah, but fo real kine, you really tink going work, o wat?

OPU-NUI: Everyday! [*Makes shaka sign*]

KUKANA: Well, if you tink so, les check it out when he goes see my lady, Mahealani. He going come to her in yellow stockings, which is her worse color; and cross gartered, a fashion she always hate; den mo worse, he going smile at her, which

of course is wrong already because of her situation wid da
deaths in da family. So all Malolio going do is make one fool
of himself and get Mahealani all salty at him. Come on kids,
step right dis way!

OPU-NUI: To da pits of Pele, you tuff little tita!

[*Exeunt*]

Curtain

ACT THREE

SCENE I

[*Enter* LAHELA *and* LOPE]

LAHELA: Bless you, keia, and your music. Do you live by your
drum?

LOPE: No, bra, I stay live by da church.

LAHELA: Oh, so you one churchman?

LOPE: No matter such, bra. I live by da church, and my house
stand by da church!

LAHELA: Hmm, not bad! By da way, you Lady Mahealani's
fool, eh?

LOPE: Not me, Lady Mahealani no mo one folly. She no keep one
fool, until she get married. I no stay her fool but instead her
corrupter of words.

LAHELA: Eh, I neva see you at Prince Amalu's place da odda day?

LOPE: Eh, foolery walks around da orb like da sun; it shines every-
wea. But, yeah, I wen spark you wisdom dea too.

LAHELA: Nah, you stay making fun at me, hia, take dis and make
it. [*Gives* LOPE *a coin*]

LOPE: Tanks, eh. By da way, next time tell him send you one
beard!

LAHELA: By my life, bra. I tell you I stay sick fo one, even do' I no
would have it grow on my chin. Is Mahealani in da house?

LOPE: Yup. Spock you lata. [*Exits*]

LAHELA: Mahalo, brada. Chee, dat brada is smart fo play one fool,

and fo do dat, you gotta be real sharp. I mean, he mus check
out dea mood befo he make fun of dem, check out da goodness of da peopo, da time, den like one hunting hawk, spock
every feather dat comes befo his eyes. Dis kine work is tuff like
one wise man's art, because folly dat he shows wisely is perfect, but wise men who fall in jolly jam up dea heads.

[*Enter* OPU-NUI *and* ANDREW]

OPU-NUI: Good day, gentoman.

LAHELA: Good day, sirs.

OPU-NUI: You going in da house? My niece stay desirous of you, if
   you like trade wid her.

LAHELA: I stay bound to your niece, sir. I mean, she is da list of my
   voyage.

OPU-NUI: Taste your legs, bra, and put om in motion.

LAHELA: My legs betta undastand me den I undastand wat you
   mean by "taste my legs."

OPU-NUI: I mean, to go o to enter, bra.

LAHELA: Shoot! But look who stay coming. [*Enter* MAHEALANI]
   Aloha to you lady, may da heavens rain odors on you.

ANDREW: Dis baga is full of tirty-cent poetry. "Rain odors"—
   well!

LAHELA: My business no can be told to anyone but your own ear.

MAHEALANI: Let da garden door be shut, and please, go excuse us.
   [*All exit except* MAHEALANI *and* LAHELA] Try give me your
   hand, bra.

LAHELA: Shua. Das my duty and most humble service.

MAHEALANI: Wat's your name?

LAHELA: Dey call me Kimo, fair Princess.

MAHEALANI: Oh, and you stay one servant fo Prince Amalu, eh?

LAHELA: Yeah, and he is yours.

MAHEALANI: Eh, bra, come on, no talk about him o his tawts. I
   really wish his tawts was big blanks radda den filled wid me.

LAHELA: But dear Princess, I come to sharpen your gentle tawts on
   his behalf.

MAHEALANI: Eh, I no like talk to you. Afta da las time you was
   hia, I wen send one ring to go chase fo you. Now I tink I wen

do myself in and I fear you too! All you do is talk about Amalu's unmuggled tawts. Ho, you no can get it together, o wat?

LAHELA: I pity you.

MAHEALANI: Yeah, das one side of love!

LAHELA: No, I not talking about dat side, because most of da time we only pity our enemies.

MAHEALANI: Den I tink it's time to smile again. Chee, how come da poor always ack proud? If you going be one prey, mo betta fall befo one shark den one barracuda. You know wat I mean, mo class, eh? [*Clock strikes*] Auwe! Da clock stay reminding me dat I wasting time. And so, dea lies your way, due west.

LAHELA: Den westward ho!

MAHEALANI: Try wait. Eh, tell me wat you tink of me.

LAHELA: I tink dat you tink dat you no stay wat you are.

MAHEALANI: Den if I tink, I tink da same of you.

LAHELA: Den you tink right. I not wat I really am.

MAHEALANI: I wish you was wat I want you to be.

LAHELA: I hope stay betta den I really am.

MAHEALANI: Oh shucks! Even one murderous guilt shows less den love dat seems to hide. Kimo, by da pikakes of Palolo, by maidhood, by honor, by truth, and by everyting, I love you so dat even my pride, wit, and reason my passion no can hide.

LAHELA: Oh wow! Ah . . . ah . . . I swear by innocence and by my yout dat I get one heart, one bosom, and one truth dat no woman has; plus no one eva going be mistress to it except me alone. So real quick, I spock you lata, lady, and . . . take it easy! Oh, I won't even bodda you wid my masta's tears. [*Exits*]

MAHEALANI: Eh, but no scared, come again, okay?

SCENE II

[*Enter* OPU-NUI, ANDREW, *and* KOHALA]

ANDREW: One mont longa, I'm not going stay.

OPU-NUI: How come, brada, tell me how come.

KOHALA: At least go tell us why.

ANDREW: Because I wen see your niece do mo favors fo Prince
Amalu's main boy den she eva did fo me. I saw dem not in
but next to da bushes down da river.

OPU-NUI: She wen see you, too, o wat?

ANDREW: As plain as I see you.

KOHALA: Ah, dis was her proof to you dat she stay in love wid you.

ANDREW: Eh, come on, no make me laugh, I trying to be mad!

KOHALA: Eh, I'll prove it true wid da testimony of judgment and
reason. Firs, Mahealani wen show favor to da yout only fo get
you jealous, to make you wake up, to put fire in your heart,
and ginger up your you-know-wat. So wat you should have
done was to give him one whack wid some good kine remarks,
den you should have banged dat yout into dumbness. Dis is
wat she was looking fo, but you wen let om slide. So now, wat
you gotta do is redeem yourself by some good attempt at valor
o policy.

ANDREW: Well, if we gotta do om one way, I like do om in valor,
because I no can stand policy.

OPU-NUI: Oo, write om as if you stay all mad. Make like you all
huhu wid him, and no need bodda to ack wise and witty. No
scared, because on paper you can write anyting. Eh, and no
call om thou, thoust, or thy; jus say you dis and you dat, and
make shua you tell as many lies as will fit on da paper. Hurry
up, go, and rememba, no scared om, even do' you scared om,
but ass awright. Oo! Oo! Oo!

ANDREW: Okay, Okay, Okay. But wea you guys going be?

OPU-NUI: We going be some place wea you can find us, hurry up
now, go!

[*Exit* SIR ANDREW]

KOHALA: Chee, Opu, you wen foget to give him one biscuit.

OPU-NUI: Eh, no ack. I always good to him, some two thousand
dollars strong o so.

KOHALA: I bet dis brada going write one strange letta. But you no
going deliver om, eh?

OPU-NUI: Nah, you tink I going stand dea and wait fo da yout to

answer? Eh, ten to one, one ox and wagon ropes no can pull
om together. And Andrew, if he got cut and if you could find
enough blood in his liver dat could clog da foot of one flea, I
would eat da rest of him.

KOHALA: And da odda one too, I no tink he one mean bagga.

[*Enter* KUKANA]

OPU-NUI: Surprise, it's Miss Twit in person.

KUKANA: Eh, if you guys like crack up and laugh yourself into one
stitch, follow me. Lolo Malolio wen turn heathen and stay all
hot up. Yeah! He stay acking jus like one Christian meaning
to be saved wid tree tons of misinformation. He in yellow
stockings.

OPU-NUI: And cross gartered?

KUKANA: Jus like one villain. Man, dat baga wen listen to everything I wen put in da letta dat going betray him. And wen he
smile, auwe! He get mo lines on his face den da new map of
Molokai! I mean, you neva see anyting like dis befo. I no can
hardly hold back from trowing tings at him. I know Mahealani going whack om, and if she do, he going smile and say,
"Whoi, tanks, eh."

OPU-NUI: Auwe! I like see, quick, I like see!

[*Exeunt*]

SCENE III

[*Enter* LOKA *and* KOA]

LOKA: Brada, I no like make trouble fo you, but since you make
like your pleasures is your pains, I no going trouble you
any mo.

KOA: No worry, I no could stay behind you. I like go wid you
because, look bra, you don't know da place, you one stranger,
and besides widout one friend, dis place might be hard fo

take. So radda den worry all da time, I figure I might as well go and help you find wat you looking fo.

LOKA: Okay, but all I can say is tanks, because I no mo money even do' I wish you could find someting else to do radda den hang around wid me. Anyway, wat you like us do? Should we check out all da ol buildings, o wat? Okay, so hia we are. Wea we going start?

KOA: Nah, firs you should find one place to sleep.

LOKA: Eh, I not dat tired, plus going be one long night, so les go check dis place out and see wat's happening.

KOA: Sorry, but I no can go.

LOKA: Gee, but you jus said you was going come wid me.

KOA: I walk dese streets wid all kine danger creeping around. Once in one sea fight against Prince Amalu's ships, I wen do some fighting dat was so sharp dat if I was captured hia, well . . .

LOKA: You wen kill somebody, o wat?

KOA: No, not dat dea was lots of blood in da matter, jus dat da time and place was wrong, and so, jus like one foolish hero, instead of being cautious radda den chicken, everybody wen spock me out. Das why if I get caught in dis city . . . *(gulp)* . . . well . . .

LOKA: Okay, yeah, das all right.

KOA: Hia, go hold my kala. Da bes place fo stay is dis small inn called da Royal Hawaiian, owned by some haoles. So take a look around, get someting fo eat, and I go meet you dea lata.

LOKA: How come you like me hold dis?

KOA: Neva mind, partner. Jus take om and enjoy.

LOKA: Okay, den I'll hold dis fo you, and I see you lata. Mahalo plenny.

KOA: To da Royal Hawaiian.

LOKA: Easy, bra.

[*Exeunt*]

SCENE IV

[*Enter* MAHEALANI, KUKANA, *and* ATTENDANTS]

MAHEALANI: I wen send fo Kimo and he said he going come. I
wonda wat fo give om. Yout is bought much mo often den
begged o borrowed. Ho, man, I talk too much. Wea Malolio?
Da baga he all sad and moody, which is perfect fo one servant
wid my fortunes. Eh, wea he stay?

KUKANA: Oh, he stay coming, madam, but he acking kinda funny, you know. Actually, I tink he nuts.

MAHEALANI: Why, wassamatta wid him? Is he raving, o wat?

KUKANA: No, sweetheart, all he do is smile. If I was you, I would
watch dat one, because someting wrong wid his head.

MAHEALANI: Go call him, Kukana. Poor ting, I staying sad and
make jus like him. [*Enter* MALOLIO] Hi, how you, Malolio?

MALOLIO: Oh, jus fine, sweetheart.

MAHEALANI: Full of smiles, heh? I wen call you fo one sad occasion.

MALOLIO: Sad, lady? Oh, I could be sad but do sun's rays stay
showing me da prettiest picture in da islands? How you,
sweetheart?

MAHEALANI: Wat? Wassamatta wid you?

MALOLIO: Oh darling, life is filled wid sweet fragrances and count-
less pastels. I wen come into dese hands, and da commands
going be executed. We do know da sweet Malolio.

MAHEALANI: Eh, go sleep, Malolio!

MALOLIO: To bed so soon? Oh, I'll come fo you . . .

MAHEALANI: Oh, wow! Eh, how come you smile like dat and kiss
my hand so much?

KUKANA: Well, speak up, bra!

MALOLIO: No worry, tita, you lucky I let you look at me.

KUKANA: How come you acking wise in front of my lady?

MALOLIO: "No go be afraid of greatness." Dat one was sharp.

MAHEALANI: Wat you mean by dat, Malolio?

MALOLIO: "Some stay born great."

MAHEALANI: Ha?

MALOLIO: "Some get some greatness."

MAHEALANI: Wat you tryna say?

MALOLIO: "And some get greatness trown on some of dem."

MAHEALANI: Eh, you need help.

MALOLIO: "Rememba who wen commend your yellow stockings . . ."

MAHEALANI: Yellow stockings?!

MALOLIO: " . . . and also wen wish to see you eva cross gartered."

MAHEALANI: Cross gartered?

MALOLIO: "Hele on and you got it made, if dat's wat you desire to be."

MAHEALANI: You betta hele on!

MALOLIO: "If you no like, den let me see you always as one servant."

MAHEALANI: Eh, you was smoking dat pakalolo, o wat?

[*Enter* KOHALA]

KOHALA: Princess, get one man from Prince Amalu's court who stay hia fo see you.

MAHEALANI: I going come. [*Exit* KOHALA] My sweet Kukana, go get dis fellow looked at o someting. Wea is Uncle Opu? Go let some of da peopo take special care of him. I no like anybody harm him fo da half of my dowry.

[*Exit* MAHEALANI, KUKANA, *and* ATTENDANTS]

MALOLIO: Dis jus wat da letta said would happen. She going send fo Count Opu fo watch me so dat I can be stubborn wid him. It said, "Go be opposite wid you kinsmen, fo shua wid servants." And den, "Let your tongue tang arguments of state, and put yourself above da rest." Da letta even said how fo ack. Like fo instance: one sad face, use one slow tongue, and walk as if my shoulder was going touch da ground. I tink I already got her in da bag; but dis is God's work, so tanks, eh, God. And jus now she wen say, "Go get dis fellow looked at." "Fellow." Not Malolio o my servant but "fellow." Shucks, everyting stay coming together jus perfect. I mean, wat can I say? Nutting can come between me and Mahealani except air. One mo time, tanks, eh, God.

[*Enter* OPU-NUI, KOHALA, *and* KUKANA]

OPU-NUI: How is he acking in da name of Loloists? If all da devils of hell was in one place and one troop of friends wen possess him, still I would like to talk to him.

KOHALA: Dea him, dea him. How you stay, ''sir?''

OPU-NUI: Yeah, how you?

MALOLIO: Make it. I like enjoy my private moments, so again . . . make it!

KUKANA: Seem jus like I wen tell you. Dear Opu, my lady prays dat you take care of him.

MALOLIO: Oho, she does, eh?

OPU-NUI: Eh, quiet, we gotta deal gently wid him. Make it, leave me alone wid him. Well, ah . . . how you stay, Malolio? How come you like defy da devil? Rememba, he is one enemy to mankind.

MALOLIO: Eh, you know wat you talking about, o wat?

KUKANA: Shaa you, and you like talk ill of da devil. Shame on you. Eh, God, I hope he no stay bewitched.

KOHALA: Eh, deliver his shishi to da kahuna fo samples!

KUKANA: No worry, going be done tomorrow if I still stay living. My lady no like lose him fo mo den I can say.

MALOLIO: And how you, sweetheart?

KUKANA: A, da shame!

OPU-NUI: Eh, hold on. Dis not da way. Look, you getting him all salty. Try lemme talk to him alone.

KOHALA: Go be gently, eh. Easy, easy, dis baga is rough and no like be roughly used.

OPU-NUI: Eh, how are you, my pigeon? Wat's your peep?

MALOLIO: To peep on you?

OPU-NUI: Try come wid me. Eh, you not supposed to play games wid da devil. Hang om and have some class.

KUKANA: Try aks om fo pray. Keia, aks om fo pray.

MALOLIO: Look, Emma, you betta pray!

KUKANA: Huh-uh. He no like hia of godliness.

MALOLIO: Go drown yourselves. No bodda me wid your lowtide tawts. I am one new person. You guys going see wat I mean. [*Exits*]

OPU-NUI: He fo real, o wat?

KOHALA: Auwe, if dis was one play, I could condemn da show fo malpractice.

OPU-NUI: Yeah, but look how he performs—hook, line, and sinka! [Laughs]

KUKANA: Les follow him befo he expose da show.

KOHALA: But we might make om go nuts.

KUKANA: But da house going be quieter.

OPU-NUI: Les go put him in one dark room and tie om up. My niece already tink he mad, so we can keep om dea until we feel mercy fo om.

KOHALA: Ah, look some mo matter from beyond da reef.

[Enter ANDREW]

ANDREW: Hia is da challenge. Read om. I warn you now, it is full of vinegar and chili peppa.

KOHALA: Da baga dat good?

ANDREW: Da baga is excellent. Try read om.

OPU-NUI: Lemme see. [Reads] "Yout, I no care who you are, you one ugly scab."

KOHALA: Good, plus valiant.

OPU-NUI: "Neva mind aksing questions like, why I saying dese tings about you, because I no mo any reasons."

KOHALA: Ooo, one good note dat would keep da law outa dis.

OPU-NUI: "You wen come to Princess Mahealani and in my eyes, her eyes look kindly on you. Howeva, even do' you one liar, ass not why I going challenge you."

KOHALA: Very brief, plus it exceeds in senselessness.

OPU-NUI: "I going broke your ass when you going home, and if by any chance you kill me . . ."

KOHALA: Brada.

OPU-NUI: " . . . catch you lata, and God have mercy fo one of our souls. He might have on mine, so me, if I was you, would watch out fo myself. Yours eva longingly and hateful sworn enemy, Sir Andy Waha." Yup, ass one heavy letta. I going give it to him.

KUKANA: You can do dat pretty soon, because he stay talking now to my lady and going come by any minute.

OPU-NUI: Hele on, Sir Andrew. Look fo me and him at da taro patch, and make like you one officer. As soon as you spock us, draw your sword and swear horrible tings like one warrior, so dat he get mo scared of you. Rememba, at firs sight, da louda you yell da bigga you get. Now go!

ANDREW: Okay, but no can swear because I am Catholic.

OPU-NUI: Hmmm . . . I no going deliver dis letta, because if da young man wen read dis, he would know dat dis guy was one okole and deafore wouldn't be afraid. So, I going make someting else up and tell om wid my own warmth. Dis way dey going kill each odda on sight.

[*Enter* MAHEALANI *and* LAHELA]

KOHALA: He coming now wid your niece. Let dem go until dey break up, den we'll get him.

OPU-NUI: Good. Den it going give me one chance to make up one horrible message fo one challenge.

[*Exit* OPU-NUI, KOHALA, *and* KUKANA]

MAHEALANI: I already have talked too much and wen give my honor to one heart of stone.

LAHELA: And wid da same passion my masta fall jus like you.

MAHEALANI: Hia, wear dis fo me, ass my picture. No tell me "no," 'cause no can harm you. And please, no feel shame aks me fo anyting and come again tomorrow.

LAHELA: Da only ting I ask is your true love fo my masta.

MAHEALANI: How I going give him dat if I already give om to you?

LAHELA: No worry, Princess, you have all da permission I can give you.

MAHEALANI: Well . . . come back tomorrow. Mahalo and aloha. [*Exit* LAHELA] One friend like him could take me to hell any time. [*Exits*]

[*Enter* OPU-NUI, LAHELA, *and* KOHALA]

OPU-NUI: Eh, bra, howzit?

LAHELA: Okay, and you?

OPU-NUI: If you get one defense, use it, 'cause wateva you wen do
to my friend, he salty and like beef wid you. Like one shark,
he smells your blood, is foaming at da mout, and is waiting fo
you at da taro patch. So get ready and draw your sword,
because he is quick, skillful, and DEADLY!

LAHELA: I tink you wen figure me wrong. I shua nobody huhu at
me. I no rememba making anybody mad at me.

OPU-NUI: Oh, but you will, bra, I promise. So if I was you, don't
think about it any mo and get ready already, fo your oppo-
nent get all da yout, da strength, skill, and wrath dat any man
could ask fo.

LAHELA: But who is he?

OPU-NUI: He one warrior, who is kind to everyone except when
get om mad. Already he wen kill tree guys wid one swish of da
sword dat even God couldn't see.

LAHELA: I going back in da house and get some help from da lady.
I not one fighter. I heard of guys who say tings about odda
guys so dat dey fight fo valor. Well, I tink dis one is like dat.

OPU-NUI: Not dis one. He like beef you, so you betta get ready
and give him his desire. You ain't going back into da house
unless you come through me firs. I going come right back, so
stay hia. [Exits]

LAHELA: Excuse me, but you know why dis guy is all huhu at me?

KOHALA: All I know is dat da guy like wring your neck, even if he
gotta off you; but I don't know why he like do dat.

LAHELA: But wat kine man is dis guy?

KOHALA: Nutting. I mean, when you firs look at him, dat is.
Actually, bra, he is da most skillful, bloody, and fatal oppo-
nent you could eva face in Hawaii. But no worry, I go try
make friends wid him fo you.

LAHELA: My sweet friend, I going owe you my life if you do. Like
da ol saying, "Cautious, not chicken." [Exits]

[Enter OPU-NUI and ANDREW]

OPU-NUI: Man, dis baga is one devil, I neva wen see such strength.
One time I wen beef wid him and he wen hit me wid one
club, den showed me how he would stab me wid his knife if I

wen try ack big again. He used to be in da Royal Hawaiian Army!

ANDREW: I change my mind, I no like fight wid him.

OPU-NUI: Yeah, but he no can be calmed down. Kohala no can even hold om back.

ANDREW: But I already calmed down—see?! Tell him let da matter slip 'cause I no mo mad juice in me; plus, I'll even go buy him one horse.

OPU-NUI: Okay, I going try. Wait hia and make it look good. Dis going end widout any killing. [*Aside*] I going ride your horse mo betta den I ride you. [*Enter* KOHALA *and* LAHELA] I get his horse fo settle da quarrel. I wen persuade him dat da yout is one devil.

KOHALA: He is da same, and he pants and looks sick as if one shark was afta him.

OPU-NUI: Eh, bra, sorry but he still like beef wid you fo oath's sake. But no worry, 'cause he said he not going hurt you, so you betta draw your sword.

LAHELA [*aside*]: Auwe, God defend me. One little ting would make me tell dem how I lack of one man.

KOHALA: Geev ground if you see om get furious.

OPU-NUI: Come, Sir Andrew, I no can stop it. Da gentoman fo honor's sake still not going hurt you, so come on and geev om.

ANDREW: Pray, God, I hope he keeps his word.

[*Enter* KOA]

LAHELA: Dis is against my will!

KOA: Put dat sword away. If dis gentoman wen do you wrong, give me da blame; if you wen offend him, den I going give you licking.

OPU-NUI: Why, ah . . . eh, who you?

KOA: One, sir, dat if you tink he can do you harm, watch me, 'cause I can do mo. [*Draws his sword*]

[*Enter* OFFICERS]

KOHALA: Try wait, Opu, hia come da officers.

OPU-NUI [*to* KOA]: Catch you lata.

LAHELA [*to* ANDREW]: Pray, bra, put away your sword.

ANDREW: I am glad to hia you say dat, I'm so glad I'll even stop da wind from making it move.

FIRST OFFICER: Dis is da man, nail om.

SECOND OFFICER: Koa, I arrest you at da suit of Prince Amalu.

KOA: Bra, but you mistaken.

FIRST OFFICER: Not me. I seen your map befo, even do' you no mo your seacap on. Take da baga away. He know I know om.

KOA: I gotta go. [*To* LAHELA] Dis is because I wen come to look fo you. Wat you going do since now I gotta aks you fo my money back? Mo worse, I feel kinda bad because now I no can help you. You look amazed, but no worry, you be all right.

SECOND OFFICER: Let's go.

KOA: Okay! [*To* LAHELA] But firs I need my money I gave you.

LAHELA: Wat money? Eh, I know you was kind to me hia, so even do' I no mo too much, I going lend you half of wat I get. Hia, dat's fo you.

KOA: Wat? You going back out on me now? I mean, all da good stuffs I wen do fo you no mean nutting to you now? Chee, dat's pretty rotten, heh?

LAHELA: I don't know anyting, plus I no even know your face o voice. I myself no like ingratitude, but lying and babbling drunkenness is mo worse almost.

KOA: Eh, no make like dat!

SECOND OFFICER: Come on, les jus go.

KOA: Try wait, I like talk some mo. You know, dis baga, I wen pull om out da jaws o death and wen take care of him till he was healthy again, and dis is how I get repaid.

FIRST OFFICER: Auwe, he getting mad, take om away.

KOA: Les go, I salty! [*Exits with* OFFICERS]

LAHELA: Chee, da way he was talking to me wid all dat passion, he really believe himself. But imagination, please go prove true! Please make true dat he really tawt I was my brada!

OPU-NUI: Eh, knight, Kohala, les go. Les go talk about some wise sayings, o someting.

LAHELA: He wen name Loka. When I look in one pond, I know he stay living. My brada was like me because he is da one I imitate. Please, if dis prove true, den da tradewinds are soft and kind and da tumbling surf stay fresh in love! [*Exits*]

OPU-NUI: Dis is one dishonest kane. He mo coward den one sand crab. Look like he wen leave his friends when he wen need him da most.

KOHALA: One coward, one most devout coward—religious in it.

ANDREW: Maybe I should give him licking afta all.

OPU-NUI: Geev om, but no draw your sword.

ANDREW: No worry, I nail him wid my bare hands.

KOHALA: Come, we go see.

OPU-NUI: I bet you any money, he no going do nutting.

[*Exeunt*]

ACT FOUR

SCENE I

[*Enter* LOKA *and* LOPE]

LOPE: Eh, try make believe I no was sent fo you.

LOKA: Make it, you one foolish fellow. Lemme alone.

LOPE: Shoot, wateva. No, I don't know you. Plus I no was sent hia fo you by my lady 'cause she like talk to you; your name is not masta Kimo; plus again, dis not my nose either. Nutting dat is so is so.

LOKA: Eh, go vent your folly on somebody else. You don't know me.

LOPE: Wat? Vent my folly! You wen hear dat word from some mitchenary and now trows it at one fool. Vent my folly! "I am afraid dis great lubber, dis world, will prove a cockney." Oh, sorry! Eh, no ack weird. And tell me wat I should "vent" to my lady. You tink I should vent to her dat you coming, o wat?

LOKA: Hoo! Dese wise men dat give fools money, chee, you feel good, heh, bra.

[*Enter* ANDREW, OPU-NUI, *and* KOHALA]

ANDREW: Howzit, bra. Seems like I no can avoid you. Dat's fo
     you! [*Strikes* LOKA]

LOKA: Chee, bra, dea's fo you [*strikes* ANDREW] and dea, and
     dea! All peopo mad, o wat?

OPU-NUI: Slow down, brada, o else you going get it! [*Seizes*
     LOKA]

LOPE: Whootah! Dis I going tell my lady. I no like wear your lei fo
     nutting. [*Exits*]

OPU-NUI: Come on, bra. I said stay still.

ANDREW: Let him go. Dis not ova yet. I going have one action of
     battery against him, if dea is any law in Hawaii like dat. Even
     do' I wen strike him firs, dat is no matter.

LOKA: Lemme go!

OPU-NUI: I no going let you go. Come on, draw your sword; you
     all nuha, eh, come on.

LOKA: Den I will be free. [*Frees himself*] Wat you going do now?
     If you going try tempt me, draw your sword. [*Draws*]

     [*Enter* MAHEALANI]

MAHEALANI: Stop, Opu! On your life, I said stop!

OPU-NUI: Sweetheart.

MAHEALANI: Always da same. You ungracious baga, you only fit
     fo da mountain and caves wea good kine manners neva was
     tawt. Go, hele, get outa my sight. No be offended, Kimo.
     Eh, Rudesby, take your gang home. [*Exit* OPU-NUI, ANDREW,
     and KOHALA] Sweetheart, no go let your emotions sway you
     in dis matta. Go home ova to my house, and I'll tell you wat
     kine stuff Opu did befo dat would make dis look lomi. No say
     "no"; jus come and let's go.

LOKA: But wat is dis? Which way does da stream go? Either dis
     one dream o I stay mad. But if dis is one dream, ho man! still
     let me sleep!

MAHEALANI: Nah, jus come, please. You like me rule you, o wat?

LOKA: Sweetheart, fo eva.

MAHEALANI: Oooo, I like talk to you some mo.

     [*Exeunt*]

SCENE TWO

[*Enter* KUKANA *and* LOPE]

KUKANA: Hia, go put dis gown and dis beard and make believe
   you one kahuna. But hurry up, eh? I going go call Opu, okay?
   [*Exits*]

LOPE: Hmm . . . I going put dis on, but I know I going look
   funny. Man, I bet I must be one fo da firs fo eva do dis. Mo
   worse, I not tall enuff fo do da job well, and I not skinny
   enuff to look like one good student; howeva, I can look like
   one honest man who is one good housekeeping neighbor,
   which would also mean dat I one careful and one great
   scholar. Da playmates enter.

[*Enter* OPU-NUI *and* KUKANA]

OPU-NUI: Hi, how you, Masta Kahuna?

LOPE: Howzit, Sir Opu, because as da ol hermit of Makapuu who
   neva saw one pen and ink once wen say to King Kamehameha, "Dat dat is, is so. So I, Masta Kahuna, am Masta
   Kahuna; for wat is "dat" but dat, and "is" but is?

OPU-NUI: Sounds good! Go get om.

LOPE [*whistles*]: Eh! Howzit in da prison? [*Whistles*]

OPU-NUI: Chee, he ack some good, eh. Check om.

[MALOLIO *within*]

MALOLIO: Eh, who dat?

LOPE: Masta Kahuna, dat comes to visit Malolio da lunatic.

MALOLIO: Masta Kahuna, Masta Kahuna, good Masta Kahuna,
   please go to my lady.

LOPE: Out, you nut! Why you talk like dat? All you talk about is
   ladies, o wat?

OPU-NUI: Geev om, Masta Kahuna.

MALOLIO: Oh, Masta Kahuna. No man was eva wronged mo den
   me. Oh, please, no tink I mad. Dey wen put me hia in hideous darkness . . .

LOPE: Shash up, you lying devil. Eh, I call you by da most modest terms. Heh, and no tink I one gentle one dat going use da devil wid courtesy. So you say da house dark, o wat?

MALOLIO: As hell, Masta Kahuna.

LOPE: But it has mud-smeared windows to da sout, nort, mo beautiful den ebony, and you still complain of abstruction?

MALOLIO: I no stay mad, Masta Kahuna, and I tell you dis place is dark.

LOPE: Madman, you mistake. I said no mo darkness but ignorance, which you stay mo puzzled in den English in dea fog.

MALOLIO: But dis house stay as dark as ignorance, even do' ignorance was as dark as hell; and I say dat all dose bagas framing me. I not any mo nuts den you. Make one trial of it and try ask me someting.

LOPE: Okay, den, in English terms, wat is da opinion of Pythagorus concerning wild fowl?

MALOLIO: Ho, no mo nutting easier. No, no, wait, wait . . . Oh, dat da soul of our grandmada can happily inherit one bird.

LOPE: And wat you tink of his opinion?

MALOLIO: I tink his soul is noble, but I no approve his opinion.

LOPE: Spock you lata. Stay right dea in darkness. You going hold da opinion of Pythagorus befo I could allow of your wits, and scared to kill one mynah bird, unless you dispossess da soul of your grandma. Take it easy.

MALOLIO: Kahuna, Masta Kahuna.

OPU-NUI: Oh, my most goodest Masta Kahuna!

LOPE: No clap, jus trow money.

KUKANA: You could've done om even widout da beard and gown. He neva see you.

OPU-NUI: Go back and talk to him in your own voice and tell him how he stay. [*To* KUKANA] I like get outa dis. If he could be easily freed, I wish he would, 'cause I stay in enough hot water wid my niece already, and no can do dis sport any mo wid any safety. [*To* LOPE] Catch us lata at my chamber. [*Exits with* KUKANA]

LOPE [*sings*]: "Hey, Nene, jolly Nene,
       Tell me how da lady does."

MALOLIO: Fool.

LOPE: "My lady is unkind, fo shua."

MALOLIO: Eh, come on, Lope.

LOPE: "She loves one nodda." Who calls, eh?

MALOLIO: Eh, pal, I like you do one favor fo me. Can you get me one candle, one pen, one ink, and one paper . . . please. I one true friend and if you help me, you neva going regret it.

LOPE: Masta Malolio?

MALOLIO: Yeah, dis me.

LOPE: Eh, bra, how come you stay down hia halfway outa your mind?

MALOLIO: Eh, dey wen wrong me. I stay well in my wits, jus like you, fool.

LOPE: Den you gotta be mad if you stay no betta den one fool.

MALOLIO: Dey wen put me hia in darkness, send da kahuna to me, and try to do everyting dey can to drive me mad.

LOPE: Watch out wat you say now. Da kahuna is hia. "Malolio, Malolio, may da heavens restore your brains. Endeavor yourself to sleep and always rememba oranacanapuna!"

MALOLIO: Masta Kahuna . . .

LOPE: Das enuff already. Masta Kahuna, who, me? No, not me. God bless you, Masta Kahuna. Amen, amen . . . I will, I will.

MALOLIO: Fool, fool, fool! Lope!

LOPE: Eh, no get all wet. Jus be cool head.

MALOLIO: Please get me da pen, paper, and light. I promise I be your friend.

LOPE: I neva going believe one madman until I spock his brains. But no worry, I'll get da stuffs fo you.

MALOLIO: Oh, tanks, bra. Now please go get om.

LOPE [*sings*]:

>I going go, sir,
>So wateva, sir,
>I'll spock you again, sir!
>In a short while,
>Plus he back wid style
>Dat you need to sustain

Like to da oldest wid his knife,
Who in his rage and his wrath
Cries "shaka" to da devil
Like one mad lad.
"Cut your nails, dad."
      Every day, goodman devil.

[*Exeunt*]

SCENE III

[*Enter* LOKA]

LOKA: Dis is da air, dat is da sun; dis da pearl she wen give me. I feel it and see it. Still, I know I not mad! Den, wea's dat Koa? He no was at da Royal Hawaiian . . . Oh, I wish he was hia to help me tink. 'Cause even do' my soul say my senses mistaken, my head tell me dis is too favored, and make me tink I nuts, o else da lady is. Still, if dis not true, she no could rule her house, command her followers, take and give back tings fo do wid such a smooth style dat I tink she has. Dea must be someting in dis dat stay all jam up. But hia comes da wahine.

[*Enter* MAHEALANI *and* KAHUNA]

MAHEALANI: No blame dis haste of mine. Eh, sweetheart, if you mean well, go come wid me and da kahuna to da church. Den dea, befo him and underneath my roof, dea my anxious and doubtful soul can stay at peace. He going keep it until you and me stay ready fo tell everybody about da celebration. Wat you tink?

LOKA: Sweetheart, I going wid you and dis kahuna, and having sworn da truth, I going be true.

MAHEALANI: Den please take us dea, and let da heavens shine so dat dey may rate dis ack of mine.

[*Exeunt*]

ACT FIVE

SCENE I

[*Enter* KOHALA *and* LOPE]

KOHALA: Eh, you my friend, eh, lemme see da letta.
LOPE: Brada Kohala, I'll do someting else fo you.
KOHALA: Anyting?
LOPE: Jus no ask me fo see da letta.
KOHALA: Eh, bra, no make like dat.

[*Enter* AMALU, LAHELA, KAWIKA, FRIENDS, *and* ATTENDANTS]

AMALU: Howzit? You guys belong to Mahealani?
LOPE: Das us, we all bit da hook.
AMALU: I know you. How you stay, my friend?
LOPE: I must admit, da betta fo my foes and da worse fo my
    friends.
AMALU: Nah, jus da opposite—da betta fo your friends.
LOPE: No, bra, da worse.
AMALU: How can dat be?
LOPE: Because my friends praise me and make one ass of me. But
    my foes tell me straight—I one ass, period! Deafore, by my
    foes, I stay profit in da knowledge, and by my friends, I stay
    abused; so dat, if conclusions was kisses, and if four negatives
    make two affirmatives, den da worse fo my friends and da
    betta fo my foes! Not bad, eh?
AMALU: Eh, you tuff, bra!
LOPE: In truth, no doubt, it please you to be one of my friends.
AMALU: Eh, no going be da worse fo me. Hia's some puka shells.
LOPE: But das like deceiving me, bra. Why no give me someting
    else?
AMALU: Now you giving me ill advice.
LOPE: Bra, jus put your title in your pocket and obey your flesh
    and blood.
AMALU: I not going be one sinner to deceive you. Hia's some mo
    shells.

LOPE: Junk-ena-po is one good game, and tree strikes, and you
   out. Hawaii Pono get one good tripping measure, o maybe
   even Aloha Oe might make you tink. Ready? Junk-ena-po, I-
   kena-sho!

AMALU: Eh, no trow your mossy jokes at me fo money. Jus go tell
   your lady I stay hia fo talk wid her, and bring her hia wid you,
   den it going awake my bounty further.

LOPE: You know wat, sing to your bounty till I come back, I
   going; but I no like you tink dat my desire is da sin of covet-
   ousness, eh. But, like you say, let your bounty take one nap; I
   wake om up lata. Okay? Okay? Bye. [*Exits*]

   [*Enter* KOA *and* OFFICERS]

LAHELA: Eh! Das da man dat wen rescue me.

AMALU: I rememba dat guy. But da las time I saw him was all
   black, like when you kalua one pig. He wasn't even wort half
   a pound of one ahi. Wassamatta now?

FIRST OFFICER: Amalu, dis is da same captain dat wen cause all da
   trouble in Waikiki when your young nephew wen get da
   puka-head. Dis time we wen catch om down Kakaako side in
   one private beef.

LAHELA: But he wen do me kindness and was trying fo help me.
   But he also was talking funny kine tings dat even I neva
   undastand.

AMALU: Eh, mana, you dodo-kai baga, how come you make silly
   and come back to one place wea nobody like you?

KOA: Amalu, kind Prince, I not all dose names you calling me,
   but I will confess dat I am your enemy. Some strange wind
   wen blow me hia. And dat ungrateful boy ova dea I wen go
   save from da mad and foamy sea. He was past hope and ready
   fo make. His life I wen save, gave him all my love and aloha,
   and wen follow him into dis town; wen fight and defend him,
   den when I was captured, he wen make believe he neva know
   me and neva even give me back my purse, which I wen give to
   him only half hour ago.

LAHELA: Dis no can be.

AMALU: When he wen come to dis town?

KOA: Today, good Prince, and fo tree months widout one minute fo spare, both day and night we wen keep company.

[*Enter* MAHEALANI *and* ATTENDANTS]

AMALU: Hia come da princess. Oo-la-la, heaven walks on earth. But fo you, bra, your words stay mo tangled den woodrose on one hau tree. Limbs fo days! He was wid me fo tree months already. But lata on, you. Take om on da side.

MAHEALANI: Aloha, and wat you like, except dat you no can have dat Mahealani can do fo you? Honeyboy, you not keeping your promise wid me.

LAHELA: Wat?

AMALU: Eh, sweetheart . . .

MAHEALANI: Wat you say, Honeyboy?

LAHELA: My prince like talk—duty tells me to hush.

MAHEALANI: If it's like one old tune, Amalu, it is fat and ugly to my ear like howling afta music.

AMALU: You still cruel, eh?

MAHEALANI: You still constant, eh?

AMALU: To wat, to perverseness? You uncivil lady, whose ungratefulness wen turn every bit of faithful offerings of devotion I had to nutting. Auwe! Wat I going do?

MAHEALANI: You can do wateva you like. I no care.

AMALU: Why should I not, if I had one heart fo do it, like one thief, kill wat I love. But hia me out. Since you no like my true faith, and I know why you no favor me, live like da stone-hearted tita you are. And because he your favorite, and because I know you love om, I going take om away from your cruel eyes, wea he stay sit like da beautiful snow-capped Mauna Kea. Come, les go, I like make mischief. I'll sacrifice da garland I love to spite one raven's heart in dat dove. [*Leaves*]

LAHELA: And me most willingly and happily should follow you to da depths of da great Pacific to give you one rest. [*Follows*]

MAHEALANI: Honeyboy, wea you going?

LAHELA: Wid him dat I love mo den I love dese eyes, mo den my life, oh, mo and mo den all mores den eva I going love one wife. If you tink I only making believe, den punish me wid softness fo da rest of my life fo stepping on my love.

MAHEALANI: I stay stepped on! How come I stay cheated?

LAHELA: Who stepped on you? Who wen cheat you?

MAHEALANI: Is it dat long dat you wen already foget. Call da kahuna.

[ATTENDANT *exits*]

AMALU: Too much forty-weight grease. Les go!

MAHEALANI: Wea you going? Honeyboy, husband, stay hia!

AMALU: Husband?

MAHEALANI: Ass right. Aks om.

AMALU: You her husband?

LAHELA: Not me, Prince.

MAHEALANI: It's because of fear dat makes him say dat. Eh, Honeyboy, no scared. Take up your fortunes and by yourself, den you can be great as da one you scared of. [*Enter* KAHUNA] Aloha, Kahuna. Dear one, please tell dem wat we wen intend fo do when da fruits was ripe between me and dis yout.

KAHUNA: One contract of eternal bond dat was confirmed by your lips and hands and was strengthened by da exchange of rings; and all dis was done wid me in front, sealed by my office and my testimony. Since den, da sun wen tell me I wen walk only two mo hours toward my grave.

AMALU: Eh, I no like see how you going be when you grey and ol if you like dis now. [*To* LAHELA] Den, aloha, and take her; and make shua dat weaeva you go dat we no meet again.

LAHELA: No, Prince Amalu, I no stay lying!

MAHEALANI: Honeyboy, no need be scared now. He no can touch you.

[*Enter* ANDREW]

ANDREW: Fo love of God, one doctor.

MAHEALANI: Wassamatta?

ANDREW: I got one puka-head and Count Opu-nui got one Charlie-horse on his ear. I tell you fo da love of God, help us. Mo worse I wish I was at home.

MAHEALANI: Who wen do dis, Sir Andrew?

ANDREW: Dat one who work fo Prince Amalu, da one dey call

Honeyboy. We tawt he was one coward, but, ay soos, he is da devil.

AMALU: Who, Honeyboy?

ANDREW: Das him, hia he is. You wen broke my head fo nutting; dat dat I did, I was tol fo do it by Count Opu.

LAHELA: Why you talk to me? I neva wen hurt you. You wen draw your sword on me fo nutting, and I wen talk you outa it and neva hurt you.

[*Enter* OPU-NUI *and* LOPE]

ANDREW: If one puka-head is one hurt, den you wen hurt me. Look, hia comes Count Opu; you folks going hia some mo. But if he no was drinking, you would have seen da lights, pal.

AMALU: Howzit, gentomen. How you stay?

OPU-NUI: Ass easy! He wen hurt us and das da end! You wen call da surgeon, o wat?

LOPE: He already drunk about one hour ago. His eyes stay set fo eight in da morning.

OPU-NUI: Ooo, da rotten baga! I no can stand drunk peopo!

ANDREW: I'll help you, Opu. We can be patched up together.

OPU-NUI: Bullshit. You know you baga . . .

MAHEALANI: Take om to bed and go look at his hurt.

[*Exit* LOPE, OPU-NUI, ANDREW, *and* KOHALA. *Enter* LOKA]

LOKA: Sweet Maile, I wen hurt your uncle and his friend, but even if it was my brada, I would do da same fo my own safety. You look like you salty at me. I guess all I can say is dat I sorry. Sorry, eh?

AMALU: One face, one voice, one habit, but two peopo. One natural mirror dat wen lost you.

KOA: Loka?

LOKA: Yeah, ass me, brada.

KOA: How you wen split in two? One papaya chopped in two no stay mo twin den dese two keikis. Which is Loka?

MAHEALANI: How wonderful.

LOKA: I stand dea, o wat? I no mo one brada. I had one sista dat was eaten by da sea. Eh, aikane, wat you stay to me? Wat island, wat name, and who your fada?

LAHELA: I from Maui, eh, and my fada's name was Loka; dat was also my brada's name, too, but he was drowned into da cold seas dat surrounds us. If da spirits can return to da earth, den you come back to make us scared.

LOKA: I am one spirit as you all are, and born from my mada's womb, like you all did. Yet, if you was one woman, I would cry and go let my tears fall on your cheek and say, "Welcome back, my little lost sista!"

LAHELA: My fada had one mole on his eyebrow.

LOKA: Mine too.

LAHELA: And he wen die when Lahela was thirteen years old.

LOKA: Dat memory is lively in my soul.

LAHELA: Den if nutting hinders us, us both happy, except dis masculine usurped outfit, no go embrace until each circumstance of place, time, and da kine . . . oh, fortune do stick together dat I is Lahela. To prove dat, I going show you da fisherman wea my maiden clothes stay who wen also save me from dat always hungry ocean. And dis is da prince who I wen work fo dat helped to preserve me. Everyting else dat wen happen to me since den was between him and her.

LOKA [to MAHEALANI]: So it looks like you was greased, Princess. But nature wen draw you into one natural course. You was almost contracted to one maid, but you stay deceived; you stay betrothed to both one maid and one man.

AMALU: No go be amazed, his blood stay noble. If all dis stay true, I like have one share in dis most happy confusion. [To LAHELA] Boy, you wen tell me one thousand times dat I neva should love one woman unless was someting like you.

LAHELA: And all dose tings I said are true, and will always be true like da sun dat cuts nights from day.

AMALU: Gimme your hand, and lemme spock you in your wahine attire.

LAHELA: Da fisherman dat wen bring me firs to shore, he get my wahine attire. But now he stay doing someting to, fo, o wid Malolio, who is one gentoman dat work fo da princess.

MAHEALANI: He going free him. Do get Malolio. But yet, I tink, I rememba dat dey said he all twisted, o someting. [*Enter* LOPE *with letter and* KOHALA] Eh, you guys, how Malolio stay?

LOPE: I figure he stay holding off da devil as good as any man in his condition. Hia is one letta fo you dat I wen foget to give you dis morning. But since one madman's epistles is no gospels, I neva tink I had fo give om to you right away.

MAHEALANI: Neva mind unrolling all your paper—just read om.

LOPE: Okay, den clean your ears because da fool going speak fo da madman. [*Reads*] "By da Lord, Madman . . ."

MAHEALANI: Try wait! You crazy, o wat?

LOPE: Uh-uh, but I read madness. And my lady going have om jus as it should be read.

MAHEALANI: Oh please, jus go read om in da right wits.

LOPE: But I do, and to read om in his right wits was to read om like dat. So jus listen, please!

MAHEALANI [*to* KOHALA]: Okay, you read om.

KOHALA [*reads*]: "By da Lord, Madman, you wen wrong me and da world shall know it. Even do' you stay put me in darkness and wen give your drunken uncle to rule ova me, I still get da benefit of my senses. I still get da letta you wrote to me telling me wat fo put on. Tink wat you like of me. I not trying fo ack sassy to you and deafore speak out of my hurt. Da Madly Used Malolio."

MAHEALANI: He wen write dat?

LOPE: Yup.

MAHEALANI: Kohala, go and get him. [*Exit* KOHALA] Dear Prince, we'll deal wid dat lata, but I was hoping from now on dat you would tink of me as one sista, and hope dat some day you and I can make one alliance of houses at my cost.

AMALU: Princess, I stay most happy fo accept your offer. [*To* LAHELA] Looks like your masta going let you get go, and since you wen call me masta fo so long, hia is my hand; so from dis time on you going be your masta's mistress.

MAHEALANI: Den you going be my sista.

[*Enter* KOHALA *with* MALOLIO]

AMALU: Is dis da madman, o wat?

MAHEALANI: Ass him. How you Malolio?

MALOLIO: My lady, you wen do me wrong, plenny wrong.

MAHEALANI: Me, Malolio? Not me.

MALOLIO: Yes, you! Hia, look at dis letta. You no can tell me dat's not your handwriting. Okay, den, tell me, in da name of honor, why you wen give me so much flavor; tol me fo smile in yellow stockings, and to frown on Count Opu-nui and his circle of idiots; and den trow me in prison, in one dark house, visited by da kahuna, and made da biggest fool dat invention eva wen play on? Tell me why!

MAHEALANI: Eh, Malolio, dis not my writing. But I must confess it look like mine; howeva, I tink Kukana wen go write dis. Actually, I tink was her dat firs wen tell me you was nuts. Anyway, jus be cool head. Dey wen grease you and did you all kine wrong, but when we find out all da angles, you can be da plaintiff and judge of dea own punishment.

KOHALA: Dear Princess, I like say someting, but I no like quarrel o start one beef. I confess dat was me and Opu dat wen start dis and was written in Kukana's hand, afta which Opu wen marry Kukana. Anyway, we wen do dis because Malolio always tink he big shit and he always boss us around, so we wen do one to him fo laughta and not fo revenge. So wat I was trying to say is, if you look at both sides, I figure we even.

MAHEALANI: Eh, brada, look like you was duck soup!

LOPE: Why "some stay born great, some achieve greatness trown upon dem." I was involved in dis too, but dat's pau. "By da Lord, fool, I no stay mad." But you rememba, "I marvel dat you take delight in one barren rascal? O, unless you laugh, and minister occasion to him, he get stuck throat." And deafore, peopo, in time, brings on his own revenges.

MALOLIO: I going revenge da whole pack of you. [*Exits*]

MAHEALANI: Eh, you guys, you wen shua do him in!

AMALU: Follow him and make om peaceful. He neva tell us wea da captain stay. Meanwhile, sweet sista, les all go to my place and plan one big luau. My beautiful Lahela, we go. And from now on you are Amalu's mistress and his queen.

[*Exeunt all but* LOPE]

LOPE [*sings*]:

> Sand between your toes,
> Feeling all your woes,
> Picking ripe mangoes,
> Baking new bread.
>
> You're in and den you're out,
> But wat are you worrying about?
> Go have some crack seed,
> We're a new breed.
>
> It's an ol Hawaiian feeling
> Dat keeps running through us all
> Jus a kind of laid-back breathing
> That makes someting look pretty small.
>
> Climbing an ol tree,
> Looking fo love, free.
> Let me tell you now,
> It's open, it's free, it's free.
>
> Wateva, wateva, wateva
> Wateva you want.

Curtain

GLOSSARY

BY
CAROL ODO

DEFINITIONS of Hawaiian words are adopted from Mary Kawena Pukui and Samuel H. Elbert's *Hawaiian-English, English-Hawaiian Dictionary* (Honolulu, 1971). Definitions of all other words are from Carol Odo's *Dictionary of Hawaiian Pidgin and Creole English* (in preparation). Not all words that deviate from English spelling are listed in the glossary. Only the commonly used ones are listed, as well as those that might not be readily understood.

Pronunciation Features of Pidgin

1. The sequence *str* as in 'strong' is pronounced *shchr*, as in *shchrit*, 'street'.

2. The sequence *tr* is pronounced *chr*, as in *chri*, 'tree'; in fast speech the *r* is often dropped, as in *chi*.

3. The sequence *dr* is pronounced *jr*, as in *jraiv*, 'drive'; again, the *r* may be dropped in fast speech.

4. The sounds represented by SE *th* are replaced by *t* or *d*, as in *tink*, 'think', and *dis*, 'this'.

5. Consonants at the end of a word are often dropped when they occur in clusters of two or more, as in *fers*, 'first', or *neks*, 'next'.

6. The sound *r* is dropped when it follows the vowel *a* in the same sylla-

Carol Odo holds a doctorate in linguistics from the University of Hawaii. Her specialty is sociolinguistics, and she studies varieties of English. She has published several reports and articles on Hawaiian pidgin and creole, and is presently working as a consultant and researcher. In 1975 she was co-instructor and pidgin consultant in a pidgin playwriting course in the Department of Drama at the University of Hawaii. She is presently preparing a dictionary of Hawaiian pidgin and creole English.

ble, as in *stat*, 'start'; *r* is substituted by *a* in certain cases (*sista*, 'sister') and by *e* in other cases (*reked*, 'record').

7. The contrast between long and short *i* and *u*, as in SE *bit*, 'bit' : *bit*, 'beat', and in *pul*, 'pool' : *pul*, 'pull' tends to be minimized. The long form is generally used.

8. The vowels *e* and *o* tend to be pure unglided vowels, in contrast with SE (*de*, 'day', SE *dey*; *go*, 'go', SE *gow*).

9. The contrast between SE__ and *a* as in *hw__t*, 'what', and *wat*, 'watt', tends to be minimized; *a* is used for both sounds in pidgin.

10. Syllabic *l* in words like 'people', 'handle', and 'bottle' is pronounced *o*, as in *pipo*, *haendo*, and *bado*, respectively; *l* that follows a vowel in the same syllable in some words like 'real' and 'small' are pronounced as *w*, as in *riw* and *smaw*.

Pronunciation Guide: a, f*a*ther; æ, c*a*n; ey, l*a*te; e, l*e*t; i, w*e*; u, sh*oe*; o, gl*o*ry; aw, c*au*ght; ay, l*i*ne; au, c*ow*; oy, t*oy*; sh, *sh*in; ch, *ch*in; ', glottal stop.

Abbreviations: Many of the words used in pidgin are loan words. The languages from which these come are identified as follows: *H*, Hawaiian; *J*, Japanese; *F*, Filipino; and *K*, Korean.

ack /æ/ Act.
adobo /adóbo/ Pork or chicken dish. [*F*]
afta /ǽfta/ After.
ahi /áhi/ Tuna fish, usually the yellow-fin tuna. [*H*]
aikane /aikáne/ Friend; smart, clever. [*H*]
aks /æks/ Ask. Variant: *ass.*
ali'i /alí'i/ Chief or member of Hawaiian nobility. [*H*]
aloha /alóha/ Love, affection; hello, goodbye. [*H*]
aole pilikía /a'ole pilikía/ No need to bother. [*H*]
ass /æs/ That's; ask.
auwe /áuwe/ Oh! Alas! [*H*]
ay soos /aysús/ Alas! [*F*]

baga /bága/ Person. [From English 'bugger'; mildly derogatory]
bagong /bagóng/ Fish sauce made by fermentation. [*F*]
baimbai /baymbáy/ Later. Variants: *bambai, bumbye.*
beef /bif/ Fight. [Noun or verb; from English slang]
befo /bifó/ Before.

betta / béda / Better.
bia / bía / Beer.
bukbuk / bukbúk / Person of Filipino ancestry. [Derogatory]
bodda / báda / Bother.
bra / bra / Form of *brada*, 'brother'. [Term of address]
brada / bráda / Brother. Cf. *bra.*
buddha-head / búdahed / Person of Japanese ancestry. [Nonpejorative]

chee / chi / Gee.

da / da / The.
das / dæs / That's. Variants: *dats, ass.*
dea / dea / There or their. Variant: *dere.*
dem / dem / Them. (Used also as a proper name suffix to mean 'and associates', as in *John-dem*, 'John and friends'.)
den / den / Then or than.
dey / de / They.
dis / dis / This.
dese / diz / These.
do' / do / Though.
dono / dono / Don't know.
dodo-kai / dodokái / Stupid.
dose / doz / Those.

eesalay / isalé / It's in the bag. [From 'easily']
eh / e / Form of 'hey!'
eva / éva / Ever.

fada / fáda / Father.
fo / fo / For, to; in order to, as in *he wen call me fo go out*, 'he called me to go out'.

giv / giv / Give.
giv om / gívom / Give 'em hell. Variant: *geev.*
going / góing / Future marker: *we going eat lunch*, 'we're going to eat lunch'. Variants: *going, gon.*

haftu / hǽftu / Have to.
haimakamaka / haymakaḿaka / High mucky-muck.
hale / hále / House, building. [*H*]

haole /háule/ Caucasian. [*H*]

hapa /hápa/ Half.

hele on /hele áwn/ To go. [Hawaiian *hele,* 'come', plus English *'on'*]

hia /hía/ Here; hear.

hohana /hohána/ To work with a hoe.

ho /ho/ Wow.

howzit /háuzit/ Common greeting. [From English]

huhu /huhú/ Angry, offended. [*H*]

hui /húi/ Expletive equivalent to 'look here!' or 'hey!'

imua /imúa/ Forward! [*H*]

junk-ena-po, i-kena-sho /jankenapó, aykenashó/ Words for choosing-up
    game using paper, scissors, stone. [*J*]

kahuna /kahúna/ Priest; expert in any profession. [*H*]

kala /kalá/ Money. [From 'dollar']

kalua /kalúa/ To bake in a ground oven. [*H*]

kamaaina /kama'áyna/ A person born in Hawaii or a long-time resident;
    lit. 'child of the land'. [*H*]

kane /káne/ Male, husband, male sweetheart, man. [*H*]

kapakahi /kapakáhi/ One-sided, crooked, lopsided. [*H*]

kaukau /kaukáu/ Eat; food. [Possibly from 'chow chow']

keia /keía/ Child, offspring, descendant. [*H*]

kim chee /kimchí/ Pickled vegetables. [*K*]

kine /kayn/ Kind. Also *da kine,* a filler word similar to 'whachamacal-
    lit'; also used as a suffix to adjectives (as in *small-kine,* 'small kind
    of' or 'small type of').

koa /kóa/ Largest and most valuable of native trees. [*H*]

kokua /kokúa/ Help; assistant. [*H*]

kotonk /kotónk/ Japanese-American born on the mainland.

la dat /ladǽt/ And things like that.

lata /léyda/ Later.

lepo /lépo/ Dirt, earth, ground. [*H*]

les /les/ Let's.

letta /léda/ Letter.

limu /límu/ Seaweed. [*H*]

lolo /loló/ Brains, bone-marrow; feeble-minded. [*H*]

lomi /lómi/ To rub, press, mash fine, massage. [*H*]

luau /luʻáu/ Hawaiian feast; named for the taro tops always served at one. [*H*]

mabuhai /mabúhay/ Greeting. [*F*]
mahalo /mahálo/ Thanks. [*H*]
mahu /mahú/ A homosexual. [*H*]
mai /may/ Hither; toward. [Hawaiian *hele mai,* 'come in, come here']
maka /máka/ Eye, face. [*H*]
make /máke/ Dead, to die, faint. [*H*]
mana /mána/ *Lit.* supernatural divine power. (Used colloquially in *Twelf Nite O Wateva!*)
manong /manóng/ Older brother. [*F*]
maua /máua/ Ungrateful; close-fisted. [*H*]
menehune /menehúne/ Legendary race of small people who work at night building roads, bridges, temples, etc. The work remains unfinished if not completed in one night. [*H*]
moemoe /moemóe/ Sleep, lie down. [*H*]
molowa /molówa/ Lazy. [*H*]
moopuna /moʻopúna/ Grandchild, great niece, or nephew. [*H*]
mo /mo/ More. (Used before adjectives to express comparative form, as in *mo nice,* 'nicer'.)
mo betta /mobéda/ Better. Also equivalent of English 'ought to', as in *mo betta you stay home,* 'you ought to stay home'.

nene /néne/ Hawaiian goose, official state bird of Hawaii. [*H*]
nesan /nésan/ Older sister. [*J*]
neva /néva/ Never. Also used as a negative past marker for any verb, as in *we neva see om,* 'we didn't see it/them'.
no /no/ No. Also used as a negative marker with certain words, as in *no like,* 'don't/doesn't like', or *no can,* 'can't'.
no mo /nomó/ There isn't/aren't any (as in *no mo rice,* 'there isn't any rice'); don't/doesn't have (*she no mo money,* 'she doesn't have money').
nuff /naf/ Enough.

o /o/ Or.
odda /áda/ Other.
okole /okóle/ Anus, buttocks. [*H*]
okolehau /okoleháu/ Hawaiian liquor made from the root of the ti plant. [*H*]

om /om/ Third person singular or plural pronoun. Similar to English ' 'em.'

ono /óno/ Delicious, tasty, savory. [H]

opu /ópu/ Stomach, belly. [H]

oronacanapuna /oranakanapúna/ Nonsense word.

ova /óva/ Over.

peopo /pípo/ People.

plenny /pléni/ or /plǽni/ Plenty, many.

pakalana /pakalána/ The Chinese violet, which has yellowish green flowers. [H]

pakalolo /pakalólo/ Marijuana. [H]

pake /paké/ Person of Chinese ancestry.

pali /páli/ Cliff, precipice, steep hill. [H]

pau /pau/ End, finish (as in *pau school*, 'finished school'; *pau work*, 'finished work'; *pau sick*, 'over being sick').

Pele /péle/ Volcano goddess. [H]

pikake /pikáke/ Arabian Jasmine. [H]

pilau /piláu/ Rot, stench, rottenness. (Used as adjective: *pilau baga*, 'dirty person', 'stinker'.) [H]

pilikia /pilikía/ Trouble. Cf. *aole pilikia.* [H]

pilute /pilút/ Drunkard. Also *piluted,* 'drunk'. [Possibly from English 'polluted']

poi /poy/ Staple food of the Hawaiians; made from cooked taro pounded and mixed with water. [H]

popolo /popólo/ Black person; *lit.* the black nightshade, a smooth cosmopolitan herb. Also *pope* /pop/. [H]

pua'a /puá'a/ Pig. [H]

puka /púka/ Hole, perforation. [H]

pupu /pupú/ Hors d'oeuvres, appetizers. [H]

Portagee /podogi/ Portuguese.

radda /rǽda/ Rather.

scoop /skup/ Verb meaning 'to take' or 'to goose someone'.

shaka /sháka/ Expletive equivalent to English 'right on!'; also used in *shaka weed,* 'excellent marijuana'.

shimpai /shimpái/ To arrange (as in marriage). [J]

shishi /shíshi/ Urine; to urinate. [J]

shua /shúa/ Sure.

spock /spak/ To see. [From English slang 'spark']

stay /ste/ Used as verb 'to be' in the following contexts: 1) before certain adjectives, as in *she stay sick,* 'she is sick'; 2) to indicate continuing action, as in *she stay sleeping,* 'she is sleeping'; 3) to indicate location, as in *wea you stay?,* 'where are you?' [Possibly derived from Portuguese *estar*]

tawt /tawt/ Thought.

time /taym/ Suffix equivalent to 'when', as in *small-kid-time,* 'when (I) was a small kid'.

ting /ting/ Thing.

tink /tink/ Think.

tita /títa/ Sister; tough local girl. [Hawaiianized English]

tri /chri/ Three, tree.

trow /chro/ Throw.

tutu /tútu/ Granny, grandma, grandpa. [*H*]

uku-million /ukumílyen/ Many millions.

vamp /væmp/ In hula, to take steps to the left or right.

wahine /wahíne/ Woman, lady, wife. [*H*]

wata /wáda/ Water.

wassamatta /wasamaéda/ What's the matter. Variant: *wassamalla* /was amala/ used by Chinese pidgin speakers.

wat /wat/ What, so what.

wass /was/ What's. Variant: *wats.*

wea /wéa/ Where.

wen /wen/ Past tense marker used before certain verbs, as in *Virgie wen sweep da floor,* 'Virgie swept the floor'; used interchangeably with *wen go.*

whootah /húta/ All right! [Expression of exultation]

wikiwiki /wikiwíki/ Hurry, hurry up. [*H*]

wid /wid/ With.

whacking om. Eating a lot.

wrinks /rinks/ *Idiom.* Screwed, crazy.

you /yu/ You, your.

THE PLAYWRIGHTS

Lynette Amano was born in 1949, and graduated from the University of Hawaii in 1971 with a B.A. in English. Prior to *Ashes* she wrote a pidgin sketch, "Lurleen and Joseph," which formed a segment of the experimental revue *Hemo Skin,* produced in Kennedy Theatre Lab in 1971. She also wrote a short film script called *Hotel Street* (no relation to the musical of the same title) and the play *The Winter of Summer,* and is currently working on a play about interracial marriage.

Arthur Aw was born and raised in Singapore, and graduated in journalism from the University of Hawaii in the early 1970s. He is now a part-time journalist. He was resident in Kailua until 1981, when he temporarily moved to Duarte, California. In addition to *All Brand New Classical Chinese Theatre,* Aw has written two other plays, *Caught Dead* (1977) and *Expiration of the Two Weeks Guaranteed Aloha* (1981).

James Grant Benton was born in 1949, and raised in Honolulu. He appeared in a number of productions as an undergraduate at the University of Hawaii, including *Desire Under the Elms* and *Narukami the Thundergod,* an English-language kabuki production later televised nationally. He also appeared in *Hair* in Las Vegas, but returned to Honolulu and in 1974 became a founding member of the comedy collective Booga Booga. Benton performed with them until 1978 and again when the group re-formed in 1982. He has soloed as a comedian in various Honolulu night spots. In 1980 he played Stevenson in Aldyth Morris' one-man play *R.L.S.* for the Hawaii Public Theatre. In 1981 he released an original satirical LP entitled *Unknown Moments from Hawaiian History.* Television audiences saw him on *Hawaii Five O, Magnum P.I.* and *The Jeffersons.* He is currently working on a one-man play to be performed in 1983.

Lisa Toishigawa Inouye (Bessie Toishigawa) has spent most of her professional life as an editor, journalist, and public relations worker. She has worked for the *Honolulu Star-Bulletin, Hawaii Hochi*, KHET and KTRG television, and for the University as critical editor for a 1978 Department of Ethnic Studies, University of Hawaii Oral History Project. She has worked in the State Legislature twice as an administrative assistant in 1970, and in 1975 as press secretary to the Senate president. After graduating from the University of Hawaii in 1948 with a B.A. in English and journalism, she did post-graduate work at Columbia and the New School for Social Research in New York. She wrote *Reunion* and another short play, *Nisei*, a romance between a local girl and a haole, at the same time.

Charles R. Kates was born in 1948, and grew up in the windward Oahu area. He currently lives in New York City. After playing numerous roles in UH Drama Department productions, he graduated with a B.A. in drama in 1976. He then studied acting with the American Conservatory Theatre in San Francisco and the California Institute of the Arts. He graduated from the Institute with an M.F.A. in acting in 1981. He has acted with most community theatre groups in Honolulu and directed two musicals for the Hawaii Performing Arts Company. More recently he has acted for the Cal Arts Repertory Company in Los Angeles and with the On Stage Children Company and Common Ground Chekhov Theatre in New York. He played the lead in the San Francisco Youth Film Festival Award winner *It's Your Move*. Apart from *The Travels of Heikiki*, Mr. Kates has written *Tin Can Alley*, which gained second place in the Kumu Kahua/UH Drama Department Playwriting Contest of 1979. More recently he wrote *The Killing of One Self* and *Meatloaf*. The latter had a reading at the Vineyard Theatre Workshop in New York in 1982.

Darrell H. Y. Lum has a B.A. in Liberal Studies and an M.A. in Educational Communications from the University of Hawaii, where he presently works counseling disadvantaged students in Special Student Services. He is co-editor and co-publisher of *Bamboo Ridge: The Hawaii Writers' Quarterly*, which he helped found in 1978, and co-editor of *Talk Story: An Anthology of Hawaii's Local Writers* (Honolulu, 1978). He has published a number of short stories in *Bamboo Ridge*. The fourth issue of *Bamboo Ridge* is entitled *Sun*, and is a collection of his own work. In 1982, his short play for children, *Magic Mango*, was staged by the Honolulu Theatre for Youth and published in *Bamboo Ridge*.

Robert J. Morris was born in 1945, and lives in Honolulu. He is currently an attorney and Counselor at Law. From 1964 to 1967 he worked as a missionary for the Mormon Church in Taiwan and Hongkong. In 1971 he received a B.A. and the following year an M.A. from Brigham Young University in Hawaii; he thereupon worked as an Instructor of English and Chinese language at the university from 1973 to 1977. In 1980 he received a law degree from the University of Utah Law School. Robert Morris acted in several productions at Brigham Young University, including *The Winter's Tale, Inherit the Wind,* and *J.B.* In addition to some poetry and short fiction, he has published scholarly articles in his field and on Hawaiiana. He is working on a new full-length play.

Edward Sakamoto now lives in Los Angeles where he works as a copyeditor for the *Los Angeles Times.* His first play, *In the Alley,* won the UH Drama Department Playwriting Contest in 1961 and was subsequently produced in Kennedy Lab Theatre. He graduated with a B.A. in English from the University of Hawaii in 1962, but for the next ten years devoted his energies to journalism. His recent plays, written for the East West Players in Los Angeles, include *Yellow is My Favorite Color* (1973), *That's the Way the Fortune Cookie Crumbles* (1976), *Voices in the Shadows* (1978), the double-bill *Aala Park* and *Manoa Valley* (1979), *The Life of the Land* (1980), a sequel to *Manoa Valley,* and *Pilgrimage* (1982). His plays have also been staged in San Francisco and New York. A revised version of *Manoa Valley* was presented in Kennedy Theatre, University of Hawaii, in 1982. Sakamoto has received the Rockefeller Foundation Playwright-in-Residence Award for 1981–1982. He received a smaller Rockefeller grant in 1978 and a National Endowment for the Arts grant in 1981.

Production Notes

This book was designed by Roger Eggers. Composition and paging were done on the Quadex Composing System and typesetting on the Compugraphic Unisetter by the design and production staff of University of Hawaii Press.

The text typeface is Garamond and the display typeface is Compugraphic Palatino.

Offset presswork and binding were done by Malloy Lithographing, Inc. Text paper is Glatfelter Offset Vellum, basis 45.